CULTURE IN IRELAND –

REGIONS: IDENTITY AND POWER

Nid oedd i einioes
　　y fam o fardd
binnau diogel,
　　nac cyd-ddeall
rhwng poteli babsn a pharadwys iaith...

(For the poet, also a mother
　　　　no safety-pins
to hold her life together,
　　　　nor concord
between a baby's bottles and
　　　　the paradise of speech...)

Menna Elfyn

To Eavan with love
from Proinsias/Frank

DEDICATION

The conference was dedicated to the example of Hubert Butler, a lifelong campaigner for cultural understanding in Ireland and to Patrick Kavanagh, through whose poetry we have on record, some of the greatest insights into life in rural Ireland.

'. . . Homer's ghost came whispering to my mind. He said: I made the Iliad from such a local row. Gods make their own importance'.
– Patrick Kavanagh

'. . . through my years in the county libraries, I discovered the varied beauties of my country and the rich diversity of its people. Why is it that now we look at the beauty mainly as something we can sell to tourists, and the diversity of its people, their faith and loyalties, not as an enrichment but a source of bitter antagonism?'
– Hubert Butler

Culture in Ireland –
Regions: Identity and Power

Proceedings of the Cultures of Ireland
Group Conference, 27–29 November, 1992

Edited by Proinsias Ó Drisceoil

The Institute of Irish Studies
The Queen's University of Belfast

ACKNOWLEDGEMENTS

The Cultures of Ireland Group wishes to thank the Ireland Funds for sponsoring the publication of the conference proceedings.

The International Fund for Ireland is thanked for its role as principal sponsor of the conference and for sponsoring the cost of preparing this book for publication.

First Published 1993
by the Institute of Irish Studies
The Queen's University of Belfast
University Road, Belfast

© The Cultures of Ireland Group, authors, and Tony O'Malley, 1993

All rights reserved. No part of this publication may be reproduced or transmitted in any form by any means, electronic or mechanical, including photocopy, recording or any information storage and retrieval system, without permission in writing from the publisher.

British Library Cataloguing-in-Publication Data. A catalogue record for this book is available from the British Library.

ISBN 085389 476 0

Printed by W. & G. Baird Ltd., Antrim

CONTENTS

  Page

Dedication — ii
Acknowledgements — iv
Preface — vii

Part I
MINISTERIAL MESSAGE, KEYNOTE ADDRESSES AND GENERAL DISCUSSION
Message from the Minister for Foreign Affairs David Andrews TD — 2
Conference Chairperson's Introduction — 3
Kevin Whelan: The Bases of Regionalism — 5
Rienk Terpstra: A View from Europe — 64
Myrtle Hill: A Northern Irish Perspective — 72
General Discussion — 83

Part II
REGIONS AND TRADITIONS
Chairperson's Introduction — 90
Liam O'Dowd: What is a Region? The Case of the Irish Borderlands — 91
Tony Canavan: Locality and Divided Histories — 98
Dermot Healy: Ingredients of Regional Identities (Republic of Ireland) – *Where I'm Coming From* — 102
Anne Tannahill: Ingredients of Regional Identities (Northern Ireland) — 116

Part III
REGIONS IN TRANSITION
Chairperson's Introduction — 124
Máire Uí Shíthigh: Heritage and Environment — 125

David McConnell: Regions and Minorities — 130
Tony Kennedy: Power to the Regions — 143
General Discussion — 146

Part IV
REPORTS ON WORKSHOPS
Helen Lanigan Wood: Locality and Divided Histories — 162
Gearóid Ó Tuathaigh: Locality and Divided Histories — 166
Tony Canavan: Locality and Divided Histories — 171
Terence Brown: Ingredients of Regional Identity — 176
Edna Longley: Ingredients of Regional Identity — 179
Proinsias Ó Drisceoil: Ingredients of Regional Identity — 185
Lelia Doolan: Heritage and Environment — 189
Martin McLoone: The Regions and the Media — 201
Joseph Liechty: Locality and Religion — 206
Frank Short: Sport and Culture — 211
Helena O'Donoghue: Locality and Access — 217
Fergus O'Ferrall: Local Identity and Local Government — 220
General Discussion — 223
Chairperson's Conclusion — 235

Biographies — 238
Thanks — 242

PREFACE

This book is the edited record of a conference with the theme, ***Culture in Ireland – Regions: Identity and Power***, held in the Slieve Russell Hotel, Ballyconnell, Co. Cavan in 1992 under the auspices of the Cultures of Ireland Group. The theme was prompted by the need for heightened awareness and intellectual scrutiny of cultural diversity and traditions and of the need to link up and mutually inform the debates about regional culture currently taking place in both Northern Ireland and the Republic, with the aim of bringing out the implications of these debates for wider cultural and political questions. The conference took place from November 27th to 29th, soon after the Maastricht referendum in the Republic had familiarised voters with EC regional aspirations, while their own experience continued to be one of apparent powerlessness in attempting to give validity to their identities in the face of cultural homogenisation, multinational capital and global media.

When stating the objectives of the conference, the group quoted Louis MacNeice: *As in Spain there is intense local feeling. The man from the next parish is a foreigner.* The conference 'set in border country' would 'consider cultural differences within the same locality, whether conditioned by religion, class or differing national allegiances'. This objective followed from the 1991 conference – *Culture in Ireland – Division or Diversity* – in seeking to break down division/diversity on a local and regional basis. Kevin Whelan's keynote address and the replies by Myrtle Hill and Rienk Terpstra, drawing on Northern Irish and Friesan experiences respectively, gave direction to these themes, which were explored from autobiographical, sociological, political, socio-linguistic and geographical perspectives in subsequent papers and from every imaginable viewpoint in the twelve workshop sessions.

The formation of the Cultures of Ireland Group was initiated by Constance Short, cultural adviser, Co-operation North. Co-operation North has continued to host Cultures of Ireland and joined with the International Fund for Ireland as principal sponsor of the conference. Constance's vision and dedication gave both group and conference the coherence which allowed them to be themselves instances, however modest, of democratic toleration and diversity. The members of the group are thanked for their preparatory space work, for chairing the workshops and for writing the workshop reports. The Ireland Funds are thanked for making the publication of this book possible and everyone who attended the conference – whether speakers from the podium, the floor or at the workshops – is thanked equally. This book is their creation.

Dom' thriúr mac – Cóilín, Eoghan agus Mac Dara – agus thar éinne eile dom' bhean chéile, Mary, gabhainn buíochas ar leith as ucht a bhfoighne agus mé i mbun an leabhair seo.

PROINSIAS Ó DRISCEOIL

Members of the Cultures of Ireland Group
Niall Crowley, Hon. Chairperson; Joseph Liechty, Chairperson; Constance Short, Administrator; Terence Brown, Tony Canavan, Maurna Crozier, Lelia Doolan, Barbara Sweetman FitzGerald, Mary Holland, Edna Longley, Helena O'Donoghue, Proinsias Ó Drisceoil, Fergus O'Ferrall, Gearóid Ó Tuathaigh, Kevin Whelan.

PART I

MINISTERIAL MESSAGE, KEYNOTE ADDRESSES AND GENERAL DISCUSSION

MESSAGE FROM THE MINISTER FOR FOREIGN AFFAIRS
MR. DAVID ANDREWS TD

I very much regret that I am unable to be with you at the Culture in Ireland conference. I have long admired the excellent work done by the Cultures of Ireland Group and expect that this weekend's proceedings will maintain this fine tradition.

Your intention to focus on regional identity, and the diversity of influences which help to shape that identity, is particularly timely. In all parts of Ireland there are signs of a new awareness of the richness and variety of our common heritage. Local communities are learning to appreciate their own individuality and to benefit from the sense of mutual support which this engenders. Equally, as communities come to better understand the factors shaping their past and present they gain new insights about those with whom they share this island. I am confident that this enhanced self-awareness and tolerance of difference are fully compatible. In the context of the search for peace and reconciliation on this island these are welcome developments which we must continue to encourage and foster.

We see too in the context of the European Community how difference is accommodated and where, indeed, linguistic and cultural diversity is cherished as an essential element of a true European Union. In this way, historical antagonisms have been transformed; the conflict and confrontation which characterised so much of European history have been replaced by a new solidarity. The European model, which has already helped to transform attitudes in so many areas of our lives, can act as a point of reference and inspiration to us in reconciling, on a basis of respect and equality, the traditions which co-exist on this island.

I am disappointed not to have the opportunity to attend this conference. I believe that the issues with which you are dealing are important and far-reaching, and I am sure your deliberation will cast valuable light on them. I wish you every success.

CHAIRPERSON'S INTRODUCTION

Maurna Crozier

On behalf of the Cultures of Ireland Group, may I welcome you all to this, its second conference, in Cavan.

We have come from every direction, from every part of Ireland, to this central spot, to enjoy the opportunity to discuss those ideas which are crucially important to us, as individuals and communities, in the areas from which we have come.

Last year's conference addressed the issues of division and diversity attendant on political and religious imperatives. This year the focus is on regions, since, as individuals, our experience of national structural forces comes through our local experience. It is our involvement in politics and religion – as in work, sport, music and much else – at regional level, which forms our personal and community identity, and hence, determines the nature of our response to issues of national importance.

Lest this sounds like a merely conceptual relationship between national issues and local perceptions, can I tell you that a neighbour of mine in Co. Down has completely rejected as a prospective political candidate a man who had left an excellent hay crop rotting in the field for seven months; such agricultural incompetency had shown – obviously – that he was quite unfit for public office. The point of the story, of course, is not that my neighbour was using a strange set of criteria to weigh the potential politician, but that he was doing what we all do all the time: use local and particular knowledge, which we easily translate into what we know to be true fact, to determine how we feel, and think about wider issues.

How then, if our identities and allegiances are so determined by our experience of the local, are these seminal value systems to inform the national institutions which order the affairs – political, economic and religious – of the regions?

Have regional characteristics got something particular and special to offer the country as a whole, or does a region cling on to particular identities, principally because it feels it needs the angst of marginalisation or difference in order to secure a place in the future? It would be a depressing prospect if allegiance to those strands of continuity which are so crucial to local life, committed us to trying to restore some communitarian vision from the past as our model for the future. Restoration is never a possibility – a message which is currently impinging profoundly on political traditionalists in the North, and social traditionalists in the Republic. And even if it were a possibility, our reconstructions of the past might as easily reinforce old stridencies, as foster the tolerant diversity which most of us feel is crucial to Ireland at the end of the twentieth century.

So how do we want our regional verities to survive, while adapting to contemporary realities, so that they may influence the powerful structures of nation, of state or of economic community? During this conference we will all have the opportunity to express and to consider the significant ingredients and current relevance of our varied regional identities. To launch the debate, in all its complexities, we are privileged to have Kevin Whelan, currently the Bi-centennial Research Fellow in the Royal Irish Academy, who will initiate our proceedings.

KEVIN WHELAN

THE BASES OF REGIONALISM

Epic

I have lived in important places, times
When great events were decided, who owned
that half rood of rock, a no-man's land
Surrounded by our pitchfork-armed claims.
I heard the Duffys shouting 'Damn your soul'
And old McCabe stripped to the waist, seen
Step the plot defying blue cast-steel –
'Here is the march along these iron stones.'
That was the year of the Munich bother. Which
Was more important? I inclined
To lose my faith in Ballyrush and Gortin
Till Homer's ghost came whispering to my mind.
He said: I made the Iliad from such
A local row. Gods make their own importance.

What are the bases of Irish regionalism? The most appropriate way of visualising this is as a series of allegiances, affiliations and attachments, built up in a nested hierarchy like a set of Chinese boxes.[1] At the centre of these boxes is the family farm, the smallest but most potent vector of the territorial imperative in the Irish experience. The sense of emotional attachment, the forces of generational continuity, the primary role in socialisation, the continuing valency of the kinship system – all these are well known from the anthropological texts on rural Ireland, notably that by Conrad Arensberg and Solon T. Kimball, based on work in the townlands of Luogh and Rinnamona near Doolin in west Clare.[2] The historic trajectory to owner occupancy is a well known one, but it is still worth stressing how early that revolution occurred in Ireland, and how it backboned the political ideology of the new Southern state and the family values enshrined in the 1937 constitution. In a remarkably percipient and proleptic moment, one of the Land League leaders, Matthew Harris, had pondered the potentially negative effect of achieving peasant proprietorship: 'When the farmers would be emancipated and get their lands, such men would look on the boundary of their farm as the boundary of their country, because farmers as a rule are very selfish men.'[3]

In the big farm regions of south Leinster and east Munster which have done well from the EC, the aim of keeping one's name on the land has been achieved, giving rise to a relatively stable family farm structure, where the farm is both a resource and power base. One might contrast this with the small farm zone of the Atlantic fringe and the drumlin belt, where the small family farm has had immense difficulties in surviving.[4] This is the part of the country where only two types of music are popular – country and western – perhaps because it expresses the poignancy, desolation and nostalgia of the disintegration of a cultural world when its main anchor comes adrift. The expression of this world has come memorably from J.B. Keane, John McGahern, John Healy and Eugene McCabe, and *The Field* (the play, not the film) is its literary highpoint, as *Nineteen Acres* is its journalistic climax.

The second level in this spiralling series of territorial structures is the townland which can be seen as the neighbourhood level. The island of Ireland contains sixty two thousand two hundred and five townlands, with an average size of a mere three hundred and twenty six acres. No other European country has such a remarkably close-grained territorial network, or one of such antiquity and resilience.[5] The oldest version of the townland or baile surfaces in some of the first written records of the medieval period. From an early base in landowning and land working, the townland became a convenient mapping base for land confiscation and reallocation in the seventeenth century. By the nineteenth century, it had become a unit of estate administration for the allocation and collection of rents, and it was used by the state as a unit of taxation, for postal direction, and for the collection of statistics.

But the townland also developed a distinct popular persona. It became a key structural unit in the Irish countryside, with many of the rundale villages (clachans) being townland-based. Its boundaries were etched firmly in people's minds as well as physically in the landscape, or legally on maps. Rural communities identified themselves using the townland matrix; even today, a country person is identified by family and townland : 'She's one of the Sheridans of Clough'. The enduring *dinnseanchas* (or placelore) of the countryside was townland-based, and rural people knew the country by heart through the filaments which bound the townland network to the landscape.

In social terms, the townland frame structured interaction between farm families. The neighbourhood group who co-operated in various tasks – haymaking, saving the harvest, turfcutting, sharing tools and manpower – were townland based. Four to ten families created the 'meitheal' or 'comhar na gcomharsan' group within the townlands. The principle underlying this is pithily expressed in the Donegal proverb, 'Nuair a bhíonn an bhó sa díog, caithfidh tú 'chur faoi chomhar na gcomharsan'. Economic and practical co-operation was cemented by social ties – the 'cuairdíocht' or 'bothántaíocht' at night, and by mutual celebration and grief at events in the family cycle. Thus, it was traditional for all work to cease in a townland where a neighbour died. This bonding at a townland level was also recognised in the Catholic Church's practice of basing the 'stations' on townlands.

In recent years, mechanisation of farming, increasing individualism and mobility, and the huge growth in non-farming families in the countryside have all reduced social contacts at the townland level, seriously diminishing its economic and social solidarity. Yet the townland itself is still a living social reality as is demonstrated by the recent successful campaign in Northern Ireland against their abolition in the interests of postal rationalisation.[6]

The classic celebration of the townland's centrality is Patrick Kavanagh's *Epic*, where the townland names of Ballyrush and Gortin carry the charge, authority and resonance of the poem, especially as balanced against Munich. Kavanagh deploys the intimate territoriality of the townland and the Duffys' and McCabes' micro-empire against the macro European empire and their territorial theatre of the Second World War. He does not find the townland strategy wanting.

The third of our Chinese boxes is what one might loosely term the local community zone, and here one is focusing on the parish or village base – that part of life which rotates around the local church, school, post office, pub, shop and clubs. Interaction around these hubs creates a face-to-face community, perhaps stretching for a radius of five miles around the local village or parish centre. For much of rural Ireland, this local community level is identified with the Catholic parish, and it has retained a well-developed sense of attachment. However, one should note that in Ireland the role of the parish, and especially the parish centre, has been severely curtailed as a result of the bifurcation in the system that occurred after the Reformation. The older medieval or civil parish framework was appropriated by the new state religion, and in the absence of large-scale conversions, soon became the parish system of a minority population. The loss of majority allegiance caused the decline and abandonment, or failure to develop of villages at the parish centre which is now very frequently marked by an ivy-draped medieval church ruin, and a flourishing graveyard.

When the institutional Catholic Church began its long revival in the second half of the eighteenth century, it had to build a completely new suite of parishes. At the centre of these new parishes was a Catholic chapel, and this often acted as a nucleus which attracted a presbytery, national school, pubs, shops, forges, houses, halls. Eventually, these humble crossroad accretions became the functioning heart of the community. I have termed them chapel villages, and about four hundred can be identified in the country as a whole (about one in every three parishes.)[7] In Cavan, Crosserlough, Milltown and Bellenagh and in Armagh, Dromntee, Glassdrummond, Mullaghbawn and Cullyhanna are good examples. This late flowering of a generation of villages at the centre of a new parish system is unique to Ireland – and its downside is that the traditional European village-system, based on the medieval church, has been fractured in Ireland, in both a temporal and a spatial sense. The new chapel village is often found close to the abandoned medieval parish centre.

This spatial schizophrenia has militated against the role of a rooted village tradition and this in turn has meant that the cohesive and civilising role of the village community in a wider European setting has had a limited impact in Ireland.[8] For example, the Catholic parish system, as being inherently confessional, has never been fitted into the state's administrative system. Thus, over most of southern Ireland, the basis of local community interaction in the parish and chapel village has never had any meaningful administrative connection with the state.

The inherently hierarchical structure of the Catholic Church has also militated against the use of the one thousand, two hundred and ninety eight parishes as a democratic base. Akin to the role of the TD, the parish priest is the only significant link between the congregation and the broader church, and this has led to an authoritarian and paternalistic structure of Church power. The more recent moves towards collegiality as expressed in the parish council initiative has not significantly altered these clerical facts of life; these councils have largely been assigned solely a fund-raising role, and the parish priest's 'uno duce, uno voce' still holds strong. The parish priest in my home parish commented on the parish council, 'there should be two on any committee and one of them should stay at home'! It would be very instructive to compare the community and democratic effectiveness of the non-territorially and hierarchically-based Christian Churches, especially in the Presbyterian and non-conformist traditions.

The GAA, which eventually adopted a parish rule as the basis for teams, is the most notable example of successful use of the parish system as a framework of local identity. The organisation derived great grassroots strength and durability from this adaptation to the daily rhythms and local loyalties of small communities.

If this local community level is to retain its vitality, it needs to maintain its population base and its infrastructure of services. A core population of at least two thousand is probably necessary to run a viable rural village/parish, and the basic minimum in terms of services is a church, school, shop and post office; all of which are fundamental building blocks in the design and maintenance of a compact community area. The furore over An Post's rationalisation plans of last year indicated how sensitive a community nerve was touched when the post office was threatened. A local national school is essential to renewing the sense of a highly intimate, familiar, local community. And finally, one might note that the Catholic Church, in a situation of almost universal Mass attendance, is the most significant protagonist of an ideology of communal solidarity which transcends the polarities of class, gender and generation at the local level.

Our next Chinese box, fitting over those of parish, townland and farm (or community, neighbourhood and family), is that which, following Willie Smyth, we may term the social field. This is that space or territory in which people interact in economic, social and cultural terms – the spatial reach of kinship, occupation and friendship. Effectively, the social field is now defined (but not exclusively) by the local town and its hinterland. The towns would boast a population of one thousand five hundred to ten thousand and their hinterlands would be within a ten to fifteen mile radius. The towns provide living spaces, jobs and services, and the economic and social networks are now increasingly superimposed, with convergence effectively increasing since the spread of mass car ownership. Through commuting, services and shopping, many of the important cementing institutions now operate at this level – the factory, the supermarket, the secondary school, the bank, bus and rail links, the night club. In many ways, these newly-strengthened town hinterlands are increasingly the most important level in the territorial organisation of rural communities – especially since the advent of mass participation in post-primary schools. The new patterns of social interaction can be seen in the marriage fields – those relatively cohesive territories from which marriage partners are drawn and which now tend increasingly to overlap the economic hinterlands of these towns. Thus, the more localised social field has been extended, and the traditional territorial order of the countryside has been reshaped. However, this new order has not yet had effective administrative or popular expression. Only the local newspaper offers a precise expression of the nature of these town/country interactions, and the antiquated UDC system fails to take cognisance of the functional interdependence of towns and their hinterlands, although the organisation of local administration in Northern Ireland is based on these new units. As yet, however, the sense of attachment and affiliation felt at the level of the farm, townland and parish has not transferred upwards to this fourth level, and it does not have a strongly developed sense of place, even though it is now the principal unit for the general integration and management of rural society.

Fitting over these social fields, sometimes rather awkwardly, is the county system – the next level in our spiral of territorial structures. The Irish county system represents the successful superimposition of the English shiring system initiated in the medieval period and finally completed with the shiring of Wicklow in 1606. They were units of administrative convenience created out of a collection of Anglo-Norman lordships and Gaelic 'tuatha', 'nations' or 'countries'. The county retained vitality as an administrative entity from then on, but it broadly permeated popular consciousness only after the GAA adopted it as the principal basis for national competition. A county consciousness followed, evident in the great county anthems (like *Boolavogue, Slievenamon, The Rose of Mooncoin* or *The Rose of Tralee*), and in the county nicknames both official (the garden of Ireland, the model county, the banner county), and unofficial (the Wicklow goatsuckers, the Wexford yellabellies, the Carlow scallion eaters, the Galway herring chokers, the Roscommon sheep stealers, the Waterford wheybellies). That county consciousness is a relatively recent phenomenon may be guessed at in the following transaction recorded by Peadar Ó hAnnracháin: "'An Ciarraíoch nó Corcaíoch tú", arsa mise le fear sa Ghleann Garbh. "Ní bhainim le haon taobh acu, buíochas le Dia", ar seisean. "Is Bearrach mé!'"[9] The independent radio stations have in some cases been effectively anchored to this county level – as with, for example, Clare FM.

Above the county framework, the province is now virtually obsolete with a vestigial life evident mainly only in sport (the IRFU and GAA both use it), and in the awkward and troubled overlap of 'Ulster', 'Northern Ireland' and 'Six Counties'. Whether or not the old attributes of the provinces still survive is a moot point. One Irish couplet with epigramatic precision identified 'An Laighneach lách, an Muimhneach splách, an Connachtacht béalbhinn agus an t-Ultach beadaí (the affable Leinster man, the obsequious Munsterman, the silvertongued Connacht man, and the epicurean Ulsterman).[10]

Finally, one should recognise that there are regions which survive in popular consciousness although they are not administrative units."[11] These are what the French call 'pays' – regions with a distinctive environment and way of life which are self-conscious about that distinctiveness. These run in Ireland from well-known examples like Connemara, the Burren, the Rosses, Ards, Inishowen, Sliabh Luachra and Fingal, to less well known ones like Cooley, the Glen of Imaal, the Hook, the Macamores, the Duffry, Corca Dhuibhne, the Laggan, Cois Fharraige, Fanad, the Joyce Country, or Sliabh gCua. Such regions have a fascination because they are organically derived, with a durable sense of identity based on the interaction between a human culture and an environment over time. They obviously also offer a humane and comfortable sense of scale and attachment, which is not imposed from without but arises from within a community's own sense of a shared identity.

On the Hook peninsula, a sea-based culture instinctively defined itself by excluding the 'boult-the-doors' – those inland folk who locked their doors at night and thereby rendered themselves unavailable in case their help should be needed in a sudden emergency at sea.[12] It is these particularities which give rise to the sense of a regional personality whose warmth contrasts with more clinical administrative regions – they have an affective as opposed to an instrumental purpose. It should be a policy across the board to support the regional distinctiveness of these 'petite patries'.

It is obvious that these small Chinese boxes are now increasingly stacked within ever larger boxes – those of the nation state, the EC, the global economy and media. Every individual is now linked via this ascending series to the global level, and allegiance may be attached to any, none or many of these levels. The problem of the region as conventionally defined is its increasing porosity to these territorially unrestrained influences. The question then arises: does the traditional region, statically defined in local, fixed and essentially rural terms have any continuing purchase in this diversified, mobile and dynamic world. There are obvious problems in translating the regional concept to the urban context. Can we match townland against street, parish against suburb, *pays* against city. And the very notions of place, territory and identity embedded in the regional construct may well disenfranchise those who have been displaced or alienated from it; it may also have inbuilt gender and generational biases. Stable regions with fixed boundaries may create an arbitrary, artificial sense of identity which ignores differences and individuality. The construction of regions must therefore involve their deconstruction. The notion of stable regions with fixed boundaries has to be measured against the Heraclitean flux of economy, society and culture in an age more Dionysian than Apollonian.

Looked at in this way, it is immediately apparent that our neat, ordered, spatial matrix is too neat, too ordered, too spatial to capture the ceaseless fluidity of life as it is lived in modern Ireland. While these territorial frameworks undoubtedly live as deep structures under that fluidity, they are increasingly looser, freer, less contained. Outer and inner levels now meet more frequently and spontaneously than ever before. The impact of the media and technology now transcends territorial structure and is largely independent of it. The car and the telephone have freed people to live in extended communities – communities which are acquired and aspirational, not ascribed or inherited. The traditional tight spatial structures were, for many, perhaps airless boxes, oppressive, stifling, whose only windows were squinting ones. The increasing loosening of this 'proper order' is therefore potentially liberating, an escape from the gravity of tradition, the force field of kin, place and memory. The doppelganger of rootedness is repression, of stability is inertia. The living tissue of community must continuously shed its initially protective, eventually sclerotic protective carapaces, if it is to grow. That growth may initially be wobbly, amorphous, amoeboid: eventually, newer, broader, more comfortable territorial shells will form over it too, before they in turn will also be shed in a further cycle of growth.

Adopting this perspective, we can see a problem in finding a coherent fit between different types of region – the physical (environmental), the functional (economic), the perceptual (cultural) and the formal (administrative). The very idea of regionalism, with its emphasis on inherited rather than acquired identities forcefeeds the atavistic appetites of tradition – the backwards glance, where, as in Auden's terms, tradition becomes a democracy of the dead, not the living, and in Marxian formulation, the dead generations weigh like a nightmare on the brain of the living. The appeal to regionalism can easily be construed as an appeal to conservatism, a Burkean sedative to lull the little platoons into a big sleep. In Burke's formulation, the region represents the integrity of traditional society and its local loyalties, and it can be set against abstract universalising claims, which violate the customary affections and rooted relations which make society adhesive and stable.[13] Any political system which placed abstract principles or claims above those of family, community or region would inevitably lack the crucial binding force that gives political systems their endurance – the affection and acquiescence of the people who live under them. In Burkean terms, therefore, one must weigh the primacy and potency of a particularist past against the rational, progressive and utopian claims of the enlightenment modernisation project, with its appeal to the cosmopolitan future.

For almost two centuries, the weighing of these two projects has generally favoured the modernising, Jacobin element. Recent philosophical and political trends, notably growing recognition of the limitations of the enlightenment model of modernisation, have refocused attention on Burke's ancient quarrel with it. In a sense, post-modernism has made the region intellectually respectable once more. Post-modernism's concern to disperse and decentralise power, its willingness to conjugate past and present, its emphasis on spatial as much as temporal analysis have all revitalised the concept of regionalism. One can especially clearly see post-modernism's influence in the concept of a 'Europe of the Regions'.

Europe of the Regions

The concept of a 'Europe of the Regions' has been fashionable in the build-up to the dismantling of internal barriers within the European Community.[14] In this optimistic scenario, the role of the nation-state will be weakened in a united Europe, as power is circulated upwards to the transnational EC level, and leached downwards to the regions, leaving nation-states as mere residual husks. The old destructive territorial rivalries of European nation-states will be transcended, while newly empowered and revivified regions will be woven into a richly variegated but tolerant tapestry. The new Europe will become a mosaic of regionally-based cultures, shielded by the benign EC umbrella from the deleterious effects of the centralisation and the globalisation of the world economy.[15] Under the cohesion principle, the economic cores and peripheries inevitably generated by the Single European Market will be smoothed out by transfer payments through the structural funds. The new European vision will be of a unity based on diversity. As envisaged by Neal Ascherson, for example, the united Europe will be an organism 'that will grow an outer skin around itself – an outer skin which will allow the present kind of skins which separate one nation state from another to become porous, so that eventually they will cease to matter'.[16]

Ignoring other less benign scenarios of how the Maastricht process will work itself out (such as the concept of 'Fortress Europe'), we can ask ourselves how this reading holds up against the Irish experience. Firstly, one must recognise that the Republic of Ireland and the United Kingdom are the two most centralised states within the EC; both have ignored the general European trend towards increasing the powers of local and regional government.

In both states, transnational economic or political stimuli are overwhelmingly filtered through the state apparatus. In the Republic of Ireland, the state bulks exceedingly large in economic life, with the state's share of expenditure vis-a-vis Gross Domestic Production being the highest in Europe at about 60% in the 1980s.[17] Therefore, in both states, the impact of the EC has been to strengthen the centre against the peripheries, and to weaken the residual power of local government because funding now goes completely through the state. Control of EC funds has strengthened the national bureaucracies in both countries. In the Republic of Ireland, for example, witness the role of the Departments of Finance, Environment and Agriculture, and the way in which they have been enhanced by control of Structural Funds.[18] The 1977 abolition of domestic rates emasculated local authorities, rendering them completely dependent on the centre for funding. The national bureaucracies, not the regions, have therefore been the principal beneficiaries of the EC and the states themselves have been strengthened, not weakened, by the European process. The tendency has been to remove decision-making from the hands of elected officials and place it increasingly in the hands of appointed ones, making the national bureaucracy the only effective link between the EC and local communities. The lack of effective local administration has created a vacuum at the regional level, which in turn has inhibited integrated approaches to economic development and encouraged sectorally-based decision making at the centre. The impact of the EC has therefore been to strengthen the centre at the expense of the regions; national sovereignty, national institutions and national bureaucracies have all been solidified, not weakened, and the regions have lost, not gained. In the Republic, this is ruthlessly exemplified in the decision in the 1970s to treat Ireland as a single homogeneous region for EC funding purposes. In such a situation, the benign scenario of a 'Europe of the Regions' simply does not transfer to contemporary Ireland.

Besides heavily centralised states, the other principal difficulty has to do with the role of cities in the new Europe.[19] The regions which have successfully asserted themselves in the last two decades have all been based on the thriving economies of their core cities – Catalonia is heavily dependent on Barcelona, Bavaria on Munich, Andalusia on Seville. For some of the principal protagonists of a 'Europe of the Regions', like Jacques Darras, the regions are explicitly envisaged as a return to the medieval city states which combined considerable local autonomy with a pan-European free market economy and elite culture, and which were the cradle of the European democratic tradition.[20] The rapid strides made by the Lombard League in northern Italy is one example of the revived political potential of a network of cities, consciously evoking a late medieval precedent. Powerful cities like Milan or Turin, Barcelona or Munich are also axes and hubpoints of the new transnational economy which has strengthened worldwide the role of a handful of global cities. The 'Europe of the Regions' concept can a little too easily mask this central fact of a 'Europe of the City Regions', whose success is fundamentally economically driven by an urban economy. Sir Richard Rogers, the architect, believes that 'Europe is becoming increasingly defined by its cities. It is becoming, as it was until the seventeenth century, not a national but a city civilisation'.[21] One cannot therefore separate the cultural dimensions of a regional policy from the economic realities.

How does such a scenario work out on the essentially rural European periphery? One can immediately observe the immense difficulties of translating the concept. Ireland, for example, simply does not possess a sufficiently dynamic city region to act as a pulse of this new regionalism. In the United Kingdom, London is a powerful player in the big city league; there the impetus of the last twenty years has been to create a strong regional ripple around its success in the south-east of England. However, this has meant de-industrialisation and collapse of the old northern industrial cores, like Liverpool, Manchester, Glasgow and Belfast. Thus, the London city region (at least until the recent crash) has been the principal beneficiary of the new economic order. This is a striking example of the tendency of the new global economy not to erode but to intensify regional economic differences, based around a new pecking order of successful cores and depressed peripheries. With agriculture in crisis, with peripherality if anything increased by the Single European Market, it is very difficult to see how strong city regions could emerge in Ireland around, let us say, Cork, Limerick, Galway, Waterford, Dublin, Derry and Belfast. But in their absence, 'Europe of the Regions' is likely to remain aspirational rather than actual in the Irish context. The EC project will dissolve the politics of identity, by diminishing the credibility and authority of the nation state: malevolent divisions will mutate into benevolent diversity, because cultural identity will be divorced from political allegiance, and because the EC project will allow for the replacement of exclusivist single definitions of identity by multiple and non-competitive ones.

An ancillary strand of 'Europe of the Regions' thinking is to see it as a potential solution to the Northern Ireland problem. The argument runs that economic and political integration within a federal structure will inevitably lead to a post-nationalist Europe, whose profoundly liberating effect will be to transcend and ultimately end the ideology of the nation-state. This federal Europe will deliver a stronger economy, enhanced rights for women and workers guaranteed by the social charter, and better protection of cultural minorities. The new sense of Europeanness and the enhanced power of regionalism will encourage people to shift from a simplistic nationalist identity towards a more complex and fuller set of identities, at once regional, national and European. With the EC acting as a supra-factional broker, this will eventually deliver a solution to Ireland's national problem. With the nationalist threat in retreat in a federal Europe, cultural Irishness and cultural Britishness will be divorced amicably from allegiance to their weakened nation states, and displaced from the contentious political realism into more neutral and accommodating spaces. With the increased power of the region, new types of non-sectarian, non-confrontational local identity can then emerge.[22]

This prognosis is often backed up by an economic argument: the globalisation of the world economy will also help dissolve the nation state, as money recognises no borders. After the Single European Market and the Channel Tunnel are completed, Ireland will be the most exposed and peripheral European economy, and this will heighten awareness of the advantages of a 'one-island economy'.[23] This will create a demand for co-operation and policy co-ordination to create economies of scale and to avoid mutually-damaging competition, in areas like tourism and the attraction of multi-national enterprises. In the long run, economic convergence will inevitably lead to political convergence. Some commentators have recognised a southern political strategy hidden in this discourse – technocratic anti-partitionism – especially associated with Garret Fitzgerald.[24] Others have noted its affinity with the 'Europe of the Regions' concept.

The problem with this approach can be briefly stated. First, economic integration of a one-island economy is only likely to proceed smoothly if there are no overt or covert political agendas. Secondly, the perceived decline of nationalism may be a mirage: as recent events in Eastern Europe have demonstrated, it is remarkably easy for European *fraternité* to mutate into fratricide. The most formidable challenge to nation-states has emerged not from regions but from long buried and now resurgent mini-nationalisms – Catalan and Basque in Spain, Scottish, Welsh and Irish in the UK. The federal Europe may well find it difficult to heal the hurts of history: as long ago as 1791, surveying the troubled Irish landscape, the United Irishmen noted: 'We have thought much about our posterity, little about our ancestors. Are we forever to walk like beasts of prey over the fields which those ancestors stained with blood?'[25] More recently, George Steiner has warned that 'regions too often tend to define themselves not by remembering in joy but in hatred'.[26]

Thirdly, the Single European Market is likely to increase not diminish the economic differences between the European core and European periphery. Current EC regional policy seems unlikely to be able to stem the free market forces of concentration. Cohesion funds at 1% of the total EC budget, are relatively small in comparison with other federal states (in the US for example national government redistributes 9% to the federal level). Any increase in regional differences within Europe will add additional burdens to already devastated economies and make it difficult to implement even the first steps towards a one-island economy.

Finally, as James Anderson has cogently demonstrated, arguments that stress economic integration or the hypothetical erosion of the nation state rely heavily on indirect, impersonal and automatic forces, and therefore remove the onus on politicians to provide the only solution that will ultimately work – a political solution.[27]

The Argument for Decentralisation

There is reasonably broad agreement that the centralised nature of both the southern and UK states presents a major impediment to the activation of a regional dynamic. At the periphery, it creates a dependency syndrome, stifling local initiatives and responses, encouraging a grants mentality and a sense of pervasive civic apathy. At the centre, it tends to clog the administrative system with a plethora of detail more efficiently handled at the regional level. It inhibits the development of integrated and strategic thinking, encouraging short term and sectoral responses. It also creates a mandarin class, shielded from democratic responsibility or accountability and wrapped in what Tom Barrington has called 'a cocoon of complacent centralisation'.[28] A fissure then opens up between the state and local communities, a fissure which is currently only bridged by the TD. Such a system puts immense pressure on the politician to act predominantly as a broker, a handler and a fixer, continuously interposed, like a tangler at a fair, between the state and its citizens. The politician's long-term viability depends on his success in Basil Chubb's famous phrase, in 'going around persecuting civil servants'.[29] Their role as national legislators is accordingly diminished. In the absence of any other institutions which attach the state to local institutions, the TD has therefore to become the region he represents, engaged in an endless round of shuttle diplomacy between Dublin and his constituency.

An example can be taken to show how a pervasive localism lies at the base of the Irish political system, a localism of personal bailiwicks and political fiefdoms. The series of maps illustrate the Fianna Fáil vote in the 1981 general election in the Galway West constituency plotted by polling district and based on tallymen figures.[30] These show a classic distance decay effect, with the vote peaking near the candidate's homes – Fahey in Gort: O'Conor at Leitir Mór in Connemara: Killilea in Belclare; Geoghagan-Quinn, living in Renmore but with an additional base at her family home in Carna; and Molloy with a similar power base at Salthill, and around his mother's home in Clifden. These high personal votes in privatised political spaces are maintained only by relentless massaging, and by constant preaching of the principle that only a locally-based TD will deliver the goods – from filling potholes to obtaining medical cards, from advance factories to interpretive centres. This inevitably creates a politics of clientelism and the cult of personality, not of active citizenship or participatory democracy.

All this creates a civic vacuum in the south of Ireland. The Australian poet, Vincent Buckley, put the point with characteristic clarity in his *Memory Ireland*. 'When you come right down to it, there

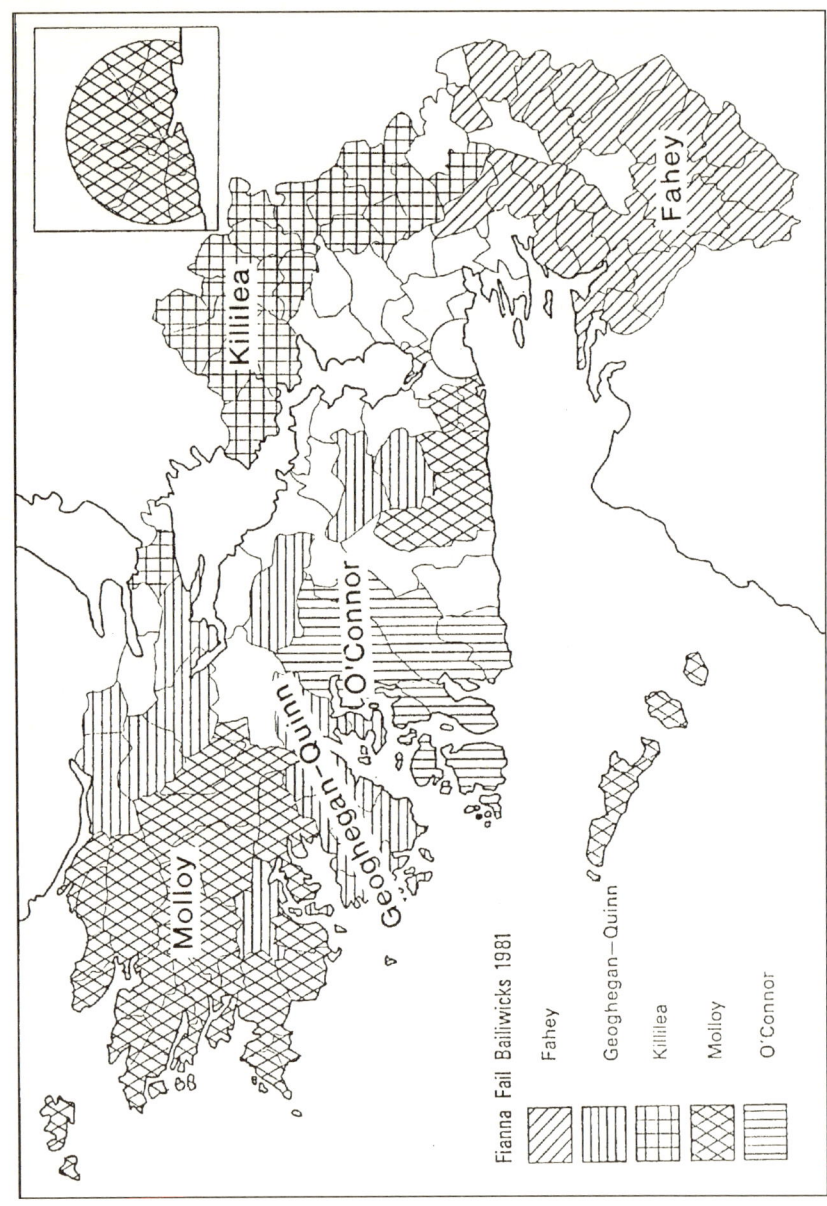

is almost no civic sense at all: the concept is too wide for people's life experience: they have little sense of a nation and none of a *polis*'.[31] The corollary therefore of a bloated centre is an anaemic vitiated local sphere. As we have seen, the principal impact of the EC in the Republic has been to enhance the already entrenched strategic position of central government as the exclusive conduit of EC funding and as the almost equally exclusive arbiter of policy initiatives. Even with EC policies specifically designed to cut out the central government nexus, as with the LEADER project, local community development initiatives eventually end up in the embrace of the state. It is symptomatic that both the Republic of Ireland and the United Kingdom are at one in interpreting the concept of subsidiarity as applying solely to the national level; cohesion funding, under the Maastricht agreement, will go to the state, not regions.

This emphasis on top-down policies (a version of trickle-down administration to match trickle-down economics?) has had a debilitating impact on bottom-up development. There is no appropriate regional tier which can attach to or foster local initiatives, no political identity which can be comfortably fitted to community initiatives. The lack of political infrastructure at the regional level makes it impossible to empower regionally-based EC projects in the Republic of Ireland. A hasty ad-hoc cobbling together of existing nationally-based institutions has been the only response so far. There is no natural community unit with a political identity, unlike more decentralised states like Germany or France, there is no Irish equivalent of the *land, département* or *canton*. It is accordingly difficult to identify the bottom for 'bottom-up' development. The Irish tradition of rural living in dispersed, isolated houses does not create a 'natural' centre, as in the nucleated village-based rural settlement tradition of much of continental Europe.

The arguments against a regional approach can be quickly rehearsed. The most common (and cogent) one is that Ireland is simply too small, geographically, demographically and economically, to be able to support a decentralised system. As a small open economy fully exposed to the impact of a global economy which scarcely recognises national, let alone regional borders, it would be inefficient and counter-productive to indulge in a policy of regionalism. A second argument is that Ireland is both spatially compact and culturally homogeneous and that it therefore does not require regional structures to protect non-existent regional identities. A third argument is that increased decentralisation would lead to waste and corruption, as local politicians and communities would not have the requisite fiscal and moral rectitude or discipline to implement it properly. A fourth argument is that existing local government is too weak to be able to bear any additional burdens (blithely ignoring the fact that this weakness has been deliberately created by a policy of centralisation, it is ironically used by centralisers as an argument against devolution).

But there are also cogent arguments against centralisation and these have been notably stated by Barrington. There is an erosion of responsible democracy if functions that could be exercised by citizens are usurped by bureaucrats. 'The sharing of responsibilities is as much a duty of democracy as the sharing of resources'. If we wish to nourish democratic institutions, local government needs to be supported, to increase that sense of both responsibility and consensus, and to protect local autonomy. The Republic of Ireland rates very poorly on an European league table of centralisation: it spends only 5% of G.D.P. on local government. It has a ratio of one locally elected body to every thirty one thousand citizens while Switzerland, for example, has one for every two thousand citizens. There is one locally elected official for every one hundred and eleven French citizens; in the Republic of Ireland there is one for every two thousand two hundred. An indication of the seepage of power from elected to appointed representatives is that there are only one thousand five hundred locally elected representatives, but there are two thousand two hundred government appointments to state bodies. On even a conservative reckoning, Ireland is about twice as centralised as the European norm.[32]

This puts tremendous strain on the centre. One obvious result is the huge growth in the civil service, and its by-product in the growth of Dublin, as the state is disproportionately located there. Due to the size of its wages bill, total state expenditure per capita is highest in Dublin, and the capital's share of the national population (at 35% and rising) is more typical of a third world primate city than of a modern state, and is matched in the EC only by Athens' share of the Greek population. The capital's concentration of decision-making in political, social, economic, cultural and intellectual terms has generated an unease which is vaguely crystallised around the potent (if nebulous) perceptual region of Dublin 4.

Ratio of Locally Elected Bodies to Population

	Population (in millions)	No. of locally elected bodies	Ratio (to nearest thousand)
Switzerland	6.6	3,825	1:2,000
Luxembourg	0.37	126	1:3,000
Austria	7.6	2,325	1:3,000
Norway	4.2	472	1:9,000
Finland	4.9	461	1:11,000
Denmark	5.1	289	1:18,000
R. of Ireland	3.5	113	1:31,000

Source: Barrington Report (1991)

In the Republic, the Barrington report has suggested solutions to these problems in a radical reinvigoration of the system of local government. Beginning at the lowest level, this would involve the overhauling of the current outmoded system of Urban District Councils, by creating sub-county districts, based on a ten-mile radius around important towns, encompassing a population of fifteen to twenty thousand. As urban hinterlands, these districts should correspond to current natural cells of town and country living, bringing a much closer fit between administrative networks and daily life as it is actually lived. Within each county, this set of districts should feed into the existing, but much fortified, county council system. The administration of local services and functions, and increased discretion over funding, should immediately be devolved to this level from central government. The county level should also offer the most appropriate bridging point across the current chasm between the state and the community, combining sufficient size to be administratively efficient, with sufficient identity to maintain local loyalty. The county level would also be the most appropriate nexus for 'top-down' and 'bottom-up' development strategies. For this to become genuinely effective, a great effort must be made to develop links between community groups and the revamped local authority structures. The tremendous enthusiasm, drive and efficiency so frequently exhibited in local voluntary organisations, and the often vigorous community spirit at local level has so far signally failed to be transferred into local and ultimately central government. One of the principal tasks facing both northern and southern society is how better to facilitate

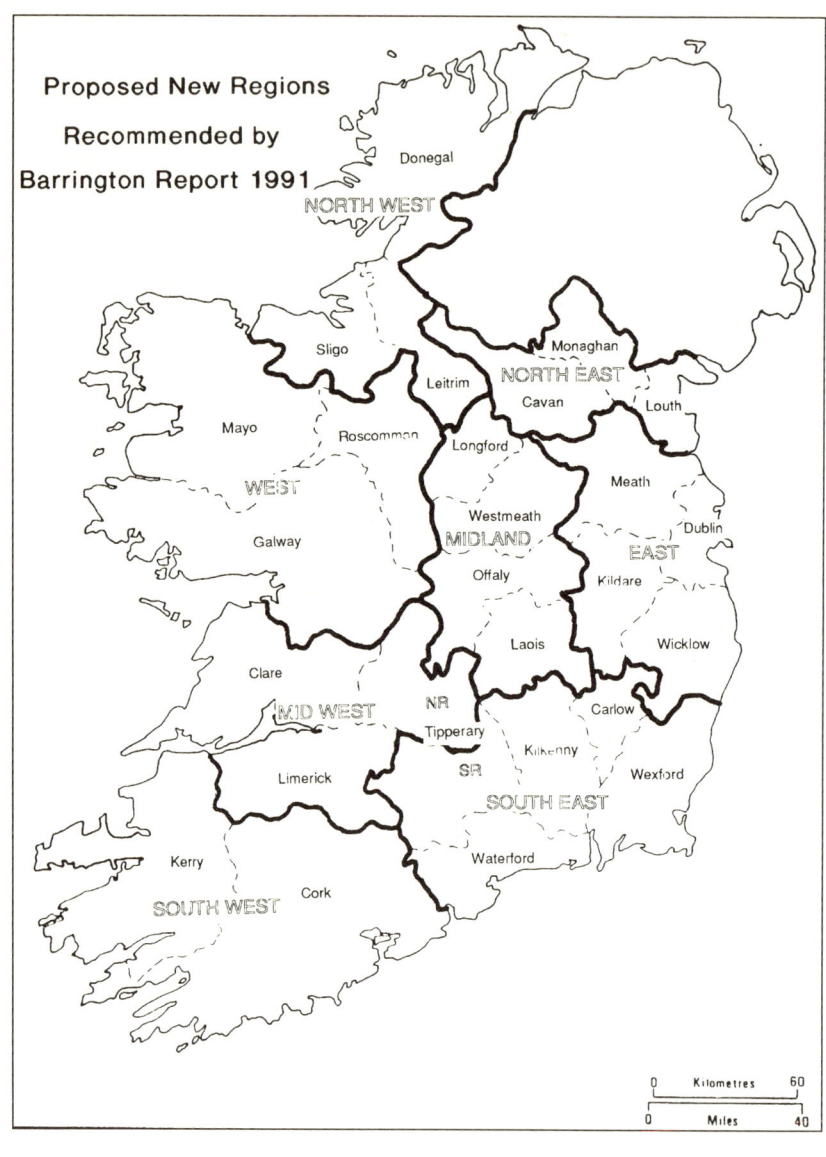

and nourish such local energies, without damaging, manipulating or altering them. The success of the County Arts Officer scheme offers one possible example.

Barrington's report also identifies a third tier in local administration, suggesting that there should be eight major regions, based on groupings of entire counties, and that these eight regions should be used as the basis for all regional planning and administration in the state sector. The new regional authorities should be given a broad strategic and co-ordinating role in policy initiation as well as policy implementation. They should have elected as well as appointed officials to increase their democratic legitimacy and accountability. They would also be the appropriate body to implement and monitor the National Development Plan. These new regional authorities could provide a genuine intermediate level on which to anchor EC regional development initiatives, and to encourage planning which meets specific and area-based, rather than broad and sectoral needs. This would require that the southern state releases its stranglehold on EC funding, allowing the regions to bypass the central government loop in dealing with Brussels. The current excessive emphasis on sectoral policies administered from the centre could then be counterbalanced by regionally-based integrated policies. By fostering local initiatives and developments, and by encouraging community participation in the process of government, this revamped local government system should diminish bureaucratic centralism and break the mould of the political culture of dependency and clientelism. To more clearly demonstrate the distinction between local and national policies, no TD or MEP should be allowed to sit at the regional or local level. In this way, by placing political power closer to the people, the twin goals of *subsidiarity* and *transparency* could be met – subsidiarity, in that public services would be administered at the lowest practicable level, *transparency*, in that decision-making would be sufficiently local to be accountable in the democratic political process.

One final reform, not suggested by Barrington, is essential if the Republic of Ireland is to move towards an effective regional policy. The decentralised system of government must not just be autonomous in a limited range of decision-making but it must be given control over appropriately funded resources. For this to happen, the relationship with the EC would have to cease to project the Republic as a whole as one region, and instead allow this new eight-fold set of regions to apply directly to Brussels for funding (within appropriate national guidelines). It is obvious, for example, that the problems of the Dublin region are not those of the West. The sectorally-based approach can cause as many problems as it solves. Consider the Irish agricultural sector. Here it is obvious that there are two distinct components – the modernising, intensive and efficient big farmers of the East and South, and the traditional low income and uncompetitive small farm area of the North and West. Any set of statistics immediately brings out the regional disparities created by the co-existence of these two sectors within Irish agriculture. In 1987, for example, average income in rural farm households in the east region was almost treble that in the north-west region.[33] Yet, state agricultural policy, through price support mechanisms, for example, actually increases regional inequalities. Two different sets of policies are needed for the two sectors, and the present sectoral policy works to disadvantage the already marginal sectors. Since EC entry, farm support has been targeted on viable farms under the EC farm modernisation scheme. As 90% of western farms are classified as non-viable, resources are withdrawn from them and pumped into the big farm areas of the east and south. This is simply one example of how different regions require different policies, of how EC and state resources transferred by a sectorally-driven administrative system can actually increase regional disparities.

The Evolution of Regional Identities

A world comes to life,
morning, the silent bog
and the God of imagination waking
in a Mucker fog.

We might wonder how such organic regions are created, and I want to take a series of case studies to illustrate this. My first example – Donegal fiddling – is used to show that regions are not just inherited, passive or inert, but are proactive, created by specific people in specific circumstances. This case study essentially draws on work by Allan Feldman and Eamonn O'Doherty[34], and more recent work by Damhnait Mac Suibhne[35] who have explored the evolution of a distinctive fiddling tradition within County Donegal, and then its further evolution into sub regional styles. A regional style can be taken to mean a musical aesthetic shared by several practitioners within the same area. In Donegal, the instrument par excellence is the fiddle, just as it might be the concertina in County Clare.

The distinctive Donegal style originates from the transfer of Highland piping techniques to the fiddle – a shared rhythmic precision, and an effort to replicate the staccato sound of the chanter. The strict tempo of the playing (albeit with an emphasis on 'lift') was derived from the fact that the music was originally overwhelmingly performed for dancing in the confined space of a country kitchen. The possibility of popularising the instrument only arose when fiddles became cheap, as a result of tin versions being produced by travelling tinsmiths, like the family of the greatest of Donegal fiddlers, John Doherty (1895–1980). Four families of travelling tinsmiths – the Dohertys, MacSweeneys, McConnells and Gallaghers – circulated predominantly in the southwest Donegal area, and they cross-fertilised and in a sense standardised the musical tradition of the area they traversed, both by their extensive repertoire and by their strong family background in the Highland pipes. There was also a pronounced Scottish influence with, for example, the popular 'Highlands' being a variation on the strathspey, adapted for dancing.

The cumulative impact of these forces produced the Donegal style of fiddling with its rich corpus of musical material and techniques. This music also had an intimate connection with the local environment. As John Doherty observed: 'The old musicians in them days would take music from anything. They would take music from the sound of the sea, or they would go alongside the river at the time of the flood and they would take music from that. They would take music from the chase of the hound and the hare!'[36] That music, evolving out of the local environment and spontaneously transferred between generations, connected the community to its own place and its own history, and became then, as with any great art form, a celebration of the community's existence.

But within this tradition, even more locally-based styles can be identified. If one takes the area stretching westwards from the Glens of Glenties to the south Rosses and then southwards to Gleanncolmcille, one can identify four distinct regions:

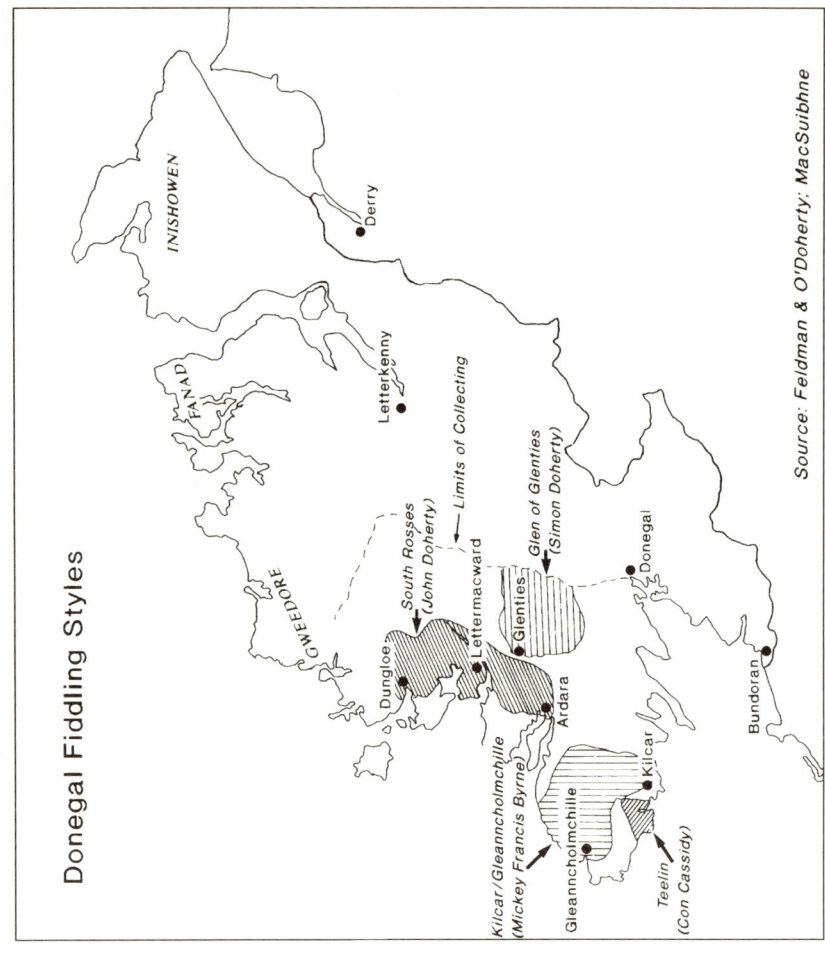

I **South Rosses** The style here was heavily influenced by the Doherty family of the Lettermacward district, and can be heard in the region stretching from Dungloe to Ardara. It is distinguished by the use of strict tempo – one bow stroke per note – and by the staccato sound, mimicked from the Highland pipes chanter.

II **Kilcar/Gleanncolmcille** The style here has more syncopated bowing, uses triplets to mimic the piper's cran and relies heavily on droning.

III **Glens of Glenties** The style (exemplified by Simon Doherty) is halfway between the Gleanncolmcille and the Rosses tradition, and utilises a greater amount of slides on the fingering than elsewhere, giving an almost 'bluesy' feel to the fiddling.

IV **Teelin** As exemplified by Con Cassidy, the music here avoids piping techniques and is created by a long, or slurred bowing style, closer to the Fermanagh/Sligo tradition. It was influenced more by the McConnell than the Doherty family tradition.

It would be intriguing to see if these fiddling regions were replicated in other aspects of popular culture – accent or dialect, for example. The sharp break between the Rosses and Gweedore seems to be evident in the general absence of traditional fiddlers in the Gweedore area – a consequence of 'the bonfire of the vanities' made by Canon James McFadden in the 1880s, when he burned every single musical instrument in the parish, as so many instruments of the devil and distractors from work and piety. As a result, the pipe band has become the dominant musical tradition in Gweedore – one more in a long line of features which distinguish it from the Rosses.[37] Regrettably, Michael Traynor's wonderful collection of seven thousand dialect words in the English of Donegal does not distinguish the undoubted dialect regions which exist within the county.[38]

The various styles of Donegal fiddling and their regional variations can be seen as an example of the bottom-up creation of regional identities. But these are now exposed to immense homogenising stresses. Most obviously, the availability of commercial recordings, beginning in the 1920s with those of the great Sligo fiddler, Michael Coleman, tended to create a unified style and repertoire, and a consequent loss of regional distinctiveness. A second erosive factor on the plurality of styles was the co-option of traditional music as a cultural expression of national identity, and associated efforts to disseminate the music in the public sphere via

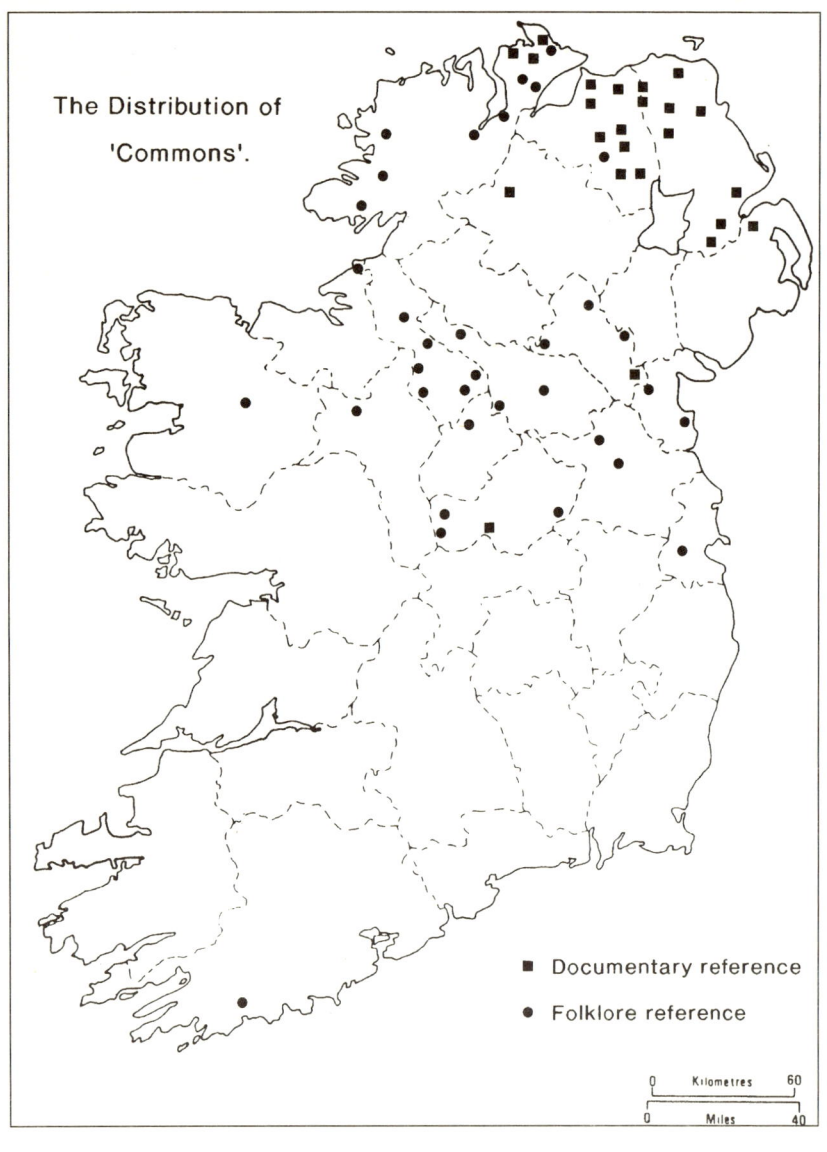

organisations. This folk revival, as with all such efforts at external manipulation of tradition, tended to be highly selective, creating a preferred 'national' musical style, compounded out of the Sligo and Clare traditions. Inevitably, legitimation by public recognition popularised this tradition at the expense of others, and Donegal music especially suffered due to its obvious contamination by Scottish influences. Thus, traditional music's *caighdeán oifigiúil* had the same imperialist effect of blurring or erasing local traditions, as did the linguistic *caighdeán* on the vigour of Irish language dialects. A similar standardisation occurred in Irish dancing in the early twentieth century, and it is only with the relatively recent (and bottom-up) resurgence of set dancing that the variety of regional styles has reasserted itself. It would therefore appear that co-option by the state or nationalist movements has an inbuilt dynamic of standardisation which is inimical to the heteroglossia of regional styles and traditions in popular culture. Nonetheless, the Donegal fiddle tradition is still, in the words of Damhnait Mac Suibhne, alive, vibrant and wholly indigenous, with its corpus of musical material surviving intact, to a large extent.[39]

The Creation of a Region: The example of hurling

> *Rugby is a game for ruffians played by gentlemen, soccer is a game for gentlemen played by ruffians, Gaelic football is a game for ruffians played by ruffians but hurling is a game for gentlemen played by gentlemen.*

A second, and broader, example of how a region can be created is offered by the game of hurling. If we wish to understand how it is that the game is popular in a compact region based in east Munster and south Leinster, we must look at the interrelationship between environment, history, politics and community life. Let us look first at the historical roots of the game.[40] By the eighteenth century, it is quite clear that there were two principal, and regionally distinct, versions of the game. One was akin to modern field hockey, or shinty, in that it did not allow handling of the ball; it was played with a narrow, crooked stick; it used a hard wooden ball (the 'crag'): it was mainly a winter game. This game, called camán (and anglicised to 'commons') was confined to the northern half of the

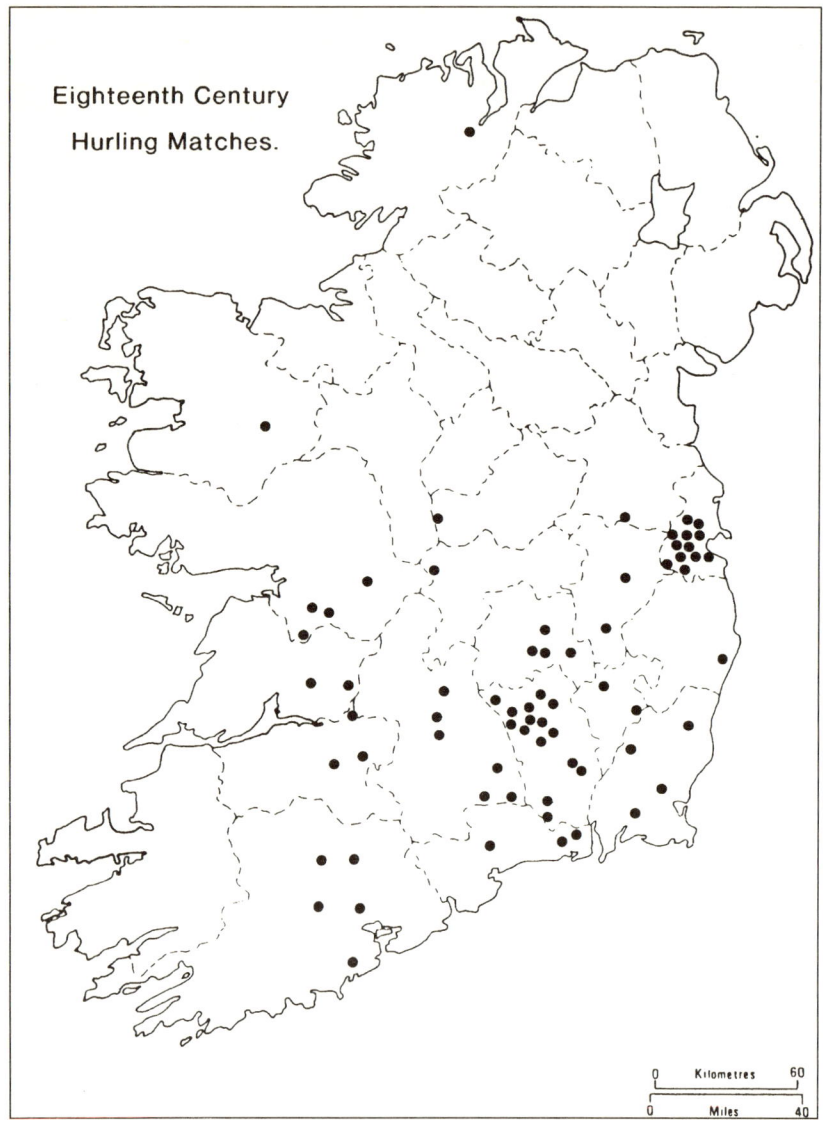

country: its southern limits were set sharply where the small farms of the drumlin belt petered out into the pastoral central lowlands.

The second version of the game (iomáin or báire) was of southern provenance. The ball could be handled or carried on the hurl, which was flat and round headed: the ball (the sliotar) was soft and made of animal hair; the game was played in Summer. Unlike commons, this form of hurling was patronised by the gentry, was a spectator and gambling sport, associated with fairs and other public gatherings, and involved a much greater degree of organisation (including advertising) than the more demotic 'commons'. A 1742 plug for Ballyspellan Spa in Kilkenny noted that 'horseracing, dancing and hurling will be provided for the pleasure of the quality at the spa'.[41]

If we were trying to interpret the distribution pattern of this southern version of the game, we would have to draw on a number of factors:

1. Landlord patronage was essential – from families like the Cosbys and Barringtons in Laois, the Colcloughs and Carews in Wexford, the Purcells and Mathews in Tipperary.
2. The distribution was closely linked to well drained low-lying level terrain – in effect, very seldom moving off the dry sod of the limestone areas. Ash, for example, the best material for making hurls grows best on limestone.
3. The game is closely linked to the distribution of big farms areas with a comfortable lifestyle.
4. The hurling zone is the area where in the late medieval period, the older Norman and Gaelic worlds fused to produce a vigorous hybrid culture reflected, for example, in the towerhouse as an architectural innovation.

By the mid-nineteenth century, for a variety of reasons, hurling declined so steeply that it survived only in three pockets, in Cork city, in south-east Galway and in the area north of Wexford town. Amongst these reasons were the decline of gentry patronage in an age of political turbulence, the rise of Sabbitudinarianism, modernisation and the dislocating impact of the Famine. Landlord, priest and magistrate all turned against the game. As one hostile observer put it: 'A hurling is a scene of drunkeness, blasphemy and all kinds and manner of debauchery and faith, for my part, I would liken it to nothing else but to the idea I form of the Stygian regions

The Hurling Region.

where the daemonic inhabitants delight in torturing and afflicting each other.'⁴²

Once landlord patronage was removed, the structures which supported the game crumbled and the game collapsed into a shapeless anarchy. If we place this in a broader perspective, we know that the progressive separation of the manners and language of the elite from the common people is a pan-European phenomenon in the modern period. The gentry's disengagement from immersion in the shared intimacies of daily life can be seen not just in hurling, but in other areas of language, music, sport and behaviour, as the gradual reception of metropolitan ideas eroded the older, and more particularist loyalties.

The model of elite participation in popular culture, as specified by Peter Burke, is a three-fold process: first immersion, then withdrawal, and finally rediscovery invariably by an educated elite, and often with a nationalist agenda.⁴³ 'Rediscovery' usually involves an invention of tradition, creating a packaged, homogenised and often false version of an idealised popular culture – as, for example, in the cult of the Highland kilt.⁴⁴ The relationship of hurling and the newly established Gaelic Athletic Association in the 1880s shows this third phase with textbook clarity. Thus, when Michael Cusack set about reviving the game, he codified a synthetic version, principally modelled on the southern 'iomáin' version that he had known as a child in Clare. Not surprisingly, this new game never caught on in the old 'commons' area, with the Antrim glens being the only major exception. Cusack and his GAA backers also wished to use the game as a nationalising idiom, a symbolic language of identity filling the void created by the speed of anglicisation.⁴⁵ It had therefore to be sharply fenced off in organisational terms from competing 'anglicised' sports like cricket, soccer and rugby. Thus, from the beginning, the revived game had a nationalist veneer, its rules of association bristling like a porcupine with protective nationalist quills on which its perceived opponents would have to impale themselves. Its principal backers were those already active in the nationalist political culture of the time, classically the IRB. Its spread depended on the active support of an increasingly nationalist Catholic middle class – and as in every country concerned with the invention of tradition its social constituency included especially journalists, publicans, schoolteachers, clerks, artisans and clerics. Thus, hurling's early success was in east Leinster and south Munster, the very region which pioneered popular Irish nationalist politics – from the O'Connell campaign to the devotional revolution in Irish Catholicism, from Fr. Matthew's Temperance campaign, to the Fenians, to the take over of local government. The GAA was a classic example of the radical conservatism of this region – conservative in its ethos and ideology, radical in its techniques of organisation and mobilisation. The spread of hurling can be very closely matched to the spread of other radical conservative movements of this period – the diffusion of the indigenous Catholic teaching orders, the spread of co-operative dairying (based on the older 'meitheal' or 'comhar na gcomharsan' tradition).[46]

It would, however, be a mistake to see the spread of hurling under the aegis of the GAA solely in nationalist terms. The codification and success of Gaelic games should be compared to the almost contemporaneous success in Britain of codified versions of soccer and rugby. All these were linked to rising spending power, a shortened working week (and the associated development of the 'weekend'), improved and cheaper mass transport facilities which made spectator sports viable, expanded leisure time, the desire for organised sport among the working classes, and the commercialisation of leisure itself. The really distinctive feature of the GAA's success was that it occurred in what was still a predominantly agrarian society. That success rested on the shrewd application of the principle of territoriality.

Irish rural life was essentially local life. Hurling was quintessentially a territorially-based game – teams based on communities, parishes, counties, pitted one against the other. The painter Tony O'Malley has contrasted this tribal-territorial element in Irish sport to English attitudes:

> *If neighbours were playing like New Ross and Tullogher, there would be a real needle in it. When Carrickshock were playing I once heard an old man shouting 'come on the men that bate the tithe proctors' and there was a tremor and real fervour in his voice. It was a battle cry, with hurleys as the swords, but with the same intensity.*[47]

Similar forces of territoriality have been identified behind the success of cricket in the West Indies and rugby in the Welsh valleys. The GAA tapped this deep-seated territorial loyalty, of the type which is beautifully captured in the rhetorical climax of the great underground classic of rural Ireland, *Knocknagow or the Homes of*

Tipperary by Charles J. Kickham – a book which has been continuously in print since its publication in 1874 and has gone through over fifty editions. It is the scene where Matt Donovan (Matt the Thresher), the village hero, is competing against the outsider Captain French in a sledge-throwing contest. In the absence of steroids Matt is pumping himself up before his throw:

> *Some one struck the big drum a single blow, as if by accident and, turning round quickly, the thatched roofs of the hamlet caught his eye. And, strange to say, those old mud walls and thatched roofs roused him as nothing else could. His breast heaved, as with glistening eyes, and that soft plaintive smile of his, he uttered the words. 'For the credit of the little village!'... His eyes dilated as, with quivering nostrils, he watched its flight, till it fell so far beyond the best mark that even he himself started with astonishment. Then a shout of exultation burst from the excited throng; hands were convulsively grasped, and hats sent flying in the air; and in their wild joy they crushed around and tried to lift him upon their shoulders.*[48]

The territorial allegiance and communal spirit celebrated and idealised by Kickham have died hard in Ireland. GAA club colours, for example, were often drawn from old faction-favours and, even now, an occasional faction slogan can still be heard. 'If any man can, an Alley man can'. 'Squeeze 'em up Moycarkey and hang 'em out to dry!'. Lingering animosities can sometimes surface in surprising ways: it is not unknown, for example, for an irate and disappointed Wexford hurling supporter (and what other kind of Wexford supporter is there but a disappointed or irate one?) to hurl abuse at Kilkenny, recalling an incident that occurred in Castlecomer to indignant Wexford United Irishmen: 'Sure what good are they anyway? Didn't they piss on the powder in '98?'

As well as this territorial principle of pride in the parish and county, hurling also requires sympathetic nurture at the childhood stage. Because a highly complex array of skills are required for proficiency, it is extraordinarily rare for even a teenager who takes up the game to be a good hurler. By then it is too late. From early childhood on, the hurl needs to become a natural extension of the hand. And as hurling is a team sport, the young hurler requires companions. Willie Nolan describes the scene in a Tipperary childhood.

The child was introduced to hurling in a slow, almost languid fashion. The progress was gradual. As he learned to talk, he learned to hurl. Young lads hurled because it was the thing to do and were informally coached in the field of experience. The open countryside, a level field, a sympathetic farmer, a couple of geansaí-draped stones as imaginary goals and a band of young lads striking, pulling and soloing.[49]

But that field of experience had also to be a field of dreams, nourished by both community support and external stimuli, like the magical voices of Micheál O Hehir or Micheál Ó Muircheartaigh. Bobby Rackard of the celebrated Wexford hurling dynasty describes the effect of such stimuli in his childhood at Killann:

There were very few radios and about the only one in the village at that time was the one in our huge kitchen. So on a Sunday afternoon that a match was being broadcast, the kitchen was cleared out by my mother, and there were extra seats put in to accommodate the locals to come in and listen to the match. As young lads we couldn't get a seat but we'd be down on one knee, crouched around the radio. We'd have the hurlies parked just outside the door and the minute the match was over, we'd grab the hurlies and you'd be out in the field, and you'd be Mick Mackey of Limerick or John Keane of Waterford. And it was that which helped to fire our imagination![50]

Hurling also required a strong base in the schools to survive. The great nurseries of the game have been the secondary schools, like St. Kieran's in Kilkenny, St. Flannan's in Ennis, Mount Sion CBS in Waterford, or the 'North Mon' and Farranferris in Cork. The recent revival in Offaly fortunes owed much to the work of Birr Community School, while Galway's revival was predicated on intense work on the game in the county's vocational schools. Conversely, the decline in Wexford's fortunes may at least partially be attributed to the demise of St. Peter's College as a major hurling academy.

With the notable exception of Cork, the game has not been successfully transplanted into the cities. In Cork, close knit working-class neighbourhoods like Blackrock and Gouldings Glen (home of Glen Rovers), and the strong antagonism between the hilly northside and the flat southside of the city nourished the territoriality and community spirit so important to the game's health. In Dublin, however, the modern suburbs, based on diversity, newness and mobility, have not proved hospitable receptacles of the game.

If one looks at the present hurling core region, it is remarkably compact.[51] It also exhibits striking continuity with the earlier 'iomáin' region. The hurling heartland is focused on the three counties of Cork, Tipperary and Kilkenny, with a supporting cast of adjacent counties – Limerick, Clare, Galway, Offaly, Laois, Waterford and Wexford, and only an handful of enclaves. In the hurling core, the game is king, and very closely stitched into the fabric of the community. Describing the situation in Rathnure, Billy Rackard claimed that in the absence of hurling, 'the parish would commit suicide, if a parish could commit suicide!' The boundaries of the hurling region are surprisingly well-defined. To the north, the midland bogs act, as in a way they have done throughout history, as a buffer zone, resolutely impervious to the spread of cultural influences from further south. The western edge of the hurling zone can be traced over a long distance. In County Galway, for example, its boundaries run along a line from Ballinasloe to the city; north of this line is the Tuam–Dunmore area, and west of it is Connemara, both footballing territories. In County Clare, the boundary runs from Tubber on the Galway border through Corofin and Kilmaley to Labasheeda on the Shannon estuary. Last summer, the tremendous achievement of Clare in winning a Munster football championship was most thoroughly relished in the footballing bastion of west Clare, from Kilkee and Doonbeg to Miltown Malbay. One could easily establish this pattern by looking at the thickening density of the forest of flags as one drove from east to west in August.

Across the Shannon in Limerick, the football–hurling divide runs clearly along the scarp dividing hilly west Limerick from the lush limestone lowlands of east Limerick. West of this is an enclave of hurling parishes in the footballing kingdom of Kerry in the area north of Tralee, in Ardfert, Ballyheigue, Causeway and Ballyduff. From Limerick, the hurling boundary loops through County Cork from Mallow to the city and then to the coast at Cloyne – home to the maestro Christy Ring, who famously expressed his strategy for promoting the game in Cork – by stabbing a knife through every football found east of that line.

The interesting question then is how these boundaries formed. In almost every case, that boundary divides big farm and small farm areas. This also tends to be superimposed on a transition from fertile, drift-covered limestone lowland to hillier, hungrier, wetter shales, flagstones, grits and granites. In County Galway, for example, hurling has not put down roots in the bony granite outcrops of Connemara, and in Clare the poorly drained namurian deposits are equally inhospitable. If ash is emblematic of hurling areas, the rush is the distinctive symbol of football territory.

Outside this core region, there are only the hurling enclaves in the Glens of Antrim and on the tip of the Ards peninsula, where the clubs of Ballycran, Ballygalget and Portaferry backbone Down's hurling revival.

I have spent some time in considering the origins and development of the hurling region as an example of how such regions come into being and how they are sustained. The final point I want to make concerns the relationship between regionalism, sport and ideology. In the case of hurling, one can clearly differentiate between the attitudes of those who play as opposed to those who administer the game. Players (and the bulk of spectators) enjoy the game as a fast, highly skilled contact sport, with a strong territorial element. It is only at the administrative level that the ideological superstructure was, and is, imposed. The game itself does not depend on the ideology, and would not in any way be diminished or damaged by losing its contact with it. Hurling is inherently a regional, not a national phenomenon.

The Image of the West of Ireland: Construction and Deconstruction

So far, we have explored the origins of two types of region – the micro region of the type associated with the Donegal fiddling tradition, and the macro region associated with the game of hurling. As a third example of the concept of the region, I want to look at the west of Ireland, with the aim of showing that the sense of a region need not be fixed or rooted in immemorial continuity but is instead, fluid, flexible, unstable in its meaning, formed, reformed and deformed by changing ideologies and perceptions. I also want to look briefly at the dialectic between insider and outsider in the creation of a sense of region.

Until the beginning of the nineteenth century, in outside perceptions, the west of Ireland was seen in negative terms. Even the sympathetic Jacobite, Nicholas Plunkett, noting in 1698 its 'want of improvement', described Connacht as 'a waste country, thin peopled, having not one Corporation of note but Galway, small improvements, no money, no markets, for all are sellers, no buyers'.[52] A more hostile observer, Samuel Molyneux, looked at Iar-Chonnacht in 1709 and dismissed both its landscape and people: 'nor could I conceive an inhabited country so destitute of all signs of people and art as this is: yet here I learn, lived multitudes of barbarous, uncivilised Irish'.[53] Thus, Connacht was conceived of as uncivilised, whose natural landscapes rebuked the domesticating, rationalising principles of Augustan taste; this image of barbarity and of being outside the pale of law and civilisation clung to it right through the century, the 'wild Irish' matched to a wild landscape. In 1794, Richard St. George Mansergh St. George observed: 'Conamara is the asylum of outlaws, deserters and persons escaped from justice, the stronghold of smugglers etc'.[54]

It was only in the first half of the nineteenth century, when romantic principles began to spread, that what had previously been seen as negative now was seen in a positive light. Interestingly, the reception of romanticism was considerably slower in the west of Ireland than in Highland Scotland or Wales – due to the sheer density and poverty of the people. The American tourist, William Balch, commented: 'The beauty of the green isle is greatly marred and our journey at every advance made painful by the sight of such an amount of degradation and suffering'.[55] Unlike the relatively empty Scottish Highlands (conveniently cleared), the traveller literally could not see the picturesque in Ireland because it was screened by swarms of people. Thus, the romantic perception of the West had as its shadow its perception as a problem region, which required special administrative and legislative treatment. As early as the 1820s, the Board of Works were developing special infrastructural projects in the West – especially road and pier building. This was the precursor of a long line of such initiatives, stretching through from famine relief, the Congested Districts Board, the Land Commission to Údarás na Gaeltachta in the present day.

A further development in the reception of the west of Ireland came with the popularisation of cultural nationalism. This constructed an image based on the association between national identity and landscape as a confirmation of that cultural identity.[56] This stressed the West as the bearer of the authentic, quintessential Irish identity, encoded in a landscape different to the industrialised, modernised landscapes of contemporary Britain. The cultural nationalist project viewed the West as an idyllic prelapsarian blending of culture and environment, creating a distinctive society and landscape, which had been saved from the pernicious effects of industrialisation, urbanisation and modernisation.[57] Ultimately, this viewpoint surfaced in the Irish literary revival, whose representation of the West was heavily implicated in the politics of culture. Here is William Butler Yeats writing on 'The Galway Plains' in 1903:

There is still in truth upon these great level plains a people, a community bound together by imaginative possessions, by stories and poems which have grown out of its own life, and by a past of great passions which can still waken the heart to imaginative action . . . England or any other country which takes its tune from the great cities and gets its taste from schools and not from old custom may have a mob, but it cannot have a people.[58]

It was only a short step from here to using the distinctiveness of the West as an argument for national independence. Once the southern state achieved autonomy, that view of the West as the exemplary Ireland found expression in its special treatment – notably in the 1926 creation of the Gaeltacht. It can also be seen in the western heartland of Fianna Fáil support. One can visually represent the special emphasis on the west as the most authentic Irish region by looking at a map showing those areas from which the Irish Folklore Commission has collected over five hundred pages of folklore. We can see here the notion of the 'Hidden Ireland' – which, as projected by Daniel Corkery, had a strong regional dimension in 'the hard mountain lands of west Cork and Kerry, the barren Comeraghs in Waterford, the hidden glens in the Galtees and other mountains, the wild seaboard of the south and west, the windswept uplands of Clare, the back places of Connemara, much of Donegal'.[59]

I have demonstrated elsewhere how misleading this view is of the west of Ireland, as the most 'authentic' and 'oldest' of Irish regions. Estyn Evan's work, for example, is seriously compromised by his adoption of the view that 'the centuries fall away as one approaches the Atlantic and to journey from east to west is to travel into the past'.[60] Social anthropologists too have popularised this conceptualisation of the west as an ancient peasant world, a refuge area on the rim of the European continent, a world of timeless survival which retained the oldest and most basic elements in the Irish settlement and social system. With the exception of the language, this conceptualisation is questionable. Large swathes of the west of Ireland were only permanently settled in the late eighteenth and early nineteenth centuries, a response to the surging demographic profile of Ireland, and dependent on the potato, rundale cultivation and proto-industrialisation. In this sense, much of Atlantic Ireland was covered not with the oldest but the newest settlement layer in the country, an adventitious veneer born out of grotesque, unbelievable, bizarre and unprecedented demographic circumstances. And this was not a 'to hell or to Connacht' scenario, where the hewers of wood and drawers of water further east had been moved west and mutated into the 'cute hoors' of Connacht. In the late eighteenth century, the Connacht economy was booming – based on the exquisite adaptation of the rundale system to the local environment. The prolific and never-failing potato, good prices for young cattle and oats, proto-industrialisation, fishing, kelp and poitín making. Turf was ubiquitous to provide fuel, houses could be cheaply constructed using local materials, and in the relatively open and egalitarian rundale villages, there were few impediments to parents subdividing with their children.[61]

Thus in the late eighteenth and early nineteenth centuries, Connacht must have appeared as a poor man's paradise, where there was a good chance of the poor man becoming independent. And this lay behind the population boom. As the French traveller, Coquebert de Montbret expressed it in 1791: 'Eyre Connaught is thickly populated because of the ease with which turf can be got, the pasture-lands, the seaweeds for manure and shellfish for the poor man'.[62] The local proverb succinctly expressed the same point: 'Dá mbeadh prátaí is móin againn, bheadh an saol ar a thóin againn'. A contemporary Connemara observer noted: 'If they have turf and potatoes enough, they reckon themselves provided for; if a few herrings, a little oatmeal and above all the milk of a cow can be added, they are rich, they can enjoy themselves and dance with a light heart after the day's work is over'.[63]

Looked at in this way, one can see that the west of Ireland meant something quite different to those who lived in it, than to those who created its public image. Paul Henry's canvases, with their luxuriant celebration of changing skies and elemental nature were at least as much a response to what he described as his stifling childhood in a non-conformist Belfast family, where he had to 'smoke in secret, drink in secret and think in secret'.[64] One can also say that the prevalent scholarly image of the West, as created, for example by Evans, is just as much a construct of the *perceptual* as the *actual* west of Ireland. In a scalding critique, John Andrews has rebuked those who seek ethnic and ahistorical explanations of the evolution of the west of Ireland:

> *Many people in this country have felt themselves as exiles from an Irish 'garden of Eden' and regarded historical research as a way of getting back into it. They have seen our modern culture, including our cultural landscape, as a mixture of alien with indigenous elements, and they have longed to get behind that heterogeneous facade to a world that was pure, uncontaminated and freshly minted. They longed to find back there at the far end of the historical rainbow, a crock of twenty four carat genuine Irish gold. But since this prize could never be recovered intact from any single historical source it had to be reconstructed, as an archaeologist uses broken fragments to reconstruct a beaker or food vessel – except that in this case every single fragment, nineteenth century, seventeenth century or whatever (just as long as it was not obviously English or Scottish or Welsh or Norman or Viking) had to be assembled with all the other fragments from all the other periods to make one huge Irish geographic pot – what Otway Ruthven calls 'the native system'. The idea of a single Irish settlement type with its clachans and its rundale laid out as it were for all eternity in some platonic heaven is a persuasive one.*[65]

The West, for a variety of reasons, in a variety of ways, in a variety of disciplines, came to be regarded as the authentic Irish area, an area of cultural survival and continuity which conserved cultural and settlement features swept away elsewhere. Such a view, as I have briefly shown, is no longer tenable but its extraordinary persistence is a powerful reminder of the strength and durability of regional stereotyping, not just at the popular, but at the academic level.

The Region in Historiography

How has the regional debate impacted in historiography? Firstly, one might note the renewed tension between a centralised national history, predominantly driven by political imperatives, and the fissiparous regional histories, where social, economic and cultural perspectives have been centre-stage. One might also note that this emphasis on a historical narrative in which politics is privileged, is shared by both the old nationalist and the newer revisionist approach. The post-nationalist, post-revisionist project looks increasingly to regional perspectives which contest their centralised orthodoxy and, in turn, proclaim a more genuinely pluralist message.[66]

In practical terms, the strident and increasingly repetitive debate has become locked into stereotyping of national identities and into exclusivist claims on ownership of the past. This has encouraged some to seek alternative modes of understanding the past, which step outside the narrow ground of politics and a politicised historiography. The historians' monopoly of the past has been implicitly challenged on both the academic and the popular level. The sharpening profile of archaeology in the popular consciousness has much to do with the fact that wedge tombs and Beaker folk inhabit a world beyond history, and therefore beyond politics, and yet they also allow for a sense of continuity and antiquity, removed from essentialist claims. Archaeology offered in this sense a neutral, not narrow ground, in which engagement with the past did not have as its doppelganger a political project. The successful launch of a popular magazine, *Archaeology Ireland*, in 1987, the painstaking county inventories compiled by the Sites and Monuments Record Office under the leadership of Geraldine Stout and Michael Gibbons, the high public profile of excavations like Céide fields and Knowth – all reflect this change.

As with archaeology, the rise of environmental history provided a different lens for looking at the past, a lens whose perspective was longer and radically different from those used in history. The inanimate world of stones and pollen, bogs and trees, seemed for some to offer a sense of a sympathetic engagement with a past beyond political contestation, of an enduring bedrock beneath history, a silent witness under the cacophony of competitive historical voices. This Irish movement gained impetus from the deepening global environmental consciousness, offering the possibility of an environmental ethic at once scrupulously local and yet engaged with the wider world, securely rooted in the present and yet with a satisfying sense of age-old continuities in time and tide, bird and blossom, rock and rain – in Braudel's famous words, that the flowers would bloom every Spring. Such engagements were lovingly rendered in fine books like Frank Mitchell's *The way that I followed*[67] and Tim Robinson's *Stones of Aran*[68], and in John Feehan's television series. The strengthening of the environmental voice was evident in the Mullaghmore debate in which, for the first time, a broad constituency was mobilised behind a campaign arguing for the autonomy of the environment itself. The sheer quality and commercial success of three recent books on the Burren is also indicative of this new trend – Charles Nelson and Wendy Walsh's *The Burren*[69], Jeff O'Connell and Anna Korffs *Book of the Burren*[70], and Gordon D'Arcy's *Natural History of the Burren.*[71]

Besides archaeological and environmental perspectives, a third growth area in responses to the Irish past has been in the field of family history. The momentum here was initially driven by the diaspora, but increasingly gained local impetus as well. Here, the historical sense has been removed from the public to the private sphere, and again into a world beyond politics. Most visibly of all, however, local history has been a growth area in both quantitative and qualitative terms. One can see how the disintegration, or challenges to, the prevailing historical consensus, the pace and direction of cultural change, the agonised questionings generated by the northern crisis, all worked together to clear spaces which local history could inhabit. As with archaeological, environmental or genealogical perspectives, local history could provide a sense of place, of anchoring, free of the freight of the politics of identity. With its diverse micronarratives local history acted as a defense mechanism against both the ruthless totalising claims of historical meta-narratives, and against the rootless blandness of mainstream Anglo-American consumer culture.[72] The sense of place, and of shared historical experiences, is a necessary component of a sense of community. Like any work of art, the sense of place abolishes time and establishes memory.

Within mainstream academic history, one can also see evidence of disaffection from the imperialist claims of political history as a totality. Those marginalised within these parameters of power –

women, minorities, the undocumented – have begun to undermine this conservative bastion.[73] Some professional historians have also turned to regional history to test – and subvert – the validity of national generalisations. Noteworthy examples are James Donnelly's explorations of popular protest[74], Bill Crawford's of the Ulster linen industry[75], Kevin O'Neill on pre-Famine demography[76], Cormac Ó Gráda on the impact of the Famine[77], and Louis Cullen on the 1798 Rebellion.[78] Cullen, perhaps the most influential and productive historian of his generation, has been especially alert to the significance of regional perspectives in understanding Irish history.[79]

Beyond history, other disciplines have also begun to interrogate the Irish past. Henry Glassie's sensitive Fermanagh-based piece of social anthropology, *Passing the Time*, is already a classic, notable for its respectful treatment of oral history, elsewhere so often-derided as meretricious.[80] Folklore, too, has been intensely aware of the value of local perspectives, notably in the work of Caoimhín Ó Danachair.[81] As a discipline, it has also consistently argued the common material base of Irish life, not least in Ulster, a point beautifully illustrated in Alan Gailey's *Rural Houses of the North of Ireland*.[82] The Ulster Folk and Transport Museum at Cultra is a successful effort to publicly demonstrate this, where exhibits at once attractive and authoritative are welded to an impressive scholarly base. Literary criticism has now also begun to interrogate historical narrative and, in so doing, may increasingly challenge Irish historiography's positivist obsession, and its trust in narrative as a stable purveyor of truth. *The Field Day Anthology* was three weighty stones dropped in this stagnant methodological pool; while deconstructionist or post-modern ripples still only lap on the outer shores of historiographical consciousness, their long term impact may well be to problematise text, and to force history to recognise the fundamental ontological instability of narrative itself. Only a handful of historians, notably Tom Dunne, have realised that the future of the Irish past lies in this direction.[83] For an example of its implications, David Lloyd's *Nationalism and Minor Literature* is a landmark volume.[84]

In a curious way, both nationalist and revisionist projects in Irish history have operated within an essentially English historiographical tradition. Both have remained hermetically sealed from developments in the non-anglophone world, notably in France, which

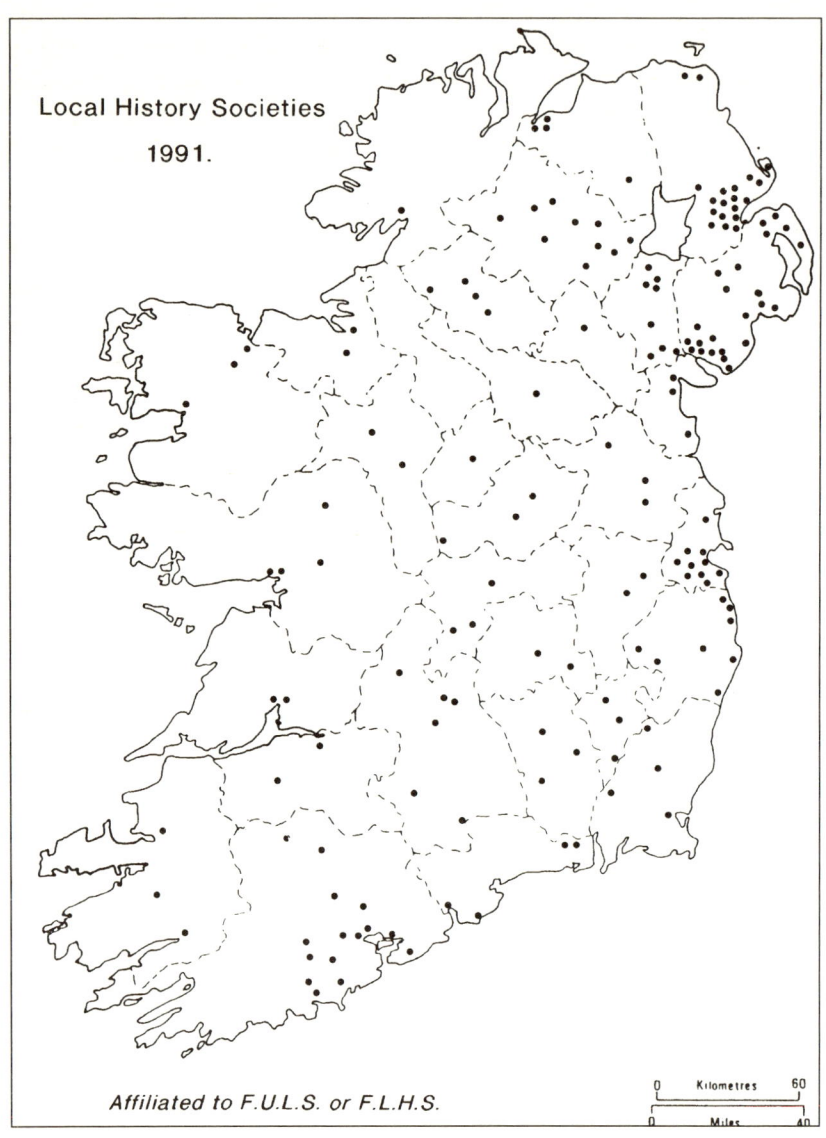

hosted arguably the most significant experiments in history writing in the second half of the twentieth century.[85] This is represented by the Annales school, and by historians like Bloch, Braudel[86], and Le Roy Ladurie.[87] In a roundabout way, historical geography has managed to smuggle some of these French concepts, such as regionalism, onto the Irish agenda. Its two most significant practitioners, Estyn Evans[88] in Queens and Tom Jones Hughes[89] in UCD, were both trained in the French *geographie humaine*, with its emphasis on the dialectic between history and environment, between *la longue durée* and *les evenements*, and on the interpretation of the cultural landscape as a text to be decoded. In this perspective, existing cultural landscapes are seen as the cumulative creation of centuries of experience, in which human desires and needs have transformed the natural environment. They are communal archives, palimpsests created by the sedimentation of cultural experience through time. The cultural landscape is therefore potentially a democratic document, from which can be recuperated the history of the undocumented. In this approach, history is reconstructed by seeing the landscape through the eyes of those who made it. This generates a broader sense of the past than can be derived from the circumscribed and narrow perspective of *écriture* on its own.[90] Under the tutelage of Evans and Jones Hughes, landscape became a braille over whose surface the geographical mind passed the tips of its understanding and sympathy to arrive at a reading of what lay behind the landscape. Such perspectives succeeded in revealing a rich mosaic of regional diversity, even in the relatively confined space of a small island. Evans' *Mourne Country* is the classic of this tradition, and is a compelling expression of how the power of place can enrich the historical consciousness.[91]

At the creative level, there is still considerable vitality in the sense of place as an inspiration. Neil Jordan, for example, while alert to 'the huge pressure of tradition', was nevertheless keen to use his own childhood landscape around Bray and Wicklow in his films, and to make it as 'resonant and familiar' to a mass audience as any Hollywood set.[92] In popular music, talents as diverse as Van Morrison, the Saw Doctors, Sharon Shannon and Gerald Barry all derive creative energy from the encounter with place. Donegal looms massively in the theatrical work of Brian Friel and Frank McGuinness and Billy Roche's work could not be understood without its Wexford town setting. In literature, McGahern's Leitrim,

Keane's north Kerry, McCabe's Monaghan are all umbilically linked while in painting the sense of place – of internalised landscape or inscape[93] – is powerfully immanent in work as diverse as Tony O'Malley's, Cathy Prendergast's, Camille Souter's and Brian Bourke's. Poets above all have been nurtured by, and in turn nurture in a reflexive process, the sense of regionalism. Heaney's south Derry, Muldoon's Moy, Mahon's Glengormley, Coady's Carrick-on-Suir, McGuckian's north Antrim, Carson's Belfast, are all good examples of this.

In one case a whole town's recent identity has been created around the art nucleus. Spearheaded by the Druid Theatre Company, Galway city has made a huge contribution to Irish drama in the last two decades. At once inward looking and outward looking, Druid held up a two-way mirror to the West of Ireland: while exploring local life through the work of Tom Murphy, M.J. Molloy and J.M. Synge, it also worked in a broad theatrical context, stretching from the classics to the most contemporary European drama.[94] Druid also slowly nurtured a new theatre-going audience in Galway, coaxed out of the city centre to the down-at-heels Spanish Arch. They were noticeably successful in breaking the class and age barriers which elsewhere seem to fence off the theatre from a broad engagement with local life. They also encouraged collaboration with locally-based artists like Joe Boske or Brian Bourke, and musicians like Seán Tyrell, and succeeded also in developing new Irish playwrights like Kenneth Burke and Vincent Woods. Maelíosa Stafford's recent powerful production of Woods' *At the Black Pig's Dyke* broke new ground in exploring the dramatic potential of the stylised vernacular dramatic tradition of mumming, allied to an exact and intimate use of traditional music, dance and rhyme – used not to celebrate but to interrogate that tradition.

Druid had three impacts on Galway. Their example stimulated other local theatrical initiatives, which blossomed in the success of Macnas, the Galway Arts Festival, Punchbag and more recently The Galway Youth Theatre. Secondly, Druid was a physical catalyst in transforming the decrepit Spanish Arch area and a cultural catalyst in creating a sense of vibrancy in the city, which ultimately contributed to its self-confident regeneration in the last decade. Thirdly, Druid's example encouraged the breakthrough of bands working in a self-consciously Galway idiom – notably the Saw Doctors, the Stunning and the immigrant Waterboys.

The future of the Irish rural landscape

One of the most visible signs of changing attitudes to the Irish past is the increased emphasis on tourist-directed interpretation, notably in the heritage-centre concept. While the rush to interpret the Irish past and the Irish countryside has proceeded apace, the destruction of the regional cultures, communities and landscapes which they claim to interpret has accelerated at an even greater pace. From the 1960s, there has been unprecedented transformation in the Irish countryside. Unease over the scale of change has crystallised around the 'Bungalow Bliss' debate. The ubiquitous bungalow has swathed the Irish countryside in an incongruously suburban and increasingly uniform idiom.[95] The failure to acknowledge distinctive regional traditions and to respect environmental standards was in part due to the sheer rapidity with which the modernisation project struck rural Ireland, after more than a century of stagnation. It was also due to its advent in the 1960s and '70s, at a time when the architectural profession worldwide and their clients were still wedded to modernist *hubris*, their necks and their buildings set in concrete, gazing relentlessly to the cosmopolitan future. In Ireland, the response by the architectural profession to Fitzsimon's pattern book was bilious rhetoric, condescending dismissal, or a wringing of aesthetic hands: there was no effort made to provide competitive alternative pattern books and, in the absence of choice, young Irish couples wishing to build a cheap bungalow simply had no option but to resort to Fitzsimon's, whose bungalows now festoon Irish roads, like flies along a sticky tape.

This architectural failure to protect and develop the particularity of the vernacular tradition was also symptomatic of the tendency of planners, conservationists and geographers to see the rural landscape, not as a complex and unified assemblage, but as a series of discrete elements which could be planned for in isolation – archaeological and historical sites, nature reserves, national parks, bogs, forests, houses and infrastructure . . . This fragmented approach led to conflicts, misunderstandings, overlaps and an overwhelming neglect of any holistic view of landscape. This explains the lack of interest in producing plans for the overall sustainability of wider cultural landscape assemblages – the Burren, or Inis Oírr, or the Mooncoin farm villages, for example.[96]

Given these developments, and given the plethora of competitive planning agencies, maintaining the coherent character of Irish regions and their landscapes is obviously a problem of great political and managerial complexity. The most crucial question facing Ireland as a whole in the post-CAP and post-SEM Europe is the continuing viability of rural life. If, as is commonly argued, two million of the current nine million European farmers could produce sufficient food for the EC's needs, then a very large part of the European landscape could, for the first time in history, be simply withdrawn from agricultural production. The question of what to do with that vast freed landscape and how to absorb the seven million farmers displaced in the process has not been sufficiently broached at the European, let alone Irish, level, but the scale of the problem is hinted at in recent French events. In a deregulated environment, agricultural production would inevitably be located in the fertile and accessible European core. The corollary of this concentration would be immense dislocation in the peripheral agricultural regions, the impoverished European crescent that sweeps from Scotland via Ireland to Iberia, and thence to southern France, Italy and Greece. One result can already be seen in the French Midi – complete desertion of large-scale rural areas and consequent landscape dereliction. We stand at the verge of a quantum leap in the evolution of rural Europe, a revolution equivalent to the Mesolithic–Neolithic transition, or the agricultural revolution of the eighteenth century. For many rural communities, that leap is a leap into oblivion, given that it is estimated that only 20% of the current one hundred and eighty thousand Irish farmers are economically viable.

In the absence of intervention, two results will evolve from this massive upheaval: (i) large parts of marginal Europe will abdicate from agriculture, with consequent depopulation, reafforestation and the turning over of the countryside solely to recreational use. (ii) In the fertile, intensively farmed core, a homogeneous, machine friendly monoculture will evolve, the agricultural landscape dissolving to a blandscape. The argument against intervention in this process is that 'preservation' of rural communities by legislative and redistributive instruments is in effect an embalming, a sterile end-to-history which artificially impedes the dynamism of communities and landscapes, and creates a mere ghost-world, a rural caricature, maintained not for the benefit of those who live within it but for nakedly exploitative tourist reasons. The argument for intervention is that non-intervention is also an end-of-history, in that large-scale change will irrevocably scour away inherited communities which were for centuries the cradles of European culture.[97]

Before one consigns these rural communities and their regional cultures to the crowded dustbins of European history, we should bear three points in mind. Firstly, the growing strength of the ecological movement worldwide will generate awareness of the problems and create a more favourable milieu for both conceptualisation and implementation of planning. As yet the Republic of Ireland has the most feeble conservation legislation of any EC country. Secondly, tourism is the most vital 'renewable resource' within the Irish economy and much of it is generated by the visual amenity value of the Irish landscape. Conservation and maintenance of that landscape character therefore becomes of strategic importance for tourism. Awareness of total landscape character can extend the focus beyond 'heritage centres', many of them only displaying artefacts in a context-free setting. Thirdly, EC agricultural policy (hitherto the most powerful influence on Irish landscape change) is consciously moving away from grant-led production policies. Other activities (agri-tourism, for example, environmental conservation, pollution control) will be of enhanced, and perhaps central, importance in a future European policy.[98]

In the post-CAP move to extensify rather than to intensify agricultural production, to support individual farmers rather than production, and to phase out subsidies except in cases of environmental benefit, a new environmental ethic may be inculcated, alongside considerations of the social desirability of maintaining small-farm communities. Income support in return for practising farming methods which are environmentally friendly may be one practical possibility. If, in the interests of environment, an ecological infrastructure needs to be constructed, then surely this can be done through enhancing the existing cultural landscape, rather than by starting *de novo*, or by excluding the human dimension. It is dangerous, and misleading, to dichotomise 'nature' and 'culture' and to strive to preserve or create solely 'natural' landscapes. In the deeply humanised European territory, most 'natural' landscapes are in fact anthropogenic, and require human maintenance. The concept of ASIs (Areas of Scientific Interest) now covers areas of specific ecological, floral, faunal or ornithological interest, thereby encouraging a rigid human/natural dichotomy in their delimitation. 'Static' conservation, with the aim of freezing an area in one moment of time in conformity to contemporary (and possibly ephemeral) canons of taste or priority, should be avoided. Instead, living landscapes should be encouraged, with a more generous sense of conservation possibilities within the inherited cultural landscape and existing communities.

This would involve a widening of the current Environmentally Sensitive Areas (ESAs) scheme, to include not just conservation of natural habitat, but to encompass regional landscapes of outstanding interest, as expressions of ways-of-life. This would then permit the support of agricultural practices compatible with the maintenance of the cultural landscape, while providing an adequate income for farmers, and encouraging ecological diversity. This 'green modulation' (trading income support for management prescriptions) would be ideally suited to areas like the Burren, underpinning farming practices which benefited the environment, simultaneously supporting rural communities in a living landscape. Such a scheme has already been successfully implemented in the Mourne mountains. The other positive dimension of such a 'green' agricultural policy would be its labour-intensive nature and its capacity to absorb more equitably the distribution of capital support. At present 80% of all EC aid to agriculture goes to 20% of the farmers; this aid encourages mechanisation, intensification and displacement of labour. A 'green modulation' would redeploy this highly selective targeting, and would help redress the gross misalignments in standards of living across the EC. Therefore, as well as helping environment, it would help redress the issue of regional inequalities and inequities in distribution within the agricultural community.

The problem with treating rural landscapes as an adjunct to tourism – in effect, commodifying it – is that it runs the risk of turning its creators and custodians – rural communities – into mere objects in the landscape. Instead of producing food, the onus would be on agricultural communities literally to produce landscape, like any other consumer item. Within such a scenario, the developed, urbanised European core would require its periphery to preserve the nature, environment and rural communities which they themselves have destroyed in their own modernisation projects. Obviously, such an asymmetrical relationship would ultimately be exploitative. As far back as 1961, R.S. Thomas's 'Welsh Testament' summarised the problem of being the objectified other of the tourist industry:

> And always there was their eyes' strong
> Pressure on me: You are Welsh, they said;
> Speak to us so; keep your fields free
> Of the smell of petrol, the loud roar
> Of hot tractors; we must have peace
> And quietness.
> Is a museum
> Peace? I asked. Am I the keeper
> Of the heart's relics, blowing the dust
> In my own eyes? I am a man:
> I never wanted the drab role
> Life assigned me, an actor playing
> To the past's audience upon a stage
> Of earth and stone; the absurd label
> Of birth, of race hanging askew
> About my shoulders[99]

Conclusions

The regional level potentially offers the best fit between territorial identities, economic imperatives, ecological sustainability and an appropriate scale for decision-making within the EC. Questions of scale in decision-making have traditionally been treated solely within econometric parameters of functional efficiency and viability in production, distribution and consumption. The debate about ecological sustainability defines a different set of scale parameters, based around ecosystem dynamics. This tension between economic and ecological rationality may be resolved by looking at historically-rooted practical experience in specific regions. Long term economic and ecological needs may best be met at the regional level; embodying minimum levels for economic sustainability and adequate bases for ecological sustainability, the regional level may also empower the concept of subsidiarity. Traditionally, European peoples have identified emotionally with the region, and the resurgent vitality of the regional concept can easily be grasped in Catalonia, Brittany, the Basque country or Macedonia. To maintain the allegiance of its citizens, EC policies and principles must be responsive to specific cultural and regional contexts; it must be recognised that they cannot be transposed without modulation from one region to another. The regional dimension would also be essential to any genuine commitment to principles of subsidiarity within the EC.

Any argument for conservation of landscape and of the rural communities which sustain them always runs the risk of being a retreat into provincialism, or a conservative clarion-call to the faded nationalist pieties of hearth and home, blood and land. However, an alternative argument might seek to support regional distinctiveness which, in European terms, is frequently encoded in landscape. Stripped of meta-narrative and divested of Herderian melodrama, regional cultures are a powerful vernacular force. The valency of the vernacular derives from its salubrious democratic tendency. The stress on the region is potentially a stress on multiculturalism. And diversity in culture may be just as necessary and healthy as diversity in ecology.

The importance of the view from below, of subsidiarity, may be central to the health and vigour of the EC. The poet Seamus Heaney has recently summarised this regional imperative, the power of place, updating Patrick Kavanagh's version of the parochial imagination:

> *Empowered within its own horizons, it looks out but does not necessarily look up to the metropolitan centres. Its impulses and possibilities abound within its boundaries but are not limited by them. It is self-sufficient but not self-absorbed, capable of thought, undaunted, pristine, spontaneous, a corrective to the inflations of nationalism and the cringe of provincialism.*[100]

His fellow poet, Derek Mahon, invokes the same values in his poem, *A Garage in County Cork*, a powerful plea for particularity and for the human dignity of the individual life in place and time:

> *But we are in one place and one place only,*
> *One of the milestones of earth-residence*
> *Unique in each particular, the thinly*
> *Peopled hinterland serenely tense –*
> *Not in the hope of a resplendent future*
> *But with a sure sense of its intrinsic nature.*

As long ago as the 1880s, a celebrated banner was unfurled, reputedly at a Land League meeting in County Kerry. 'Arise Knocknagashel and take your place amongst the nations of the earth'.[101]

Within a restructured EC, in which due weight was given to regional imperatives, is it possible that this banner might once more float, at least conceptually, in the Kingdom breeze?

References
1. This discussion of the social and territorial frameworks of Irish life is based on W.J. Smyth, 'Continuity and change in the territorial organisation of Irish rural communities' Part I *Maynooth Review*, i (1975), pp. 51–73; Part II, pp. 152–201; *ibid.*, 'Social geography of rural Ireland: inventory and prospect' in G. Davies (ed.) *Irish Geography Jubilee Volume* (Dublin, 1984), pp. 204–36; *ibid.*, 'The changing scale of social networks in rural Ireland', lecture at UCD, 10 Dec. 1992. P. Gulliver and M. Silverman, *In the valley of the Nore. A social history of Thomastown, County Kilkenny 1840–1983* (Dublin, 1986). D. Hannon, *Displacement and development. Class, kinship and social change in Irish rural communities* (Dublin 1979).
2. C. Arensberg and S. Kimball, *Family and community in Ireland* (Cambridge, 1940); C. Arensberg, *The Irish countryman* (New York, 1937).
3. Cited in P. Bew, *Land and the national question in Ireland 1858–82* (Dublin, 1978), p. 229.
4. D. Hannon, 'Kinship, neighbourhood and social change in Irish rural communities' in *Ec. Soc. Rev.* iii (1978), pp. 163–89; N. Scheper-Hughes, *Saints, scholars and schizophrenics. Mental illness in rural Ireland* (Berkeley, 1979); L. Millman, *Our like will not be there again. Notes from the west of Ireland* (Boston, 1977); H. Brody, *Inishkillane. Change and decline in the west of Ireland* (Harmondsworth, 1973); J. Healy, *Nineteen Acres* (Galway, 1978).
5. K. Whelan, 'Beyond a paper landscape. J.H. Andrews and Irish historical geography' in F. Aalen and K. Whelan (ed.), *Dublin city and county. From prehistory to present* (Dublin, 1992), esp. pp. 400–403. See also T. Jones Hughes, 'Administrative divisions and the development of settlement in nineteenth-century Ireland' in *University Review*, iii (1964), pp. 8–15.
6. T. Canavan (ed.), *Every stoney acre has a name* (Belfast, 1992).
7. K. Whelan, 'The Catholic parish, the Catholic chapel and village development in Ireland' in *Ir. Geog.*, xv (1983), pp. 1–16.
8. K. Whelan, 'Village and town in Ireland 1600–1900' in A. Verhoeve and J. Vervloet (ed.), *The transformation of the European rural landscape and economy in the modern period* (Wageningen, 1992), pp. 298–305.
9. Cited in S. de Fréine, *Croí Cine* (Dublin, 1990), p. 221.
10. *Ibid.*, p. 220.
11. T. Jones Hughes, 'Regionalism in Ireland' in *Rural Ireland* (1963), pp. 65–71.

12. B. Colfer, *The promontory of Hook* (Wexford, 1978).
13. See S. Deane's superb distillation in *Field Day Anthology*, ii, pp. 807–9 and C. Cruise O'Brien, *The Great Melody. A thematic biography and commented anthology of Edmund Burke* (London, 1992).
14. *Europe sans rivage. L'identité culturelle Europeene* (Paris, 1988).
15. R. Kearney (ed.), *Across the frontiers. Ireland in the 1990s* (Dublin, 1988); *ibid, Visions of Europe* (Dublin, 1992).
16. N. Ascherson, 'Nations and regions' in Kearney, *Visions*, pp. 13–22.
17. R. Breen, D. Hannan, D. Rothman and K. Whelan, *Understanding contemporary Ireland: state, class and development in the Republic of Ireland* (Dublin, 1990), p. 268.
18. J. Lee, *Modern Ireland 1912–1985* (Cambridge, 1991), pp. 559–62.
19. R. Jacobs, *Cities and the wealth of nations* (Harmondsworth, 1984).
20. Cited in Kearney (ed.), *Visions of Europe*.
21. Cited in A. Sampson, *The Anatomy of Britain* (London, 1992).
22. L. O'Dowd, 'Borders in the new Europe', unpublished paper, 1992; L. O'Dowd and J. Corrigan, 'National sovereignty and cross-border co-operation: Ireland in a comparative context', unpublished paper, 1992; A. Giddens, *The nation-state and violence* (Cambridge, 1985).
23. J. Anderson, 'Problems of inter-state economic integration: Northern Ireland and the Irish Republic in the Single European Market', unpublished paper, 1992; J. Anderson and J. Goodman, 'European integration and the national conflict in Ireland' in *Ireland, Europe and the Single Market: geographical perspectives* (Dublin, forthcoming); J. Lundy and A. Mac Poilin (ed.), *Styles of belonging. The cultural identities of Ulster* (Belfast, 1992).
24. T. Lyne, 'Ireland, Northern Ireland and 1992; the barriers to technocratic anti-partitionism' in *Public Administration*, Lxviii (1990), pp. 417–33.
25. United Irishman Declaration, Christmas 1791 in *Report of the Secret Committee* (Dublin, 1798).
26. G. Steiner, 'Culture. The price you pay' in Kearney, *Visions*, pp. 43–54.
27. Anderson, *loc. cit.*
28. T. Barrington, 'Ireland: the interplay of territory and function' in R. Rhodes and V. Wright (ed.), *Tensions in the territorial politics of western Europe* (London, 1987); *ibid*, 'The situation of Irish government' in *Irish Review*, iii (1988), pp. 18–25.
29. B. Chubb, *The government and politics of Ireland* (Dublin, 1991).
30. A. Parker, 'Geography and the Irish electoral system' in *Ir. Geog.*, xviv (1986), pp. 1–14.
31. V. Buckley, *Memory Ireland* (Harmondsworth, 1985), pp. 48–50.
32. [Barrington report], *Local government reorganisation and reform* (Dublin, 1991).

33. J. Phelan and A. Markey, 'An examination of farm income in Ireland' in *Jl. Ag. Economy* (1992), pp. 1–20.
34. A. Feldman and E. O'Doherty, *The Northern fiddler. Music and musicians of Donegal and Tyrone* (Belfast, 1979).
35. D. Mac Suibhne, 'The Donegal fiddle tradition – a social history' in M. Dunleavy and L. Ronayne (ed.), *Donegal, History and society* (Dublin, forthcoming).
36. Feldman and O'Doherty, *Northern fiddler*, p. 50.
37. J. Coll, 'Continuity and change in the parish of Gaoth Dobhair 1850–1980' in W. Smyth and K. Whelan (ed.), *Common ground. Essays on the historical geography of Ireland* (Cork, 1988), pp. 278–95.
38. M. Traynor, *The English dialect of Donegal – a glossary* (Dublin, 1953).
39. Mac Suibhne, *loc. cit.*
40. L. Ó Cathnia, *Scéal na h-iomána ó thosach ama go 1884* (Dublin, 1980); A. Ó Maolfabhail, *Camán. Two thousand years of hurling in Ireland* (Dundalk, 1973).
41. *Faulkner's Dublin Journal*, 22 June 1742.
42. *Freeman's Journal*, 21–25 Aug. 1764.
43. P. Burke, *Popular culture in early modern Europe* (London, 1973).
44. T. Ranger and H. Trevor Roper (ed.), *The invention of tradition* (London, 1983); B. Anderson, *Imagined communities. Reflections on the origins and spread of nationalism* (London, 1983); S. Deane (ed.), *Nationalism, colonialism and literature* (Minnesota, 1990).
45. M. de Búrca, *Michael Cusack and the GAA* (Dublin, 1989).
46. K. Whelan, 'The regional impact of Irish Catholicism 1700–1850' in Smyth and Whelan, *Common Ground*, pp. 253–77.
47. T. O'Malley, 'Inscape: life and landscape in Callan and County Kilkenny' in W. Nolan and K. Whelan (ed.), *Kilkenny. History and society* (Dublin, 1990), pp. 617–32.
48. C. Kickham, *Knocknagow or the homes of Tipperary* (Dublin, 1874), p. 473.
49. W. Nolan, 'Rus in urbe: Hurling in the city', unpublished paper, 1992.
50. Interview with Bobby Rackard, Killann, County Wexford, December 1991.
51. K. Whelan, *The geography of hurling*, Ollscoil Video, UCD 1992.
52. P. Kelly (ed.), 'The improvement of Ireland' in *Anal. Hib.*, xxxv (1992), pp. 47–84.
53. S. Molyneaux, Tour in Connacht in 1709, TCD. MS.606.
54. Nat. Archives, 620/21/18.
55. W. Balch, *Ireland as I saw it* (New York, 1850), p. 43.
56. L. Gibbons, 'Identity without a centre. Allegory, history and Irish nationalism' in *Cultural Studies*, vi (1992), pp. 358–75.

57. C. Nash, 'Embodying the nation. The west of Ireland landscape and Irish identity', unpublished paper, 1992.
58. W. B. Yeats, *Collected Prose* (London, 1968), p. 46.
59. D. Corkery, *The hidden Ireland. A study of Gaelic Munster in the eighteenth century* (Dublin, 1924), p. 6.
60. E. Evans 'Some survivals of the Irish open-field tradition' in *Geography* xxiv (1939).
61. K. Whelan. 'Landscape, settlement and society in the west of Ireland in the pre-Famine period' in J. Plettenberg (ed.), *Proceedings of the Connamara Seaweek Conference* (Clifden, 1991), pp. 1–25; *ibid.*, 'Settlement and society in eighteenth-century Ireland' in G. Dawe and J. Foster (ed.), *The poet's place* (Belfast, 1991).
62. S. Ni Chinneide (ed.), 'Coquebert de Montbret's impressions of Galway city and county in 1791' in *Galway Arch. Soc. Jn.* xxv (1953), pp. 1–14.
63. H. Blake, *Letters from the Irish highlands of Connemara* (London, 1825), p. 68.
64. P. Henry, *Self-portrait* (London, 1952). See Sean O Faolain's comments, *Sunday Independent*, 12 May, 1980.
65. Cited in K. Whelan, 'Beyond a paper landscape', p. 412.
66. K. Whelan, 'The recent writing of Irish history' in *UCD History Review* (1991), pp. 27–35.
67. F. Mitchell, *The way that I followed* (Dublin, 1990).
68. T. Robinson, *Stones of Aran. Pilgrimage* (Dublin, 1986).
69. C. Nelson and W. Walsh, *The Burren. A companion to the wild flowers of an Irish limestone wilderness* (Aberystwyth, 1991).
70. J. O'Connell and A. Korff (ed.), *The Book of the Burren* (Kinvara, 1991).
71. G. D'Arcy, *A natural history of the Burren* (London, 1991).
72. P. Nora, 'Between memory and history: les lieux de memoire' in *Representations*, xxvi (1989).
73. M. O'Dowd, M. McCurtain and M. Luddy, 'An agenda for women's history in Ireland 1500–1900' in I.H.S. xxviii (1992), pp. 1–37.
74. J. Donnelly, 'Irish agrarian rebellion: the Whiteboys of 1769–76' in *RIA Proc.*, lxxxiii (1983), C (and further articles cited therein).
75. W.H. Crawford, 'The political economy of linen: Ulster in the eighteenth century' in C. Brady, M. O'Dowd and B. Walker (ed.), *Ulster. An illustrated history* (London, 1989), pp. 134–57 (and articles cited therein).
76. K. O'Neill, *Family and Farm in pre-Famine Ireland: the parish of Killeshandra* (Madison, 1984).
77. C. Ó Gráda, *Ireland. A new economic history 1780–1939* (Oxford, forthcoming) (and further articles cited therein).

78. L. Cullen, 'Politics and rebellion: Wicklow in the 1790's, in K. Hannigan (ed.) *Wicklow. History and society* (Dublin, forthcoming) (and further articles cited therein).
79. L. Cullen, *The emergence of modern Ireland 1600–1900* (London, 1981).
80. H. Glassie, *Passing the time. Folklore and history of an Ulster community* (Dublin, 1982). For two excellent oral history projects, see K. Kearns, *Stoneybatter. Dublin's inner-urban village* (Dublin, 1989), and D. Donnelly, *On Lough Neagh's shores. A study of the Lough Neagh fishing community* (Galbally, 1986).
81. For Ó Danachair's work, see A. Gailey and D. Ó hÓgain (ed.), *Gold under the furze. Studies in folk tradition presented to Caoimhin Ó Danachair* (Dublin, 1984).
82. A. Gailey, *Rural houses of the north of Ireland* (Edinburgh, 1984).
83. T. Dunne (ed.), *The writer as witness. Literature as historical evidence* (Cork, 1988).
84. D. Lloyd, *Nationalism and minor literature. James Clarence Mangan and the emergence of Irish cultural nationalism* (Berkeley, 1987): ibid., *Anomalous states. Irish writing and the post-colonial moment* (Dublin, forthcoming).
85. P. Burke, *The Annales school of history* (London, 1990).
86. F. Braudel, *Civilisation and capitalism from the fifteenth to the eighteenth century* (London, 3 vols, 1981).
87. E. Le Roy Ladurie, *The territory of the historian* (Chicago, 1979).
88. R. Buchanan, 'The achievement of Estyn Evans' in G. Dawe and J. Foster (ed.) *The poet's place. Ulster literature and society* (Belfast, 1991), pp. 149–56.
89. J. H. Andrews, 'Jones Hughes's Ireland: a literary quest' in Smyth and Whelan, *Common Ground*, pp. 1–21; W.J. Smyth, 'T. Jones Hughes and twenty-five years of geography at UCD' in *Baile* (1977), pp. 3–7.
90. K. Whelan, 'The future of the Irish landscape' in *The future of the European rural landscape* (Lyons, forthcoming).
91. E.E. Evans, *Mourne country. Lanscape and life in south Down* (Dundalk, 1951).
92. Cited in Kearney, *Across the frontiers*, p. 198.
93. O'Malley, 'Inscape', *Loc. cit.*
94. Interview with Maelíosa Stafford, December 1992.
95. P. Duffy 'Rural settlement change in the Republic of Ireland: a preliminary discussion' in *Geoforum*, xiv (1983), pp. 185–91.
96. K. Whelan, 'The power of place' in *Irish Review*, xi (1992), pp. 21–8.
97. P. Claval (ed.), *Les paysages culturels Europeens. Heritage et devenir* (Paris, 1990).
98. J. Meldon, *Structural funds and the environment* (Dublin, 1992): J. Feehan (ed.), *Environment and development in Ireland* (Dublin, 1992).

99. R.S. Thomas, 'Welsh Testament' in *Tares* (London, 1961).
100. S. Heaney, 'Foreword' in Canavan, *Every Stoney Acre: Ibid*, 'The sense of place' in S. Heaney, *Preoccupations* (London, 1980), pp. 131–49: *Ibid*, 'The sense of the past' in *Ulster Local Studies*, ix (1985), pp. 109–15.
101. S. O'Connor, *Tomorrow was another day* (Tralee, 1970), p. 28.

CHAIRPERSON

Kevin Whelan's paper has wonderfully encompassed the macro issues – the social and democratic inadequacies of economic determinants, and the disabling effects for local democracy of centralisation – with proposals for the organisation of new structures, and with the detail of the crucial determinants and historical background of regional identity. His suggestion that the thrust of local history interests and an holistic approach to environment and landscape can provide a vision for the future of the regions will, I am sure, form the base for all our discussions.

However particular our own regional characteristics may seem, I think that we all know that there is a universality in our concerns – even in our believed uniquenesses. Many countries contain profound diversities of ethnic, linguistic and ideological variation, in addition to the commonalities of class, gender and economic heterogeneity. Our involvement in the issues which divide Ireland have, perhaps, intensified our identification with those areas of Europe which are currently, so tragically, re-evoking old animosities.

Our interest in areas which have taken positive steps to address diversity and regionality has increased similarly, and we are privileged to have Rienk Terpstra, policy maker in the province of Friesland, Holland, to respond to the keynote address.

RIENK TERPSTRA

A VIEW FROM EUROPE

I thank you very much for inviting me to this conference. I also wish to thank you for the warm reception you have given me.

Ireland and Friesland have much in common, such as a rich and sometimes dramatic history, which in your case began with the Celts, in our case with the Frisians. We both have our own distinctive languages, Gaelic and Frisian, and a distinct agricultural development. Another factor we have in common is the large number of people who emigrated owing to insufficient job opportunities. Both Ireland and Friesland have excellent educational facilities. Another common feature is an unemployment rate of over 25%.

The title of this conference is 'Regions: Identity and Power'. The intention is that I will respond from a European point of view. It suited me better, however, to deal with this from the perspective of European regions with minority languages and cultures.

On the whole these regions are rural in character, showing a strong decline in agricultural activities, which in turn has a negative effect on employment. The politicians are of the opinion that tourism may present a suitable alternative. They have high expectations, especially of tourism in combination with the regional, cultural identities. There are many positive aspects to tourism. It can offer a combination of regional, cultural, political, economic and ecological benefits. It's labour-intensive, generates varied employment and stimulates economic exchange.

Besides, tourism is among the few sectors expected to show substantial growth.

Tourism, especially cultural tourism, not only offers opportunities; we have to pay a price for it, socially and culturally. It may add to misunderstanding, stereotypical ideas about culture, religion and the arts and it may even lead to hatred of strangers. Another threat is visual pollution.

The cultural identity of a region is not only a force, it's also its only possession and therefore, must be treated carefully because it's unique. Naturally, this also applies to the natural resources and heritage of the region. A thorough understanding of culture is required before any tourist activities can be developed. Tourism adds to the local culture but all this may conflict with and be contrary to the values of the local population.

Therefore, it's sensible first to acquire insight into how tourism is defined by the various groups in a region. It's looked upon differently depending on the interests of these groups. The same is true for regional culture. How should it be defined? How does it relate to tourism and the other way round? Tourism has a different meaning to different people. The authorities consider tourism as an industry which brings employment. The tourist industry wants to know what revenues to expect, what marketing techniques to apply.

What interests sociologists is the host–guest relationship. What changes will tourism bring with it? What cultural adaptations will be required?

To religious groups tourism is a form of pilgrimage practised throughout the centuries.

To the local population it's important to know about the types of tourists they can expect. What impact will this have on the local culture. Will it affect their environment?

Tourists are not made alike. They have different motives and demographic characteristics. What are their expectations as to environment, ways of living and activities when they are on holiday?

Additionally, it is of major importance to us to be thoroughly familiar with the community. How is it structured? Why does it function the way it functions? It's important to be aware of the fact that culture itself is the *raison d'etre* of tourism.

Without culture there would be no tourism. Cultural tourism must reflect the characteristics of a certain region or town. No other formula would work. Besides, it has to be sustainable, correcting itself constantly. More than any other type of tourism, cultural tourism requires a community which is involved in tourism as well as in the planning and development of it. It's the culture of the host community we are utilising. It's the people themselves that attract the tourists. It is up to them to decide what they will share. They determine the dividing line between the public and the private domain and nobody else.

Cultural tourism can serve to bring out the strength of the cultural identity of a region. If we want to ensure that the impact of tourism on our cultural identity is kept within bounds, it's important that we should determine what we exactly understand by culture in general and our own regional culture.

There are some three hundred definitions of culture. You can pick and choose. The concept of culture can be understood in a narrow sense: Art with a capital A. In that case, referring to possible economic benefits is considered improper and contrary to the nature of the fine arts. Apparently, the aim of art and architectural historians is to make their studies accessible to the smallest possible public. However, I have to admit, where my own studies are concerned, that I have been interested in the pleasure I could derive from them myself rather than in letting others share in them. Museum collections are also presented in a way which leads one to think that the aim is to keep them away from the public as much as possible.

The poet T.S. Eliot understands by culture in a wider sense all the characteristic activities and interests of a people. Or to put it differently: the complex of living patterns and related values, of standards and ideas, of social relationships and structures, of spiritual and material structures and their products. This has brought me to concepts such as cultural identity and cultural entity or unity. Cultural identity, especially in a geographical context, means that a cultural entity may be a local community (a village), a regional community (a district or province), a national community (country) or a supranational community (Scandinavia, EC). Obviously, smaller cultural entities, Friesland for example, may form part of a larger one. Cultural entities are not determined by political or economic power and/or size in terms of population or geographically, but especially by their cultural production, culture being taken in its widest sense.

This reminds me of the Irish film *The Commitments*. The producer, Palmer, has the leading character, a manager of a band yet to be formed, say that the band will not just make soul music, it will make Dublin-soul. The soul of and for the working class. A perfect marketing formula in a nutshell. Besides, the band manager says that the Irish feel themselves to be the blacks of Europe, the Dubliners the blacks of Ireland and the people of the northside of Dublin feel themselves to be the blacks of Dublin. You don't have to agree with this view, it's a way to position yourself: knowing your own culture and giving it a place in a larger one.

For all these reasons and in view of developments in the tourist industry, it's necessary to define a number of cultural concepts as clearly as possible. There's another reason: developments within the European Community leading to an ever-increasing integration of our cultures within Europe. Preservation of our cultural heritage and promoting the availability of cultural facilities and events of high quality are of essential importance to be able to give shape to our own identity in an integrating Europe.

At any rate, it's necessary to assign a dynamic character to all cultural concepts. A stagnating culture is a dead culture.

The EC has also come to realise this. The 'bottom-up' approach is reflected in the current trend towards subsidiarity in the conception and implementation of EC policies. There has been a growing commitment towards an integrated rural development based on local and regional initiatives and socio-political traditions.

This suits us perfectly. The government in the Hague may not seem a centralist government compared with those in London and Paris, it nevertheless is. And as I have said earlier, it will be necessary to indicate the scope for manoeuvre at the local and regional levels. At the national level one cannot possibly be familiar with the specific cultural features and identities of the regions. Kevin Whelan rightly says that the results of the 'top-down' approach are visible in the landscape of present-day Ireland. A similar form of visual pollution can be found in Friesland. However, this is not the only reason. We also should blame ourselves. Simply because factors such as cost price and employment are always given priority over the living conditions in and environment of an area. Summarising, short-term economic planning is put first; long-term planning comes second. Besides, we should bear in mind that for the average politician a term of four years is quite a long period.

Given all this, the question is how we can succeed in preserving and realising an attractive living and working environment. First, by establishing that there's great diversity as to the users of the urban and rural environments. Inhabitants, workers and visitors, they all have their own specific demands in terms of the living climate, space, etc. When the available space is so intensively used, the layout and planning of it is essential. This is certainly true for a densely populated country such as the Netherlands.

The quality of planning and layout is determined by the utility value (suitability, unsuitability, diversity etc.), people's perception of it (attractive design, identity, illogical disturbances) and the future value (durable, controllable/possible adjustments). This means that physical changes and new developments need to be checked for compatibility with these three values. The differentiation between traffic and non-traffic areas, which was introduced long ago, is still workable. Another starting point should be that the primary user be given precedence; this primary use should also be reflected in the physical planning policy. Secondary use can be allowed to a certain extent. Therefore, it's necessary to draw up structure, outline and sector plans. Each plan should be based on the principles that the existing (possibly historical) features are respected, that the factors decisive for the identity (use of materials, waterways etc.) are strengthened and that the development of such plans is aimed at the realisation of quality.

So far, our thinking has been product-oriented. As quality, management and future value are gaining in importance, a shift from a random approach to a planned, co-ordinated approach is called for. The building process has been strongly developed, but now attention should be focused on the social and management process.

This requires networks at the local and regional levels, forming platforms where the cultural identities can be discussed and where knowledge and experiences can be exchanged. Naturally, it's good that these can be built up and obtained in many forms on the international level, but the foundations have to be laid in the regions.

With the mottoes 'saving for quality is investing in the future' and 'from ready-made to tailor-made' we have to adopt a forward-looking approach. Quality is increasingly put first. We should avoid integral policies followed for their own sake; we should also avoid doing more with less money. We should give priority to developing a cohesive, future-oriented policy covering several disciplines. Consequently, this requires a co-ordinated instead of an integral approach. Again, exchange of information is of essential importance. We have to opt for information exchange by a system of arrangements regarding the concepts to be used and the way in which this information is exchanged and made accessible. Mutual competition and taking of positions (information is knowledge and knowledge is power) should be avoided.

The quality requirement explicitly applies to the layout of the rural and urban environment as well as to the architecture. However, what does quality mean? Quality can be determined by concepts such as uniqueness, careful use of values, availability of social, technical and/or aesthetic dimensions.

Quality is the real enemy of consolidation. In this process of consolidation, now in full swing, quantities conflict while qualities complement each other.

In my opinion, what matters is that quality is formed by a combination of immaterial factors worked out and implemented with the greatest possible care, such as:

- the preservation of existing physical values and historical qualities
- awareness of cultural identity (The fact that many residential areas look alike does not mean that the people living in them are alike or have the same behaviour patterns)
- quality can only be achieved if we can realise maximum co-operation between all parties concerned
- quality is also tailor-made and especially requires inspiration – through perspiration – dedication, enthusiasm, commitment and a willingness to put the shoulder to the wheel.

This evening I have used cultural tourism as a means to link up apparently different matters. This type of tourism offers opportunities for favourable development of cultural facilities and activities. If we fail to point out the inter-relationship, then others will do this for us. In that case the price for developing tourism will be high.

We shouldn't wait any longer. Cultural tourism may not be a new phenomenon, there is a demand for it now in all sections of the population; it's no longer exclusively reserved for the small group of the well-to-do.

This demand for culture should be taken seriously. Precisely in our society, which seems to be obsessed by speed, movement and variety, perception and thought are subject to fundamental change. Film and TV are dosing information in rapidly changing pictures. We are trained to think in pictures rather than words.

The automobile, train and aeroplane reduce the landscape and the city to a monotonous desert, resulting in the traveller looking at endless sequences of pictures produced by his movement rather than at certain spots. For this purpose the French philosopher and expert on urban development, Virillo, coined the term 'dromology', derived from the Greek work 'dromos' which means race in the sense of trial of speed. This race does not allow us to linger over what happened and still happens in our direct surroundings. Therefore, 'dromology' can also be considered one of the very reasons for developing cultural tourism, which can only be achieved if the cultural identity is recognisable and is clearly brought out – not only for the visitors but even more for our own benefit.

CHAIRPERSON

Rienka Terpstra has stressed the importance of integrating past realities with present pre-occupations and future plans, and the need for a community to determine its own perception of identity – either for central government or for cultural tourists. For many people, I would suggest, it is their involvement in the field of adult and informal education which first helps them 'fix' that received knowledge, those ideas which are central to the identity of their community, into the wider framework of regional and national significance. So we could have no better person to respond to the keynote address than Myrtle Hill, an historian who is regularly involved in understanding local perceptions, at an academic and practical level, as a lecturer teaching in the Department of Continuing Education at Queen's University, Belfast.

MYRTLE HILL

REGIONS: IDENTITY AND POWER
A NORTHERN IRISH PERSPECTIVE

I would like to begin by thanking the organisers for their invitation to participate in the conference, and for providing us with a rare and welcome opportunity to discuss matters which interest us in congenial, not to say, salubrious surroundings. Kevin has begun the proceedings with a succinct and wide-ranging analysis of the major issues raised by the concept of regionalism in relation to Ireland, and has introduced some stimulating ideas which I look forward to discussing during the course of the weekend. In the north of Ireland, where the inter-related areas of politics, the economy and cultural identity are hotly contested components in an ongoing violent conflict, the opportunities offered by a regionalist approach deserve our close consideration.

The perspective I offer is both individual and non-specialist; touching on what seem to me to be at least some of the issues which are relevant in the contemporary debate around Northern Ireland and regionalisation.

As someone who is not a political analyst, an economist or a geographer, but an historian, I found the whole world of geopolitics quite difficult to grasp. The more I read – and thought – about regionalism the more slippery and elusive the concept seemed to become. Text books described regions as 'descriptive tools, defined according to particular criteria for a particular purpose', and stated that there are as many regions as there are criteria to define them.[1] They could be social, cultural, economic or administrative units which in turn could be 'formal or functional, physically or non-physically-conditioned'.[2] Regionalism could be quite simply a general system of beliefs and be regarded as a means to an end rather than an end in itself. While I feel able to relate to John Hewitt's 'area of size and significance we could hold in our hearts' I found less subjective definitions were required, at least on this occasion.

As has been pointed out, the concept of a Europe of the Regions is thought to be particularly significant when applied to the Northern Ireland situation. It is suggested that within such a structure – a European federation of interdependent, self-governing regions in which national borders would be rendered irrelevant – we would at last be able to emerge from the political stalemate which, Richard Kearney suggests, has rendered us the 'festering wound' of the European body politic and enter into a 'more extended cultural community where common heritages are celebrated and specific differences cultivated'.[3] Casting off our internal feuds and preoccupations, and embracing a new openness, we can look outward to explore our relationship with the culturally diverse regions of other parts of Ireland, Britain and Continental Europe.

This vision of the new Europe – of a unity based on diversity – has obvious appeal, but clearly relies on the premise of politically empowered regions operating within an economically and politically integrated federalist Europe. There is obviously some distance still to be travelled before that vision can become a reality. But even accepting it as a long-term goal, if it is one to be worked towards, we should perhaps look realistically at the kinds of structural problems which might prove difficult to overcome. It is clear that in the Europe of late 1992, claims that nationalism is dead are somewhat premature, and, even if it is to subside as a political force, one must agree that the 'hurts of history' cannot easily be cast aside. The divisions which underlie the conflict in the north of Ireland have many strands: economic, cultural, religious and social, as well as ethnic, all of which will continue to make the defining of the region in territorial terms a matter of critical importance. Witness the Unionist suspicion of the notion of a 'one-island economy' – based on the (not-ungrounded) fear that Europe is offering an indirect route to a united Ireland. Such anxieties and the hostility and resistance to which they give rise suggests that the lack of clarification of this difficult issue can seriously undermine the movement towards regional integration. Confidence, security and trust in the process itself are essential ingredients for its success. We talk here about moving towards a society without frontiers – but it must be recognised that we do so in the context of communities segregated by steel barriers.

While the European context can provide us with a wider framework for the discussion and resolution of our local problems, we must ensure that those problems are honestly confronted. Only by engaging in open debate over possible solutions have they any possibility of becoming viable options – the idea of an extended British-Irish agreement which would recognise Irish, British or dual citizenship alongside European citizenship – and with the rights of citizens protected by a European Court of Human Rights – is one such option.

It is important to note that structural problems relating to the creation of a 'Europe of the Regions' are not confined to Northern Ireland. It is already clear that the contrasting political philosophies and cultures embraced by the United Kingdom, the Republic of Ireland, and the nation states of continental Europe place real difficulties in the way of greater European political integration. The domestic laws of the Republic, particularly those concerning gender and sexuality, do not appear to conform with the dream of a united, liberalised Europe. There is, likewise, a wide gulf between Britain and her EC partners over issues such as national sovereignty and the concept of social partnership – Britain is the only member state not to have endorsed the European Social Charter. Recent developments suggest that rather than the radical overhaul of existing political structures in the interests of greater European unity, a looser and more accommodating alliance may be emerging. While this is more attractive and desirable than the notion of a highly-centralised European bureaucracy, it remains to be seen whether such an alliance will alter the old power structures to the extent necessary to provide new solutions to the problems of existing nation states.

If we shift the focus of our attention from the political to the economic arena, the view of and from Northern Ireland is indeed bleak. As one of the economic regions of the UK – on the periphery of a periphery – Northern Ireland is seen as 'a problem region with regional problems', and dubbed 'the sick man of the UK'. With the worst record in terms of employment, industry and general economic outlook, it was only the introduction of new, even poorer regions, into the European community which removed Northern Ireland from the bottom of the scale of regional performances. Despite government attempts to redress intra-regional imbalances, especially those between east and west in the 1960s, disparities have persisted. The position at the beginning of the

1990s is that unemployment remains high at over 14%, out-migration is running at persistently high levels; participation rates are low and incomes are falling even further behind the national average.[4] These problems tend to overshadow the advantages of Common Market membership – the opening up of new opportunities and markets, and of course, the availability of funding for regionally-based initiatives. These more beneficial aspects will be more to the fore once the current economic recession is at an end.

Reference has already been made to the highly centralised nature of the UK state, which mitigates against regional regeneration, and Kevin's persuasive arguments for a regional tier of autonomy in the Republic are equally applicable to Northern Ireland where the problems caused by top-down policies can be clearly identified at the local level. I am thinking particularly of those aspects of economic policy which have social consequences for the community – and require not only sensitivity to, but knowledge of the particular needs of a locality – housing needs and the consideration of planning applications for example. The loss of community health councils in recent years removed an important channel of communication between local people and a centralised health service. The government's rationalisation programme has deprived localities of vital community services such as local hospitals and schools; last week's *Belfast Telegraph* reported the planned closure of another nine schools in rural areas of Northern Ireland.

There is no doubt that both the region of Northern Ireland and its sub-regions are firmly in the grip of the bureaucracy of Whitehall, with negative economic and social results. Localities are drained of initiative and control as well as the communal institutions which should be their life's blood. The problems should not, however, be seen as only due to a lack of the government's political will to redistribute resources from the centre to the periphery. Wider issues such as the general economic recession, tensions between private and public finance and party political tensions at both national and local government levels are other contributory factors. These problems may prove more difficult to resolve, but their damaging effects at local level serve to reinforce the need to empower the regions. The questions of boundaries, functions and powers must be tackled in the interests of redressing the democratic deficit of the localities. Effective administrative structures must be set up in place of the accumulation of unco-ordinated agencies now operating at regional level, and more effective channels of communication between regions and central government must also be put into place.

In Northern Ireland, however, the process of decentralisation faces additional difficulties to those already outlined. Past experience has taught that in a divided community, local power can be abused, and, rather than encourage integration, the exercise of power at the local level can exacerbate existing communal divisions. The experience of regional government elsewhere suggests that this problem is not unique to Northern Ireland. In Italy, for example, networks of patronage and clientalism in local government management generate an unfair system of government – particularly marginalising ethnic minorities in areas such as social policy. We have only to consider the post-Soviet world where the collapse of the centralist state has produced new nations such as Estonia, where ethnic minorities face prejudice and disadvantage purely on linguistic and cultural grounds.

To return to our own problems, however, is there any indication of a shift in attitudes and perceptions which might suggest a more optimistic approach to the devolution of political power? Have we moved on from 1920? Having highlighted the grave difficulties I am at pains to end this section on a more positive note. There is some evidence of growing willingness to co-operate at local level, such as cross-party opposition to privatisation of electricity, in recognition of the perceived damaging consequences to the region's economy. There are encouraging signs also from some local councils, for example, Dungannon Council, in the aftermath of the Enniskillen massacre took positive action to pursue mutual understanding within the council chamber, undertaking responsibility-sharing at local level and in an attempt to marginalise the extremes 'called on the paramilitaries to declare the Dungannon District Council a 'violence-free zone', to enable the council to further improve community trust and harmony, and at the same time establish a district where the Northern Ireland political parties and the United Kingdom and Irish governments could advance discussions towards a political agreement on the totality of relationships within these islands'[5]. It is to be hoped that the sense of shared responsibility articulated here and exhibited in other councils in Northern Ireland can outlast the now-collapsed government talks.

There are those of course who argue that it is easy for these local politicians to agree when in fact they have no real responsibility. While there is still a long way to go, these local examples help to build belief in consensus politics and provide experience of co-operation to set against years of conflict and recurrent walk-outs. As one commentator has suggested, 'spatial frameworks can provide the opportunities for participation and interaction; communities decide whether such opportunities are grasped and used positively'[6].

The problem of attempting to recast our present situation in the European regional model is the interdependence of several factors: for the disputed Irish/British frontiers to 'wither away' necessitates the simultaneous strengthening of the region and of an integrated Europe. On the other hand, the dismantling of national aspirations within the community seems to be a prerequisite to the successful operation of local power. This chicken and egg dimension suggests that the process might be rather bumpier than anticipated.

The whole concept of 'Europe of the Regions' has heightened awareness of cultural peculiarity at sub-national level – as something to be preserved and promoted to offset the danger of regional culture being submerged in a wider, more bland Europeanness – although George Watson has posed the interesting question of whether Northern Ireland has an identity to be overwhelmed. The question is highly relevant because Neal Ascherson has described one of the characteristics of a region as 'a community which is confident enough about itself to accept cultural pluralism as something less than a threat to identity'.[7] Kevin has demonstrated how a wide range of regional affinities can be created. In Northern Ireland the debate about regional identity has centred on the power of place and cultural identity, the latter, predictably, closely related to history and politics.

As a result of his study of the relationship between human culture and the landscape, the historical geographer, Estyn Evans, developed the idea of a distinctive Ulster regional identity – 'a strong regional variant in habitat, heritage and history'.[8] On the basis of archaeological and folklife evidence he maintained that 'the two communities in the north, however deeply divided by religion, share an outlook on life which is different from that prevailing in the south and which bears the stamp of a common heritage'. He regarded the cross-fertilisation of the Ulster community as a potential source of enrichment, and his thesis has been developed by Ronnie Buchanan and others. This form of regional identity is firmly rooted in a sense of geographical place – in the physical differences between Ulster and other parts of Ireland and Britain. Most of us can relate to this sense of place, which is not just theoretical or abstract, though the geographical area by which we define ourselves may be more limited – the North-West, the Sperrins, the Belfast area.

In practical terms, Evans' commitment to the preservation of this rich culture was of lasting significance. His concern with the conservation of landscape and wildlife, the preservation of ancient monuments, and most visibly his study of folklife, finding expression in the founding of Ulster Folk and Transport Museum at Cultra. It is perhaps worth mentioning here that the successful development of that initiative relied on availability of funding, and thus was subjected to wider political and economic considerations. In this case, Evans' invaluable work accorded with the perception of what was acceptable/desirable in terms of the heritage industry. Previous speakers have pointed to the danger of cultural tourism being taken too far, and the danger of an over-commercialised heritage sector cannot be ignored by anybody who cares about true and valid perceptions of Ireland, Ulster or indeed of any region. However, in a time of economic stagnation, these fears must be balanced against the benefits to be gained through tourism as a means of supporting a local economy.

There has also recently been a revival of interest in the perception of regional identity put forward in the 1940s, most notably by the poet John Hewitt in an attempt to reconcile his sense of rootedness with the acknowledgement of being (as one of planter stock) 'once alien here'. Hewitt's regionalism, like that of Evans, suggests a common ground on which the divided community might build, and also articulated the multi-faceted nature of his perceived identity in a much-quoted hierarchy of values; 'I'm an Ulsterman of planter stock. I was born in the island of Ireland, so secondarily I'm an Irishman. I was born in the British archipelago and English is my native tongue, so I am British. The British archipelago is offshore to the continent of Europe, so I'm European. This is my hierarchy of values and as far as I'm concerned anyone who omits one step in that sequence of values is falsifying the situation.'[9]

While there is some vagueness and lack of precision about the actual frontiers of Hewitt's region (in itself of course attractive) his balancing of Ulster/Irish/British allegiances strikes a chord in many Northern minds. A similar combination of identities is seen in Breton/French and Basque/Spanish relations, and this sometimes fragile balance can be either positive – encouraging minority languages – or negative, creating suspicion and ill-feeling.

I would hope that in Northern Ireland we can accept the positive aspect of dual identity, embracing our common heritage and accepting our differences rather than pushing them to the point of division. A hopeful manifestation of this is the recent shifting of attitudes towards Irish identity – a recognition in the twenty-six counties of the failure of Irish nationalism to accommodate the aspirations and experiences of all on the island of Ireland – leading to acceptance of the need to accommodate uncomfortable realities within a more pluralistic pattern.

As has frequently been pointed out, however, probably only a small number of people in Northern Ireland embrace the concept of cultural pluralism. This is not to say there have not been fascinating developments within both so-called communities in the six counties at a more popular level: many Northern Irish nationalists have now found themselves able to work within a Northern Irish environment, while at the same time coming to terms with a growing sense of alienation from the political establishment within the twenty six counties.

We can perceive a shifting in the Unionist position also, as those who once felt they had been denied the Irish aspect of their identity, now struggle with what they perceive as the betrayal of their Britishness, striving for a sense of security in a largely unsympathetic world. However, we must always remember that, for some members of both communities, identity is sometimes expressed in terms which we sitting here would call extreme, violent and counterproductive. Against a background of political uncertainty and sense of increasing vulnerability, it is perhaps unsurprising that this reorientation is often expressed in narrow and exclusivist terms.

An interesting example of one current strand of Unionism can be seen on the Newtownards Road in the form of a wall mural which depicts the defenders of Ulster – Cúchulainn, the B Specials and the UDR – all now perceived as betrayed by forces alien to their sense of identity. The slogan 'Irish out of Ulster', and the claim that only the UDA remain to defend its people – can be seen as articulating a dangerous counter-nationalism promoting a narrow, exclusivist sectarianism. The Utilitarian dimension to this kind of reinterpretation of the past is of course nothing new in either British or Irish nationalism. Nor if we are honest is it unique to these islands. The history of Europe is littered with the bones of histories discarded, as new and more acceptable pasts are created to buttress presents.

Such collective belief although important is inevitably only one component of personal/group/local/regional or national identity – religion, class, gender, economics and race all create a sense of uniqueness which sets us apart from our neighbours and creates the ever-changing, open-ended categories in which we relate to others. Anthropological studies reinforce the argument that ethnicity is not static, but a resource which we actually use – we represent ourselves in different ways according to the context in which we find ourselves, and express that identity through a wide variety of visual, literary and popular cultures.

Such complex and individual definitions of identity suggest the need to seek regional cohesion in other factors. Rather than engineering artificial concepts of identity we should perhaps seek to develop a sense of communal identity based upon what is already there, building a sense of shared identity from the bottom up. A possible example of what can be accomplished has been the women's movement within Northern Ireland which has sought to transcend the narrow and often frustrating divisions within society. Catherine Shannon has noted that women's political allegiances are often more complex and varied than that of their menfolk and neighbourhood – 'Like the statue of the ancient Celtic deity on Boa Island in County Fermanagh, some Northern Irish women are able to look in two directions at once and remain whole'[10]. The network of women's organisations in Northern Ireland are not only expressions of gender solidarity, but have the potential to be well-connected, effective forces for change. Sadly, that effectiveness is often constrained by other political or religious loyalties within the region. Groups have to operate within a geographical area, and thus can risk labelling according to the sectarian identity of the area or meeting place, and with meetings held in parish, chapels and Orange halls the local difficulties are obvious.

Organisations such as the Women's Information Network, Northern Ireland with two hundred affiliated societies have realised a sense of common ground, but, with little official recognition or funding, no further channels exist to extend this process of identification or establish effective political responses to the issues of common interest – particularly in the area of welfare.

Voluntary groups, like the women's movement are regional organisations which again seek to be non-governmental, non-party and non-sectarian. Other groups in the voluntary sector, such as the Northern Ireland Anti-Poverty Network, embracing similar criteria, and committing themselves to the provision of information and lobbying beyond a narrow community, have proven capable of building alliances and coalitions throughout Ireland and across Europe. An article by Quentin Oliver concludes that 'Through their flexibility, accountability and value-based commitment to tackle disadvantage, community and voluntary groups are well placed to act as catalyst and initiate change'.[11]

Community arts and theatre groups are other forms of expressing cultural identity. Bringing new vibrancy and a feeling of self-worth to the regions, they can provide a forum for marginalised groups, helping them to create a space for themselves within the community.

Kevin has pointed to the importance of local history societies, focusing on the cultural, economic and political development of the locality and often challenging the national perspective. There is, of course, a danger that the sense of place focused upon in this instance can be constrictingly parochial, and local history, like its national counterpart, is vulnerable to misuse by its components. However, the potential for regional bonding and a wider appreciation and acceptance of diversities is there, especially in the increasingly developed links between societies, not just in Ulster, but in Ireland, Britain and further afield. Conferences, newsletters and publications increasingly reveal the cross-fertilisation of such groups. The introduction of academic courses on the methodology of interdisciplinary local studies combined with an appreciation of the contextual setting will hopefully allow this process to develop further.

Previous conferences of this group have acknowledged the important contribution increasingly made by education in Northern Ireland, and I would only note here the importance of a continuing emphasis on cross-community initiatives, for all age groups.

In all of these areas there is an urgent need to harness the very real potential for community development.

Perhaps the most positive thing we can say about regionalism, is that in our consideration of its various aspects, what comes through very plainly is the fluidity. Just as individual perceptions change from birth to death, and in relation to the myriad of circumstances in which we find ourselves so too is the concept of region and the context in which it operates changing. The map of Europe is still being redrawn with monotonous regularity; the economic basis of the world appears to change from one morning's paper to the next; political relations between the two islands is constantly under review, as is the very basis of political life in the twenty-six counties, while in the North changing demographic patterns likewise suggest that change rather than stalemate is on the agenda.

Although we may at times feel like MacNeice's bus passengers in Charon, who were instructed to 'Hold onto that dissolving map'[12], the road to regionalisation in a European context is one along which we might cautiously, but positively, proceed.

References
1. John Glasson, *An Introduction to Regional Planning: Concepts, Theory and Practice* (2nd edition) (London, 1978), p. 36.
2. J.H. Andrews, 'Jones Hughes's Ireland: A Literary Quest', in *Common Ground: Essays on the Historical Geography of Ireland* ed. W.J. Smyth and Kevin Whelan (Cork, 1988), pp. 1–21, p. 12.
3. Richard Kearney, 'A blot on the edge of Europe', *Fortnight* January 1992, p. 10; *All Europeans Now: Cultural Traditions in Northern Ireland*, ed. Maurna Crozier (Belfast, 1991), p. 48.
4. Mark Hart, 'A decade of enterprise in Northern Ireland?' in *Social Attitudes in Northern Ireland*, 1990–91 Edition, ed. P. Stringer and G. Robinson (Belfast, 1991). pp. 55–60.
5. Michael McLoughlin, *Fortnight*, May 1992, p. 23.
6. J. Neville H. Douglas, 'Spatial frameworks and community relations' in F.W. Boal and J. Neville H. Douglas, *Integration and Division: Geographical Perspectives on the Northern Ireland Problem* (Belfast, 1982), pp. 105–132, p. 132.
7. Neal Ascherson, *All Europeans Now*, p. 28.
8. Estyn Evans, *The Personality of Ireland: Habitat, Heritage and History* (Cambridge 1973).
9. John Hewitt, 'The clash of identities', *Irish Times* 4 July, 1974.
10. Catherine Shannon, 'Recovering the voices of the women of the North', *The Irish Review*, No. 12 (Spring/Summer 1992) pp. 27–33, p. 30.
11. Quentin Oliver, 'At the edge of the Union'. *Fortnight*, June 1992, p. 22.
12. *Collected Poems of Louis MacNiece* (1966).

GENERAL DISCUSSION

Chairperson:
Myrtle Hill's paper has pointed up the gap between the hopes of European integration, and the realities of local experience – but also some of the possible ways forward, including consensual political activity, and interest-based networks. She has also enumerated some of the important ingredients of identity in the north of Ireland, so she has ranged from the general to the particular and given an excellent starting point for our discussion session.

Seán Nolan (Ulster Museum):
The point I want to address is in relation to my own professional concerns with regard to heritage. Perhaps I can illustrate it by mentioning that the first time that I went to the Donegal Gaeltacht in 1944, there was a very pretty young lady known as Máire Nic Giolla Bhríde, who lived in a bungalow on the way down to Maheragallon and because that was the only bungalow between Maheragallon and Gweebarra she was known as 'Máire bhungalow'. Now, if you go back to that region today, it is peppered with haciendas and bungalows and the whole cultural landscape has been destroyed.

I retire now and again to Andalusia and if you look at that region the whole east coast around Andalusia has been damaged totally by the development on the Costa de Sol, and the Spanish have just wakened up to the fact of the damage that has been done. In the area around Malaga, hydroponic horticulture is now affecting the water-table and in the Coto Doñana National Park, Huelva is the greatest strawberry producing area in the world. The strawberries which you eat in March or October are most likely to come from Huelva – all based on hydroponic horticulture – the water-table of that National Park is now also seriously damaged. The flamingos, and the other wild life are in danger; to remedy that the Spanish have limited access to the park and visitors must give forty-eight hours notice to get into the park. Now, this means that the whole question of tourism and its effect on heritage sites is going to be quite radical and if tourism is going to be the major industry by the year 2000 then there are concerns that must be addressed now and we only have eight years to do that. I think that what we are going to have to do is to limit access – unfortunately. So I think the message that I am trying to convey – yes, tourism is an economic benefit, but it is also a potential danger to the heritage and one that needs to be addressed.

Terry Clare (Wexford Centre for the Unemployed):
In the past – I read the book of last years conference – and it would appear that only the intelligentsia were included in the debate. You take Wexford Centre for the Unemployed with nine thousand people unemployed. They see their future not as bound up with the intelligentsia – they blame the intelligentsia of Ireland; they blame the Church; they blame their political leaders for not being able to come up with proper solutions that will give us a viable country where we can all live. We also put the responsibility on those leaders who in seventy years of the state have not been able to resolve the divisions within the communities of Ireland. So, basically, the debate is widening up and I'm sure that there is a contribution to be made there by the unemployed.

There is just one question, I would like to put to you, sir. Mr. Whelan stated that the funding of the EC is not regionally-based. Within the South-East, we in the Trades Council, through the Rosslare Harbour Development Committee, have made a submission on the basis that the next funding under Maastricht will be regional and we will hope to make an impact now particularly and each of the counties in the region have put forward proposals for that particular region. Other problems exist like, say, about Status One, under Maastricht, where we have to export through British ports, where they haven't got similar status, and so cannot develop ports like Fishguard, through lack of funding, which must develop to match ports like Rosslare Harbour, which will surely bring down the cost of our exports and create more viable employment. At the moment we are about 7% disadvantaged in transport costs and while the EC will make funding available for port development, they will not make funding available for movable assets i.e. ships – so we are arguing now that sea miles should be treated the same as land miles for the purpose of getting us into a more economically viable position to be able to compete effectively with the rest of Europe.

Dara Molloy (The Aisling Magazine, Aran Islands):
My name is Dara Molloy, I live on the Aran Islands; its really an illustration for Kevin – perhaps he would respond to it. I moved to live in Aran eight years ago and I found it easy to rent a thatched cottage on the island because the islanders have tended to move into the haciendas or the bungalows. Since living there, my landlord comes every year or two and he rethatches it with rye straw which is the traditional style of thatching on the island. When the tourists flow in the Summer, my house being about two and a half miles from the pier is the first stop for the minibuses and all the tourists pile out and take photographs of the thatched cottage which is the first they would see across the island. So on the one hand, the thatched cottage is a very attractive feature for tourists; on the other hand my landlord can get a grant to re-roof his house in any way except thatch. He can also get a grant now only because our development committee on the island pointed out that there was no grant available for thatching and got an insert put into a budget two years ago. Now we can have our houses thatched provided they were thatched before, but it turns out in the small print that they have to be thatched by reed thatching and they have to be thatched by somebody who is certificated to do that job. Now that means that the traditional rye thatching is still not being grant-aided and there is now an even stronger push on people, encouragement to people to either slate their roof or to thatch it with a non-traditional type thatch. That's just an illustration of how the 'top down' can destroy the 'bottom up'. But I would like to hear Kevin's comment on that.

Kevin Whelan:
The failure to formulate a national policy to take into account regional distinctiveness where diversity exists in vernacular architecture is a classic example of what I was talking about earlier. One of the searing sadnesses for those who know the countryside well is the degree to which it has become homogenised; now you can drive for very large distances without noting the sharp differences that used to be there in styles of architecture or of thatching. This kind of debate has focused around the 'Bungalow Blitz' notion, it

is the people themselves who tend to be blamed by cultural commentators for adopting what is seen as crass non-indigenous, non-traditional forms of housing. But my criticism would be that the professional architectural community failed in that they did not provide an alternative set of more appropriate and more regionally-based plans which would have been equally cheap and equally possible for people to build. The result was an erosion of regional diversity in architectural expression.

James Hawthorne (Northern Ireland Community Relations Council):
I hope at this conference we can clean up a few words like 'subsidiarity' which I suspect is a word that doesn't actually exist and which attempts to describe an idea which doesn't actually exist either. And I think the word 'heritage' should be challenged. In the English town of Wigan, which I'm sure you've all visited, there was at one time special financial assistance for new building in the centre of the town provided it was carried out in the Tudor style. It provided a source of amusement and effrontery to many people at the time. And what has happened to those Tudor anachronisms? Some have been granted preservation orders. They have become part of heritage so I think we've got to be a little thoughtful at times about what we are trying to preserve.

As to looking back on history, very often it's only the more uplifting ideas that are taken up and then developed by the short-term economics of what has virtually become the 'heritage industry'. In Northern Ireland we've been concerned with, and are increasing our experience in dealing with, such terminology as 'cultural heritage' and 'cultural traditions' primarily to encourage not merely the celebration but the interrogation of history. Without our assistance I can assure you, even bits of that can get out of hand – on the Newtownards Road in Protestant East Belfast, Cúchulainn is taking his place alongside King Billy within the local graffiti. But such daring revisionism, though based on certain new and slightly dubious historical research, is not entirely unwelcome. Perhaps it's the first time that the people of that area have laid claim to a piece of Irish history previously dismissed or consigned to their enemies. I see it as a cry for acceptance, a readjustment, a signal which we should welcome and respond to.

So with regard to heritage and the popularising of history mainly to serve tourism, I think we could be catering to, and encouraging, views of history which are dangerously comforting and exclusive and simplistic below which nationalism and regionalism can continue to fester. I'm sure we must reassess the aims, the real economics and the ethics of tourist-driven heritage and I would hope that these issues can be closely examined over the next two days.

Mary Banotti (Member of the European Parliament):
I am very glad the last speaker got in before me, because he raised one of the issues that I feel was very important. The words by which we are beginning to define such concepts as 'regionalism'. I am glad you threw down the dreaded word 'subsidiarity' which we have been trying to work out for ourselves in the European Parliament recently. In fact, Jacques Delors in the European Parliament last month said that if anyone came up with a definition of subsidiarity in one page, they could have his job and I don't see too many people running to get it. In theory, I think regionalism is a great idea, but we stand in great danger of us finding ourselves defining regions as being only those places that qualify for European funds. We qualify for a structural fund grant, therefore we exist. I am beginning to get very nervous about this and fear that in the end this definition is what will, in fact, define a region.

Kevin in his speech today spoke about the dreaded interpretative centres which are proliferating all over the place and people here this evening might be interested to know that the high court in Dublin today turned down the application by the Luggala Interpretative Centre on a legal point based on a concept of nineteenth century British law stating that the crown of the state cannot, by definition, be acting against the best interests of people.

I think we should look at regions beyond our own borders too, and one of the areas with whom I think we have both a cultural and economic common interest is Wales. An interesting project in economic development which could have a cultural underpinning as well is the land bridge through Wales. In exporting our products, the large majority of them still have to go through the UK. Our interests and those of the people of Wales and around Holyhead are identical and there are moves towards drafting a regional case for both Ireland and Wales because of these common interests. We have a great deal in common culturally and we certainly have similar economic problems. I think we need to be very wary of the concept of 'subsidiarity' and what it actually means, particularly in this country where we probably have the most centralised government system in the whole of Europe. We continue to run our country on the concept that 'nanny knows best' in the Department of Finance.

Harry Hughes (Willie Clancy Summer School):
There is a subtle pressure growing for interpretative centres of a musical nature. In other words, people have visions that somewhere out in west Clare, somewhere near Miltown Malbay or Spanish Point or along there, there should be some monstrosity that would house artefacts of a musical nature. Now our situation is this. We prefer living musicians to come into Miltown Malbay every year and we prefer living music followers to come in there every year and we prefer them to treat our environment the way it is. In other words, in a respectful manner, rather than have a huge monstrosity in there with people being bused in. At least, if we possibly can, we will prevent a musical Mulloughmore in Miltown Malbay.

PART II

REGIONS AND TRADITIONS

FOUR PAPERS

CHAIRPERSON'S INTRODUCTION

On behalf of the Cultures of Ireland Group, and all those attending this conference, I am most pleased to welcome our Patron, the President, Mrs. Mary Robinson. We are most grateful for her interest, particularly as illustrated by her presence with us here.

This morning starts with a series of short talks, which will inform and inspire the workshops.

To help focus on the issues which are central to the debate on regional identity and power Liam O'Dowd will start the session by addressing the problems of regional definition, concentrating on the significance of borders.

This will be followed by Tony Canavan, who will concentrate on the practical application of local history, with its potential for involving and excluding, both at a personal and group level. To complete the overview of the issues of regionality, Dermot Healy will focus on the different identities evident in the attitudes and expressions of particular counties, and Anne Tannahill will consider how the interweaving of political realities and personal experience contribute to notions of identity.

LIAM O'DOWD

WHAT IS A REGION?: THE CASE OF THE IRISH BORDERLANDS

I must confess that my first instinct was to avoid answering the question, at least directly. Too much ink has been spilt to too little effect in the social sciences in trying to define regions, localities, communities, even nations. For the non social scientist, the whole exercise often appears excessively academic, abstract and inconclusive. Much depends on who is doing the defining and for what purposes.

Nevertheless, given the title of this conference, there may be some merit in broadly reviewing ways of seeing regions. This will also serve as an introduction to the second part of this contribution which will deal with the Irish Border region(s) in the EC. As I am currently researching this topic[1], I will use it as a means of addressing the regional question more concretely.

Defining Regions

Regions generally can be defined in terms of:

(1) Natural or physical terrain;
(2) Specific types of economic activity or functions in a wider economy;
(3) Specific political consciousness or politico-legal and administrative structures;
(4) The military control and administration of territory;
(5) Cultural characteristics, customs, accents, literature, leisure pursuits or, more broadly, ethnic, national or religious identity.

While I suspect that the cultural characteristics of regions are of most interest to this conference, on their own they seldom provide clear guidelines for regional mobilisation or demarcation; in fact, they often persuade us that we partake in a fairly passive way of multiple identities, local, regional and national. The more active, durable and clearly defined a region is the more likely it is that it has succeeded in linking cultural characteristics to one or more of the elements mentioned above. The most significant and durable territorial unit of recent times, the national state, demonstrates this capacity most effectively. In the process, it claims to legitimately monopolise the means of violence and administrative control within fixed territorial boundaries. These boundaries enclose, not only defensible space but a complex of economic, political, administrative, legal and cultural institutions.

Regions, therefore, would seem to be rather less complex, less clearly defined territories subordinate to national states. For example, the Council of Europe's (One hundred and seventy-one members) Assembly of European Regions employs wonderfully imprecise criteria for membership. It defines regions as 'a level of government immediately below central government which represents territories which constitute from a geographical point of view a clear-cut entity whose population possesses certain shared features and wishes to safeguard the resulting specific identity and to develop it with the object of stimulating cultural, social and political progress'.

The flexibility of this definition is evident when we consider the diverse entities represented in the Assembly from former states such as Bavaria to would-be states like Scotland and the Basque Country, to some English counties, to Rhine-Westphalia, a region invented by the Allied armies in the late 1940s for their own convenience. There is one Irish region represented: Donegal.

The conclusion to be drawn is that regions are entities which are constructed in many different ways using a variety of resources. They may be constructed gradually over a long period of time or peremptorily through military, administrative or political fiat. They may be the product of coercion by a superior power, of prolonged negotiation or a mixture of both. They can be suppressed, revived and reconstructed. They are often forged in interaction or conflict with other regions or territorial entities. In sum, the construction of regions is an open, complex and unfinished business.

Against this background of diversity and flux in regional formations, two factors are of particular significance in my view. The first may be termed globalisation, i.e. production, consumption, finance and mass communications and popular culture are increasingly subjected to the dictates of a capitalist market organised on a global basis. The second is the growth in the importance of the national state in regulating everyday life. Some of the most potent influences on regional formation derive from the tension between the global imperatives of the 'free market' and the territorially specific strategies of national states.

Border Regions: Ireland in context
The Irish Border region(s) is caught in the tension between the imperatives of transnational markets and the territorial strategies of nation-states. Borders, in the sense of known, geographically-drawn, lines marking jurisdictional limits are characteristic markers of sovereignty in *modern* nation states. They also act as barriers to the free play of market forces. As such they would appear to be ideal arenas in which to assess the tension between global economic strategies and those practiced by states within circumscribed territories. Moreover, border regions often have distinctive historical, socio-cultural and economic characteristics which span one or more national territories.

The plan to abolish internal border controls on the movement of capital, goods, services and EC citizens has re-focused attention on border regions within the EC. Superficially at least, it appears that the Single European Market is reducing the salience of national borders, moving the EC towards a Europe without national frontiers from which Euro-enthusiasts hope a federated 'Europe of the Regions' might emerge. Many Irish observers, for example, would subscribe to Richard Kearney's contention that conflict over the Irish border, and between Britain and Ireland, will be dissolved in a wider European 'constellation of regions'.

This optimistic scenario seems to bear out the strategy of the EC's founders in employing economic means to put an end to border disputes in western Europe. Indeed, the relative success of the EC in moderating such disputes seems in marked contrast to the eruption of border conflicts in eastern Europe. On the other hand, suggestions that national sovereignty is becoming attenuated are not grounded in analysis of what is actually occurring. There is a point at which aspiration and 'vision' must be subjected to empirical analysis.

Ireland is a reasonable place to begin. It seems to be a stubborn exception to the ameliorating impact of economic integration on border conflicts. Indeed, the conflict acts as a brake on cross-Border economic links. More recently, however, the SEM and the proposed Maastricht Treaty have acted as major stimuli to cross-Border economic co-operation among business people, government agencies and local development groups. While not all of this activity is focused on the Border region, there has been a major increase in cross-Border economic initiatives in the region under the aegis of both the IFI and the EC's INTERREG programme. The latter programme is part of the wider package devoted to economic and social cohesion to offset the centralising thrust of the Single European Market (SEM).

For a variety of reasons, the political significance of the Irish Border has increased over the last two decades. Since the early 1970s, the current 'Troubles' have progressively engaged both national governments in the policing of the border. This progress has culminated in the Anglo-Irish Agreement (AIA), in a systematic policy of closing cross-border roads and, more recently, in the investment of millions of pounds by the British government in elaborate fortifications and permanent security checkpoints at the major border crossings. Militarisation, therefore, has played an important part in consolidating the Border as an international boundary.

Secondly, the growth of nationalist influence in NI local authorities contiguous to the border has encouraged interest in cross-Border economic co-operation at local level. This has been stimulated by the creation of a 'grant environment' funded by the IFI, INTERREG and other EC programmes. Our research has uncovered almost three hundred local economic initiatives in close proximity to the border, of which almost fifty are explicitly cross-Border in orientation. In a sense, proximity to the Border has been a 'resource' for groups in that it makes them eligible for specific types of grant-aid.

Increased inter-governmental co-operation and formal cross-border contacts are not synonymous with the withering away of the Border, under the impetus of EC economic integration. Nor do they lead to a decline in the political significance of the Border; in fact the opposite may be the case.

It might have been expected that the simultaneous entry of the UK and the Irish Republic into the EC in 1973 would have diminished the role of the Border as an economic and political divide. Indeed, by international standards the Border was already an open one, with no travel restrictions, no language barrier and an interchangeable currency on either side. No major national economic or strategic interest seemed threatened by a diminution of the border. Naive expectations about the decline of the Border were not to be realised however. Remarkably, even the impact of EC economic integration, i.e. the area in which national sovereignty seemed most at risk, served to accentuate rather than reduce its significance. Currency parity ended in 1979 when the Republic entered the EMS and the UK did not. Since then, fluctuations in currency values, customs regulations, and agricultural subsidies have created a volatile shopping and trading zone along the Border.

While cross-Border trade between Northern Ireland and the Republic increased in absolute terms, it declined in relative terms as the Republic's trade diversified away from the UK to other EC countries. Although, there are several examples of major firms in the Border area which span the boundary, it remains unclear if they do so because, or in spite of, the existence of different jurisdictions on either side.

Clearly, the SEM will reduce some physical barriers to cross-Border trade. Customs barriers will disappear and technical and fiscal barriers to trade will also diminish. It is not clear however that the freer movement of capital, goods and services across the border will benefit the Border region itself. EC investment in cross-Border trunk routes, canals and rail lines will not necessarily attract new firms to an area where new physical barriers are being created for policing and security purposes. The potential opportunities and drawbacks of the SEM for Border regions has led to the creation of several cross-Border regional authorities elsewhere in Europe, many of them involving elected representatives, local authorities, chambers of commerce and trade unions. Such developments have been either prevented entirely, or restricted to embryonic forms, in the Irish Border area. The major reason is that both the UK and the Irish Republic are the two most centralised states in the EC. Meaningful regional or sub-regional institutions do not exist. This in turn has hindered the emergence of economic co-operation in the Border region. The management of INTERREG funds and, to a lesser extent IFI funds, reveals the tight control wielded by both central administrations and their reluctance to allow discretion to groupings of local authorities and development associations.

The significance of state centralisation is compounded, moreover, by the huge role both states play in the economies on either side of the border. In 1990, public expenditure in the South was 49% of GDP and 60% in the North. It seems likely that these figures would be higher for the Border area taken separately. Economic co-operation is not easily separable from politics and administration in these circumstances. It often becomes redefined, not as a means of addressing economic development issues directly, but as a way of coping with the duplication or parallelism in the provision of public services by the two centralised bureaucracies. In the circumstances, significant cross-Border economic co-operation would seem to require, as in some other EC countries, a common political and administrative framework for the Border region or sub-sections of it. There is little sign of the latter emerging – it is tempting to suggest that the most coherent strategic planning for the region is military rather than economic.

EC economic integration and moves toward closer European unity certainly have not resolved the violent conflict on the Border nor prevented it becoming an increasingly militarised zone. EC economic integration, the policies of both governments, the activities of the British army and the IRA all seem to point in the same direction, to the consolidation of the Border as an international boundary. Even the AIA and the management of EC and IFI development funds have involved the re-affirmation of the administrative integrity and sovereignty of both the UK and Irish (twenty-six county) states. In Ireland, at least, an EC of national states seems a far more substantial reality than the chimera of a federated 'Europe of the Regions'.

It is now useful to return to the question, 'what is a region?', posed at the outset. Throughout, I have used the term 'Border region' advisedly. The Border area is not, of course, a clearly-bounded, pre-given region. It is best seen as a region or a number of sub-regions, 'under construction' which may or may not become consolidated as significant entities. The outer boundaries of such regions are hazy although they are centred on the inter-state boundary.

In our research, for example, the 'Border region' includes those local authority areas contiguous to the land border, as well as Down. The INTERREG programme adds Sligo and other Northern Ireland councils outside the Belfast region. On the ground, various sub-regional groupings exist such as the North-West group of councils: Derry, Donegal, Strabane and now Limavady. The Eastern Border Region committee links councils at the other extremity. Other cross-Border organisations have been formed as part of EC networks. Examples include the Irish Border Regions Association and the Derry and Donegal councils' role in ERNACT, an information technology network linking several EC regions.

There are cross-Border networks of economic activities involving clothing and textiles, tourism, quarrying and the production of poultry, eggs, mushrooms, meat and dairy products. These activities forge links across the Border establishing distinctive sub-regional economies at different points along the boundary.

Overwhelmingly, however, the Border area is shaped by the history and evolution of the national boundary and by the assertion and affirmation of state sovereignties. It is a product of coercion and political and administrative activity. Because the Border region has been largely imposed from without makes it no less real, however.

Local people have sought to use it both legally and illegally to their own advantage. It also exists to their disadvantage, increasingly so, perhaps as the SEM begins to take effect.

Although I have concentrated on the political, administrative and economic dimensions of the Border area, cultural aspects need to be taken into account too. After all, this region is more ethnically and religiously diverse than the rest of NI or the Republic. In our research definition it embraces eight hundred thousand people, 16% of the island's population. The Southern side accounts for 10% of the population of the Republic and 22% of its Protestant population. The Northern side accounts for 28% of Northern Ireland's population and 43% of its Catholic population. This diversity, the contested nature of the boundary, and the impact of EC developments, make the Border area a good place to start looking for clues to the prospects of regions and regionalism in the new Europe.

Reference

1. The QUB research *Negotiating the British–Irish Border: Transfrontier Co-operation on the European Periphery* is directed by the author and funded by the Economic and Social Research Council (Grant No. R000 23 3053). James Corrigan and Tim Moore act as researchers on the project.

TONY CANAVAN

LOCALITY AND DIVIDED HISTORIES

At about this time last year, I was at a book launch at one of the larger bookshops in Belfast, and during one of those long speeches that someone always has to make on these occasions, my eyes strayed to the floor guide which happened to be on the wall beside me. You know, the sort of list that begins with something like anatomy and ends in zoology, telling you on which floor those books are located. As I looked down I read 'Healthy Living' and then immediately beneath that, 'History'. Except that I read it as 'healthy living history'. "If only!" I said to myself, thinking of the heavy burden of history on Ireland, but on second thoughts it struck me that 'healthy living history' epitomises local history exactly. It is healthy because it depends on the commitment and enthusiasm of ordinary people. In Northern Ireland there are about ten thousand people – and I am sure the figure is comparable in the Republic – who regularly meet to listen to lectures, visit historic sites, publish journals; to explore together the history and heritage of their own community, giving up their free time without thought of material reward.

Today, local history is seen as healthy also in the sense that it is good for both the individual and the community. In this era of mass communications and rapid change, local history or local heritage, provides a centre which will hold; a sense of identity and identification with place which seems essential to us all. For any individual, local history can be a fulfilling leisure time activity and a valuable exercise in self-education. For the community, local history also provides that same sense of identity and can play a key role in being a cohesive factor among an ever-thinning rural population. In Northern Ireland in particular, local history is viewed in terms of social enlightenment as a forum where Protestant and Catholic can come together to explore their shared history and traditions. In this way it is seen as making a significant contribution to community relations and so playing a role in healing the divisions in Northern Ireland.

It is living because being local it is immediate and real. The events of the local past happened on your own doorstep, not in some far-off foreign field. Likewise, the protagonists from local history are likely to be your own ancestors or those of your neighbour. History in your own locality is immediate and real in a way that history in books cannot be: You can look out from the door of your house and read in the landscape – its place-names and its physical features such as ancient graves, forts, ruins of buildings and even field boundaries – who has been there before you, how they lived and what they left behind. The motives of the local historian are not simply a desire for knowledge or an interest in research for its own sake but a personal interest in the history of his or her own family, community or locality. It can focus on broad social developments, such as changes in public education, or on more intimate subjects such as the history of a townland or farm, but all of it sheds light on the nature of the local community, and of that heritage and identity shared by all.

This identity with place and the awareness it brings of tradition, folklore, culture, change and inheritance, also brings with it a sense of community which is vital in the rural context and is just being rediscovered in the soul-less redevelopments of our cities.

A recent study in County Fermanagh revealed that for many in rural society today a local history association may be their first experience of working within a group. In Belfast, local history projects, on the Shankill Road or the old Sailortown, have helped to resuscitate a sense of community and neighbourliness almost lost when these areas were 'redeveloped' in the seventies and eighties. For particular groups, such as the elderly, local history is not just a leisure time activity but one that gives them a sense of their own worth as keepers of local heritage and brings recognition of their status within the community from others. Interest in local history, local heritage, has engendered in many places a new sense of community and self reliance which has directly resulted in new community-based developments. I am aware of a number of important locally-centered initiatives in education, economic development and tourism in Ireland, both north and south, which have grown directly out of the activities of local history groups.

But is this all there is to local history? Some months after that book launch in Belfast I attended a meeting of curriculum advisers to the Education and Library Boards in Northern Ireland at which someone sardonically remarked that 'geography gives us our neighbours but history gives us our enemies'. That struck a chord with me, as I am sure it will with anyone from Northern Ireland. Growing up in Belfast, I learned at an early age that 'neighbours', whether the people living on the other side of the road or sometimes even next door, could be 'enemies'. As a child I soon got used to shouted insults and even physical attack from other children who lived only in the next street. This perception – viewing neighbours as enemies – is born of history: what separates a 'Taig' from a 'Prod' is not which street you live in but over three hundred years of history, or at least a particular understanding of history.

Of course, a true understanding of history will not only help us to understand why such divisions exist but will also help us understand what we have in common: that shared humanity and shared heritage which are essential to any resolution of the conflict on this island. Having said that, however, we should not underestimate the strength of divided histories. The division between nationalist and unionist is an easy and obvious example, but an awareness of the past, of an inherited identity, can also divide townland from townland in any part of Ireland. It was not so long ago when occasions like the Lammas Fair in Ballycastle would see fights between the men of one townland and another, for example. A sense of community, of the unique or characteristic heritage of one region, say the Mournes in Ulster or Connemara in Connacht, can reinforce a sense of identity which is inward-looking and resentful of outside influences, not just people buying holiday homes or the more intrusive tourists, but those who want to join the community, even the 'blow-ins' who study the local history – a not very healthy sense of history or identity.

Divided histories, or divisions in history, can mean divided communities at even the most intimate level. Which side did your father or grandfather take in the Civil War? Who used to own a particular piece of land and who owns it now? Who prospered in the past while others failed? Answers to such questions may still arouse resentment and confrontation, but they too are a legitimate part of local history. We cannot ignore, and some will not let us forget, certain episodes in our history. Old resentments and old feuds, carried on from the past, may, in certain cases, outweigh the importance of locality, neighbourliness and community.

To conclude, then, I think we should recognise that there are two sides to this matter. History or heritage, when explored and celebrated in the local context can be, and in most cases is, something healthy and living. It does foster a sense of community, an awareness of a shared heritage and a common identity. On the other hand we should not be blind to the potentially divisive effects of history – it can give us our 'enemies'. Celebration of local heritage and local identity can reinforce a sense of the 'otherness' of outsiders and encourage an introspection which is unhealthy. Even within a small community, history and the legacy of the past can divide neighbour from neighbour.

But let me not end on too gloomy a note: progress lies in avoiding the pitfalls created by a rosy-eyed optimism about the virtues and benefits of local history as well as those created by a jaundiced pessimism of seeing only the limitations in a strong sense of local identity. The reality lies somewhere in between and illustrates that locality and history – divided or shared – both have their place in creating a healthy, living, community.

DERMOT HEALY

**INGREDIENTS OF REGIONAL IDENTITIES
(REPUBLIC OF IRELAND)**
WHERE I'M COMING FROM

I was reared in County Cavan. My mother was by the name of Slacke and she was born nearly ninety years ago in Ardlogher which is four miles up the road from the Slieve Russell Hotel where this conference is taking place. Her father – James Slacke – was an old RIC sergeant, a mystic who was always buried in books and spoke in conundrums. Slacke says Protestant, but he was in fact Catholic, with all of the extremism of a convert.

The Slacke family saw the barracks they were reared in burned to the ground, the girls were taunted in school, hate mail arrived, but despite that a couple of the daughters, including my mother, married men from the new Free State Garda force.

My father's side came from Elphin in the County Roscommon. We met his family very seldom. Some lived in America, and those who lived in the West of Ireland we saw only at funerals. They were small horse-farmers and republicans and great people to pray.

I moved to Sligo without having any intention of staying but six years on I find I have bought a small cottage there alongside the Atlantic. By chance I discovered that Guard Healy's father came from east Sligo, up at Lough Arrow, and that Sergeant James Slacke's father came from Aclare in south Sligo.

This gave me a whole new perspective on things. So, I've chosen to have a look at, and to compare the counties of Cavan and Sligo in this talk, two counties that might appear to have nothing much in common.

First I had to start though with a brief account of my own family background. Family background is the first ingredient of regional identity. For your sake I had to give you some perspective of where I'm coming from, else I'll be pretending to rise above the so-called 'closed mind' of the provincial.

'I have risen above the common herd' is the underlying maxim of the new liberal Ireland, and the new liberals actually abhor those people we are here to discuss – those who actually practise their cultural and regional identity: GAA supporters, Orange marchers, Fianna Fáil supporters, soccer fans and all those who gather for stoic suffering in cold churches.

In the main, the new order are not only well removed from the life of the everyday Paddy but spend their intellectual life trying to get over their disgust with ever having been associated with it. Yet, many of our writers turn back to those deprived years for their source material, and not without a certain love. I spent years out of touch with the milieu I grew up in and yet I now believe there is another 'closed mind' than that preferred by traditional mores. The liberal too has a closed mind, which is just as infectious and false as the traditional one it is attempting to replace.

In the regions, the demarcation lines between the two sides are clearly evident. Dublin 4, which was invented by Dublin 1 which in turn was invented by Dublin 4, has satellites throughout rural Ireland, in places such as Montenotti, Rosses Point and Pontoon. A key to their ghettoes is the price of properties. Their propaganda embraces much academic work that passes itself off as high-principled and objective, though the same academics would cut each others' throats when it comes to fighting for the chair of History or English in various universities. For some, this conference will be akin to slumming for the weekend among the worst excesses of the Country-and-Western rural phenomenon.

Ireland has become European, says one voice, and soon the Northern 'Troubles' will be swallowed up as our differences give way to more universal concepts. Ireland has become very small, says another voice. The more European or international our ambitions are, the smaller we get and the less diversified we become. According to this thinking the war in the North may end when we have become uniformly bland.

But this is all shop talk. The ingredients of regional identity, which, in fact, can be read not only as those ingredients that keep us together but those that keep us apart, are going to be there for a long time to come. To get at some of those ingredients, it's time

I stopped broad generalisations. I think when you talk regions, you better be specific.

When I was young I heard a theory about the effect of environment on dialect. A Cavan man – an environmental linguist of course – told me that if a few thousand Japanese were transported to South Armagh they would in time take on the Armagh accent. I asked him: 'Would the Japanese have to mix with the Armagh folk first?' 'Not at all' he said, 'clear the inhabitants out, put in your Japanese, leave them there for a couple of generations and you'll have Zen spoken with an Armagh accent.'

A half a mile outside Cootehill on the Clones road the Niall Tóibín broad-vowelled K-avan accent ends in one house and the Northern Monaghan accent begins in the next house along. This happens all along the Cavan border with Monaghan, and the Sligo border with Donegal. Even the locals can't account for this linguistic leap, but as sure as rivers or mountains make a physical border, the change in accent marks a boundary of sorts. Once you have found a border, however arbitrary, you have found a region.

It is easy to see the difference in economic and farming traditions between the two counties. Cows and pigs in Cavan, cattle and sheep in Sligo. But their relationship with the North of Ireland differs in many respects.

Cavan, although in Ulster, has few connections with Belfast, except for those Protestant women who went up there to nurse and married in. On the other hand, Sligo which is not in Ulster, was known at the beginning of the century as Little Belfast. As the Ulster identity began ranging round for adherents over recent years, Sligo has become, like Donegal, a haven for Northerners, both Protestant and Catholic, while Cavan has nearly ceased to have a Northern dimension, unless you count smuggling, price-differences and illegal hormone-boosters for cattle, which you should.

Smuggling has always been a tradition in County Cavan. Many of the main businesses like garages, coal providers, grocery shops and latterly public houses thrived on smuggling. Cavan's Protestant businesses ran nice lucrative border trades but over the last twenty years most of these builders and providers have disappeared, yet Sligo's main Protestant family businesses, despite sectarianism and cut-backs, remain intact. Cavan sent B-Specials over the border for night duty, Sligo did not. Yet, on the other hand, both the Republican tradition and the Unionist are stronger in County Sligo.

Not that there is much to-and-froing these days between Little Belfast and its older brother. Sligo knows its Belfast through those Northerners who have made of Mullaghmore and much of north County Sligo an Ulster resort. Belfast is known to Cavan through the television. What they both share in are excursions to Enniskillen.

Outsiders not only live in a region but they can determine much of what happens in that region, good or bad. This is true of Galway city and Sligo. Cootehill, though nominally in Cavan, has such a strong Monaghan connection, that Paddy Kavanagh has become an honorary Cavan man. The MacArdle brothers have turned a Cavan town into a Monaghan fortress and this was done by-and-large through amateur drama, the same force that brought the Hawkswell Theatre into being in Sligo and has given Ireland some of its premier actors. So amateur drama, when you speak of ingredients of a region, should get a mention.

The outsider not only brings new life in, but can be the mirror in which the locals can see themselves.

The Sligo Community Arts Festival was founded and sustained by people from outside the region. The Yeats Festival, though it has a local committee, draws on people outside the region, as many local festivals do, for its success. In fact, the Yeats Festival can often strike you as an imposition on the locals but the truth is that Sligo has always had a barrage of strangers living there – English, French and German, and their unemployed make many of the street-theatre figures that fill the streets during the Arts Festival. The outsider or blow-in will contribute to a region all that he or she could not do at home, in their own locality.

Many of the people at this conference I'm sure are working and living as social workers, community leaders and academics in regions well away from their original homes. The stimulus to throw yourself headlong into saving Belfast may in part come from not having been born there. Where we come from can act as a formidable barrier against getting things done if we are to remain in our own localities. And of course strangers may enter a new region full of idealistic notions and these may be soon whittled away.

Voluntary workers, often outsiders, soon tire of the energy they expend on community and amateur theatre, community magazines, art festivals and arts centres. Culture, after the initial euphoria, is a drain on the nervous system and a thankless business for paid administrators, never mind voluntary workers. The lack of funding or economic success drives many voluntary companies to the wall. And yet the call of the community is so strong that there are always others to take their place. And community festivals do enhance a region. Regions owe a great deal to those cultural volunteers.

Cavan in the old days was not hospitable to strangers, but is now home to a Buddhist temple, thriving rock bands, arts festivals, English pike-and-bream fishermen, German bed-and-breakfasts, and a new army barracks that houses soldiers from every part of Ireland. It has an arts officer and soon will have a writer-in-residence. These appointments bring new cultural life to a region. This hotel was built by a man from Fermanagh who has single-handedly revived life in West Cavan, yet, rumour has it, that stones from a passage grave were moved from their site to the forefront of this hotel. This is unbelievable, if it is true.

The Glengevlin region is one of the last pagan fortresses in Ireland and was home to Crom Cruach. It is a region all to itself. As a matter of fact the North-West of Ireland, from the point of view of landscape, begins in Glan, as Glengevlin is locally known.

And now do you know that Glan is a region apart? On the one hand there are mountains, instead of drumlins. But most of all there's the predominant name – McGovern. If you listen to the intercom in the bar here at night, more often than not, it's a McGovern that's wanted over the phone. So another ingredient of an area is the predominant name. In Cavan it's O'Reilly, in Leitrim, O'Rourke.

You have to pay attention to names. In Cavan very little attention is paid to Christian names. The greeting in the morning is 'Hay-Ho!' Christian names are rarely used, and I met a solicitor who packed up business in Cavan and moved to Sligo because no one could ever remember his name in Cavan town. He had enough of being called 'yon fellow', 'the boy there', 'that bollax', 'what's-his-name', 'good man' and 'that tulip'.

But I was reared to this. In Sligo things are totally different. There, great attention is paid to Christian names. If you meet a local once, he will have your first name on his lips for ever after.

PART II — REGIONS AND TRADITIONS 107

Weather is an important ingredient of a region. The points of the compass give as true a reading of a region's character as do its recent history. You can never underestimate what nature can do, if you live exposed to its worst rages. If the Japanese came to Sligo they too would believe in fairies. It is no wonder Yeats thrived in the North-West.

A Cavan man, protected from the worst excesses of weather, would not be so forthcoming. If he believed in fairies, he would keep it to himself. The drumlins encourage a sense of absurd, and I suppose, riotous farces. So a further ingredient of a region is the tales people tell, and how they tell them. *Now You're Talking*, a book of anecdotes and story telling collected along the border counties, testifies to this.

In the Cavan tales there are hair-raising sexual encounters told with marvellous vulgarity. The Sligo stories are more reserved and magical.

A woman is known everywhere throughout the North-West as 'the lady', and women as 'the ladies'. A woman in Cavan is not so lucky. She will earn, from both men and women, a series of outlandish pet names, from the fairly common 'young thing', through 'trollop', to 'targe'. 'Lady' does not occur. The word 'lady' in Cavan would only be used to cynically describe a woman putting on airs.

So how sexes see each other, and the words they use for each other, is also an aspect of regional identity. 'My fellow', with its broad possessive article, is not heard in Sligo but is common in Cavan and throughout the North. The Sligo woman does not pretend to own her partner. The males are known as 'the men'. Both sides view each other as an exotic collection of gender differences.

Sligo goes in for story-telling, Cavan for theatricality. The Sligo person has little time for cursing. The only curses I hear in any conversation there are my own. Among the drumlins competition and slagging are rife. Intimacy is an enigma. You don't get too close. A bar of drinkers in Sligo sounds different than a bar of drinkers in Cavan. One has a courteous air, the other is all go. The first is often mistaken for unfriendliness, and the second covers up an outrageous sentimentality. Even the sound of the place-names – though you might not know them as specific territories – will tell you whether you are in Cavan or Sligo.

Cavan's sounds are cryptic and lovingly earthy. Sligo's are soft-vowelled and musical.

So placenames too are a key to a region. The first people who named the parts, in a way described not only the personality of the place, but their own personality, and their naming of places shaped the personality of the people who would follow them into the regions. Each region has a personality, a rhythm. After you live there for a while, these place-names – however imperfectly translated – will be on our lips, that particular accent will be around you, and bit-by-bit you inherit the rhythm of the region.

Despite yourself, if you move to live near Croagh Patrick, you will climb the reek. If as a Midlander you eventually live by the sea, one day you will find yourself out in a boat in the Atlantic. Despite whatever reserves you have about anecdotes, if you find yourself in Belfast, you'll soon be chocker-block with the black humour that tries to cover up the rampant nostalgia of the city. And once you get hooked it's hard to leave a place, as many have found who have settled in Cork, on the Aran Islands, in Connemara, in Clare. You become their spokesperson. Belonging is not just an attribute of the local. Or put another way, wanting to belong is an even more fierce emotion than just mere belonging.

The Sligo people have travelled the world. I have often sat in Austie Gillen's pub in Rosses Point and heard a crowd of Yeats scholars sharing reminiscences of events literary throughout the world, while sitting quietly beside them were local men who had lived in New Zealand, shipped out of Hong Kong, shacked up in Rio and spent winters at the North Pole. Beside these experiences, the literary life seemed strangely limited, not because the seamen were physical workers, but because they saw the foreign regions they worked in as something to set against their own; the size of boats, what was farmed there, the difference in wages, the weather, the diseases, music, sayings, the women, the men and the Irish people living there. Especially the Sligo people living there.

So another ingredient of a region is what it's people do abroad, the route they take to get there and the places they settle down in. One of the most mythical Cavan creations was the Cavan football team that won an All-Ireland in the United States of America. That will never be erased from the Cavan imagination and may singlehandedly have driven a wedge across further GAA ambitions in Cavan.

The Sligos go to the States, but more often their route abroad followed the boats from Sligo port – to Scotland, Liverpool, and from Liverpool to Australia, South Africa and South America. A Cavan traveller, having no such access, took the approved route to London or the States. In England, the Sligos settled in the East End of London near the docks, or worked in the car-factories of Luton. The Cavans were dispersed through London as barmen in Watney's public houses.

Having access to the sea can also give a regional people less reliance on the county town. There were folk from Belmullet that never stood in Castlebar or, for that matter, Ballina town. Their route by sea was Belmullet to Sligo, next stop off at Donegal to take on more labourers, and then on to Scotland for the potato picking. In time, because the boat left twice a day for Sligo, the Mullet women-folk travelled over and back in the one day to do their shopping in Sligo. So they had no need of the Mayo capitals. Neither had the folk of west Cavan much use for Cavan town. They used to head to Sligo to do their shopping. But, in this instance, the 'Cavan bus' took on other connotations in Sligo. If the Sligos say someone 'has come in off the Cavan Bus' they are being derogatory. Those who used to alight from the Cavan bus were deemed to be fairly boggish in demeanour. In fact, eegits. Each county has its fall guy, and the Cavan bus, which no longer runs, seemingly brought in a rough crowd to decorous Sligo in the old days.

Regions give each other bad names.

The North of Ireland prides itself on the craft of poetry making. Everything written South of the border is seen as uniformly loose, badly contrived and anecdotal. The Southerners see much of Northern prose as exercises in nostalgia, sentimental dialogue and covert sectarianism. How the poet from Kerry views the poet from Wexford will throw up another set of critical values. And so on. When this reaches the academic texts, of course all regional biases are well disguised. Much critical work is now an agonised attempt to purge texts of all regional, sectarian, racial or gender biases, so that a whole new transparent language has come into being.

This critical language is a regional language all to itself, inward-looking, defensive and adroitly high-principled. With Europe adding a whole new subtext to the proceedings, this conference could have done with a glossary to help the uninformed know what's going on.

An interesting question to ask of the participants at this conference would be, 'Which of ye still attend Church?' Or, 'which of ye still pray?'

Religion is getting short shrift as the basis of much of what is called regional identity. The Mass-goer and church-attender have been moved in one lump into the area known as 'conservative' – for their sins, you might say. This is at a time when we have been reassured over-and-over that the conflict in the North is not a religious war. But religion is one of the prime ingredients of the personality of a place.

The Bricklieves mountains are as religious an area as any to be found in these island. They were not selected by stone-age people at random, nor were the monuments allowed remain there to the present day just because of 'local superstition'. Respect comes into it somewhere. Some landscapes are sacred, and will continue to be so. If Mass-going is now to be replaced by therapy by one section of the populace, it does not mean that the irreligious have moved up some genetic rung on the ladder. Worship and spirituality still mix well in some modern souls.

Sligo and Cavan are home to numerous religious sects. Cavan has always tended towards an unimaginative Catholicism or Protestanism, albeit with a jovial outlook, while the Sligo region is a hotbed of evangelical religions. The Cavans frown on religious excess while the Sligos welcome it.

The Sligo Orangemen were asked to lead the 'Twelfth' in Belfast in the thirties but found, with a few weeks to go, that they were short of musicians to lead them. They contacted the local YMCA band, who gave them a number of musicians that they could train in. So the brass-players and flautists went over to the Orange hall and learned the marching tunes. The day came, and the CYMS Band and the Sligo Orangemen, to thunderous applause, led the march down the centre of Belfast. All went well till the march passed a Catholic church and the CYMS musicians lowered their instrument and came to a stop to bless themselves.

In 1991, I was footing turf under Bulben with a part-time parson. I had bought a couple of banks of turf from him and he had come out to help us because the midges were biting. And in true Sligo style he told me that years ago, he would often be out there footing turf in Ballintrillick, and the next day he'd find himself driving a Rolls Royce through the gates of Windsor Palace.

'Is that right?' I asked disbelievingly.

'Yes,' he said, 'you see, I was Lord Mountbatten's chauffeur'.

This to me is a true ingredient of a regional identity – that ability to be elsewhere and yet attend to matters at home. A regionalist is at home abroad, and is an internationalist when he's back in his region.

The same parson met his wife at a dance on the Twelfth in the Orange Hall in Farnham in the County Cavan. I knew it well from the dark pure nights during Lent when we used go out there to dance the Protestant girls. Not that we were successful in our courting. A few blonde lads kept a beady eye on us as they stood by the door with bottles of *Smithwicks Number 1* by the neck. And what were we dancing to? Sixties music and Irish reels.

Music is probably the most international language of them all. You could not have two more different musical traditional styles than those from Cavan and Sligo. They share one quality – they don't play too fast. But in Sligo, as anyone knows who has heard the recordings of Coleman, decoration is prized. Sometimes the tune may even disappear and only the decoration remain.

But in Cavan, the tunes are unadorned. Cavan is accordion country, with a deft touch of the fiddle thrown in, but the music is there primarily to dance to, and the set-dances are robust, lusty and loud.

I remember, in Belfast, going to see a group of Cavan set dancers during the Traditional Music Festival. The Cavan musicians from Mullahoran who were to accompany them had been held up at the border so a few Belfast fiddlers stood in for them. The dancers formed up, the tune took off and nobody moved. The reel died away. There was some discussion and a word in the fiddler's ear. The musicians started playing again, slower this time, and the dancers tried a few steps and then gave up in confusion.

Then at the back of the hall the Mullahorans entered, opened their fiddle cases, stood in and began to play. Only then did the dance start. Even the Belfast style was too fast for the dancers.

Every region has its own musical style and this style is often echoed in the work of the writers from that region.

After Yeats, few writers have settled in or originated in Sligo. Sligo, despite its vast horizons, is culturally insular. It has no arts officer, and its council was recently going to locate a public dump on the doorstep of the Carrarowe tomb. It's as if Yeats has freed the authorities of cultural responsibility. The poet is now one of the most important sources of tourist revenues in Ireland, never mind Sligo, so, unlike Cavan, the council does not have to rustle up artistic activity. Each morning at eight during the Summer the buses are pulling in at Drumcliffe, and the last is drawing away near nine that night.

No one of Yeats' stature arose in Cavan, unless you count Brinsley Sheridan, or that frequent visitor to his father's household in Quilca, Johnathan Swift, who had the right mix of irony, malice and exaggeration to make him an honourable Breifne man. But despite this lack of major literary figures, the literary arts are thriving in Cavan with such writers as Michael Harding, Tom MacIntyre and Shane Connaughton.

Yeats' name adorns restaurants, streets, pubs in Sligo. Culturally, he is a Mecca all to himself and then what happens? The authorities raise a sculpture to his memory outside the Ulster Bank. The sculpture is drawn from a cartoon in *Punch* and is known locally as 'the wank at the bank'. The perspective adopted is twee, patronising and not even absurd. The excuse offered for the choice of sculpture is 'pragmatism'.

On the other hand, Kavanagh whose poetry provides the motto for this conference; 'gods make their own importance', has little named after him – a lounge in a Dundalk hotel, one pub – but little else in his native area. He is more prized in Dublin, with the seat by the canal, on which is inscribed one of his finest poems. I think it is significant too that Cavan abounds in local history books (nearly every parish has one) while Sligo has hardly any, despite the fact that it contains the aforementioned Bricklieves, one of the most extraordinary monuments of ancient man in Western Europe. The Bricklieves are known only to the droves of New Age people that gather in the North-West each year, in the belief that benign ley lines align there. The Battle of the Books, known to most scholars, passes unheeded in Sligo. A new Stone Age civilization, large as that discovered in Mayo, has been unearthed above Glencar, but as yet it lies unexplored. Inishmurray Island, one of the most powerful replicas of monastic life in the Atlantic, is rarely visited. If any of these monuments to the past existed elsewhere in Ireland they would long have been turned into major tourist resorts.

It is as if Sligo, having all these constant reminders of the past, has no need of local history books. They leave it all to the professional writers from the outside world. They seem indifferent to selling their region, and when they do, they perform with an abundance of naivety and sincerity, but with a lack of passion. This is their saving grace in some eyes and a cause of frustration in others, including Bord Fáilte.

But once you look at the visual arts a different story arises. Cavan and Monaghan until recent times were visually illiterate, though they were far ahead of the West of Ireland as regards television, since from a long way back they had been receiving BBC and ITV. But always in the North-West painting has thrived. Jack Yeats and Paddy Collins come to mind. It is as if the Sligos think in pictures, while Cavan needs words. The light that depresses the inhabitants of the West is the same light that illuminates the artists. At the moment three of Ireland's greatest landscape painters – Sean McSweeney, Barrie Cooke and Camille Souter – are living and working in the North-West. Achill Island and Ben Bulben must be the two of the most frequently painted landscapes in Ireland.

Film, still one of the most popular artforms, has become a new ingredient of a region. *The Quiet Man* calls up a landscape, as does *The Playboys, Angel, The Field, My Left Foot, Ryan's Daughter* and all these landscapes and people will be there on celluloid for years to come. It is interesting too to note how Irish audiences despair of ever seeing a true version of their region on the screen. The visually dramatic has always been inaccurate as far as locals are concerned, but they have been willing to forgive certain Hollywood excesses for the sake of a good story. On the other hand modern art which used to get short shrift is a thriving business.

The blues and greens of Sean McSweeney's North Sligo bogholes sit in many a consciousness far removed from where the work was painted. There is a vast abyss between the landscape and the paintings that celebrate it. 'If I was to leave a painting of mine down on the rocks by the Atlantic,' Sean McSweeney has said, 'it would look no better than a plastic bag'.

Everywhere authenticity and illusion are at odds. And much more so when discussing a region's identity. The actual landscape is the lynch-pin of belonging and that landscape embraces both rural and urban areas. But Mother Earth, which infuses a painting with light, is also the dark terrain over which battles are fought. Human habitation is in fact a phrase born of constant tension.

Meanwhile there are day-to-day problems for the two counties of Cavan and Sligo. In one, they are fighting potholes, in the other, sea erosion. Neither are doing well in the GAA, and as a matter of fact, Sligo has never done well.

'And it's a good job we're no good at GAA, and that the soccer is going bad', a neighbour of mine in Sligo said, 'If we won anything, we've nothing to sing'.

Sligo has no songs of celebration, sporting songs and few political ones. Cavan on the other hand has *Come Back Paddy Reilly to Ballyjamesduff* or *The Gallant John Joe*, written in honour of John Joe Reilly, one of those footballers who made it to the States to win an All-Ireland.

The strange thing is that two of the most popular contemporary songs in Sligo and Cavan – *The Train to Sligo* and *The Road to Killeshandra* – were both written by an American, Tom Moore who settled for a time in Sligo and now, by the way, lives in Russia. So in fact a region can look to a total outsider to capture some of it's identity in song and in poetry.

Sligo's soccer footballers often come from Scotland and England, and many have remained there and married in after their footballing days are over. So a soccer region can encourage internationalism in a quiet way.

All regions have one weakness, they tend to see themselves as unique. Hence only the authentic is seen as true. But what is considered authentic by some can be seen by others as self-deluding. Under this premise, self-delusion is as much an ingredient of a region as actual authentic details are. The authentic is governed by certain basic laws – accent, exact observations, psychological traits, proper naming and precise physical description. If you are not authentic, you're not in, the saying goes, and yet authenticity is itself based on illusion.

But how do you know when you are deluding yourself? Recent history in western Europe gives one cause to wonder. Ethnic cleansing may seem an alien concept in Ireland, and yet small Protestant farmers in Fermanagh and Catholic working class punters in the bookies of Belfast may see it as just another form of sectarianism. Old prejudices remain dormant in a region and these prejudices are an ingredient of a region.

The Half-Acre in Cavan, the Hill in Sligo town were both deprived areas that will find it hard to forgive townplanners. Architects have a lot to answer for. But things are changing. In fact the tide is on the turn and this is primarily because our politicians, journalists, and civil service have ceased to talk down to the regions, urban or rural. Even the Republic's national television station has begun to match the expectations of its viewers. The regions have long ago been cosmopolitan, it was the media and various governments that were in fact patronising us.

The outsider and the local have blended well. No moral outrage in fact seems necessary as regard the modern mix found in the arts, in music, in literature. You soon tire of a single diet no matter whether it be traditional or contemporary.

The old garrison towns of Sligo and Cavan are host to a new era. By a quirk of politics two regionalists from Cavan and Sligo have been recently taking part in national and international affairs – John Wilson in the Northern Irish talks, and Ray McSharry as Commissioner of Agriculture in the GATT talks.

A few years ago neither of these appointments to such discussions would have been a possibility. The rest of the world, including the North of Ireland, were left to look after themselves. So things have changed in the Republic. No matter that both men have departed the political scene in Ireland. The insider has been forced out into the open, and the outsider has taken up residence.

But it is salutary to remember that though the outsiders may be coming into their own, locals are a threatened species. Wisdom can come to those who have never stirred outside their townland. Put another way, you still know your own. Knowing the others is the task at hand.

ANNE TANNAHILL

INGREDIENTS OF REGIONAL IDENTITIES (NORTHERN IRELAND)

When I began to think about this paper, I found that the more I concentrated on abstract ideas of religion and identity the more uneasy and inauthentic I felt, the less true to myself and my own experience.

So, rather than present you with airy notions masquerading as profound concepts, I thought I would attempt an examination of the smallest unit in which the ingredients of identity display themselves: the individual. The individual I know best – at least I think I do – is myself. I therefore intend to begin with some of the influences which have shaped and are still shaping me, exploring the fragmented and fluid nature of 'identity' in the individual, and to move from that to the dangers of rigid definitions where regional or group identities are concerned.

The very act of trying to disentangle personal influences, to categorise and present them coherently, almost proved the point at the outset. How can class, religion, politics, gender be examined as separate ingredients? They flow in and through and over and under each other in such an inconveniently leaky and messy way that it's almost impossible to consider one in isolation from the others.

However, I must start somewhere and I suppose religion is as good a place as any. I was brought up as a Presbyterian in the sense that I was christened at Sinclair Seamen's Presbyterian Church at the Belfast docks and attended church and Sunday school there regularly until I was about thirteen, when my family moved away from North Belfast to a new housing estate at Suffolk on the Upper Falls Road. Neither of my parents were church attenders. (I realised later that in common with other young married couples living in cramped conditions, they found that having the kids out of the house for a few hours on a Sunday afternoon had its advantages).

My memories of church and Sunday school are almost all happy: I was a studious child and loved memorising enormously long Psalms, the books of the Old and New Testaments and the hymns of Mrs Alexander. The Sunday school teachers were far from the repressed authoritarians Presbyterians are supposed to be: I remember the superintendent closing the school one Sunday and marching us outside to stand at the kerb in Corporation Square to watch a circus, just disembarked from the Liverpool boat, as it began its ungodly and Sabbath-breaking procession through the city.

I had an ideal of myself as a good girl, but all through those years I knew that there was a crisis approaching when I would, God willing, be 'saved' and become a 'Christian'. The crisis came when I was about twelve and went to the Presbyterian Assembly Buildings in Belfast to hear a Billy Graham rally being relayed from, I think, Edinburgh. I was absolutely intent on being saved that night; what saved me from otherwise certain salvation was a kind of emotional and intellectual revulsion at the crudely manipulative style of the sermon. When Billy Graham thundered, 'Brothers and sisters, tonight God and the devil are fighting for your soul. Who will win?' I remember gripping tightly on to my chair to stop myself joining the people who were flocking to the awaiting clergymen on the curiously Billy-Graham-less stage.

By the time I was seventeen I had passed through the classic stages of doubt and considered myself an achieved and completely rational atheist. I'm still an atheist, but not now so dismissive of spiritual experience in myself or others. There are many such secular people in the north – around 12% of the population according to recent surveys. Many of them act as a kind of liberal leaven in the otherwise heavy religious texture of society, but they are usually ignored by academics and media people (who are often secular themselves) and by, for example, the education authorities.

I'm still, tribally, a Protestant. I'm angry and ashamed about the discrimination, the injustice and the atrocities carried out against Catholics in the name of my tribe, but I'm also angry and disgusted at the condescension and contempt with which a mass of good and decent people is being regarded in these islands and in the outside world.

The second ingredient, class, probably shaped me even more than religion; I still feel closer to Catholics from a working-class background than Protestants born into the middle or upper classes.

My father was a housepainter, quite often out of work, especially in the winter months. He was often forced to seek work across the water, living in grim digs and returning home looking thin and ill. Before her marriage my mother had been a cigarette packer at the Gallahers' factory and my maternal grandfather, who lived with us, was an iron-turner at Harland & Wolff. We lived in a flat above a pub in North Queen Street: the family home had been destroyed in the Blitz, on my parents' wedding night.

In due course I passed the new qualifying examination and became the first child in the history of the family to go to grammar school; I think it's often forgotten that the 1947 Education Act benefited Protestant working-class children as well as Catholic ones. Years later, I read and strongly identified with Richard Hoggart's autobiographical account of the tensions generated in family and community by a working-class child going to a 'posh school' – the unspoken, and sometimes spoken, accusations of class betrayal on one side and general upstartedness on the other. I left school at sixteen; reluctantly, but I was the eldest of four and the family budget needed my contribution.

I continued the slow move away from class roots by getting what my father called 'a good clean inside job' as a clerk in the Northern Ireland Civil Service and later, when I was dismissed just before my wedding because of the marriage bar then operating, with the Northern Ireland Hospitals Authority. I left that when my son was born and after some years as a rather depressed housewife and mother I took A-levels and entered Queen's University. I was absolutely petrified; the university had always seemed like a forbidden palace reserved for the rich and brilliant and I was sure someone was going to stand up in the lecture hall and denounce me as a social and intellectual fraud. I literally had never known anyone, apart from clergymen and GPs, who had been at university. Again, this step caused some bewilderment and resentment with some of my family and friends; who did I think I was? As this was exactly what I was asking myself, it took me a few years to gain any kind of self-confidence.

After university I taught for a time – very badly – in Further Education colleges and then in 1976 a part-time job with Blackstaff Press developed into a full-time one. I sometimes wonder what social class I am now and, increasingly, does it really matter?

Politics is the next ingredient. Both my parents were socialist in that they always voted Labour; I remember my mother outraging the neighbours by scraping off Unionist posters that had been posted to our wall. My grandfather was a strong Unionist and an Orangeman; he used to waken me early on Twelfth mornings to catch the train to Ballymena, his home town, where I would be thoroughly spoiled by his relations and taken to see him march behind fife and drum with his lodge.

I met no Catholics at home or at school. There were a few Jews at the grammar school, who seemed exotic and enviable with their extra holidays, but I don't think any more exotic than Catholics would have seemed. I had a very clear tribal map in my head and knew not only which streets in our district were Catholic, but exactly where in the street the Catholic houses began. I remember feeling frightened if I crossed these invisible boundaries, although I can't recall any incident that would have justified such fear.

My first close relationship with a Catholic was with another young clerk at Stormont. Through her I learned of the discrimination against Catholics in the Northern Ireland Civil Service: her father, a very capable man, had been stuck at Staff Officer level for years while mediocre Protestants were promoted over him. When I tackled my own boss about it, there was no denial that this was indeed the case. Rather, with kindly patience for my naivety, he explained that as Catholics were sworn enemies of the Northern Ireland state, they couldn't be trusted to be loyal servants of that state.

At the same time I met Brian, my husband. Like me, he was the first grammar school child in his family. His family were Unionists and he was an Orangeman, in the same county lodge as his uncles. I had some difficulties with his membership of the Order but I also greatly enjoyed the social events, accompanying the lodge to the demonstration fields and feeling part of a warm, lively social group. He left the Order after a few years because the spread of housing estates into the area brought Belfast Orangemen whose harsh brand of sectarian politics completely changed the atmosphere of the lodge. He remains unionist and anti-nationalist in his politics and living with him has kept me in closer contact with unionist thinking than would otherwise have been the case.

When I worked with the Northern Ireland Hospital Authority, I again saw anti-Catholic discrimination in operation. I succeeded as recruitment officer a genteel old Unionist lady and discovered that for years she had been withholding applications from qualified Catholics from the screened selections she presented upwards. Her senior officer believed in all good faith that appointments were free of all bias and indeed took some pride in it; this was in the early 1960s.

But it was university which really exposed me to Catholics and nationalism. Many of my best friends, as bigots always say, were Catholics. And of course the years 1970 to 1976 when I was at Queen's were turbulent and terrible; our year sat their finals during the Ulster Workers Strike and to get me there my husband drove straight at and scattered the loyalists paramilitaries who had sealed off our housing estate. It was a bizarre experience to be writing a paper on the English metaphysical poets and wondering when and if paramilitaries would allow me back home to swot for the next day's exam.

In spite of all this, or perhaps because of it, I was never an activist. I was, I think, liberal, but always very cautious, terrified of violence and social unrest. We lost our home in the Lenadoon estate in the aftermath of internment in August 1971, becoming a statistic in the biggest forced movement of population in Europe since the Second World War. The trauma of that, and a scepticism about rumour and propaganda, made me break the Bloody Sunday protest strike at Queen's the following January. If I had known the facts about Bloody Sunday as I do now, I probably would have tacitly supported the strike by staying at home. But I can't imagine ever being part of the howling, bullying picket line that I and other students and lecturers had to face to get to classes and the library; I'm still revolted when I think of it.

Like my parents, I continued to vote Labour until the Northern Ireland Labour Party ceased putting up candidates. I had a very brief flirtation with the Alliance Party but since then have felt effectively disenfranchised. I recently castigated an English Labour backbencher for abandoning people like me and he replied that his party felt that they had a very strong sister party in Northern Ireland in the SDLP. I think my point that the Catholic and nationalist nature of the SDLP made it difficult for Protestant socialists to vote for them seemed to him irrelevant and indeed faintly distasteful.

One of the strongest political influences on me has been working at Blackstaff Press; hammering out a publishing policy with Michael Burns, the Catholic owner of the company; listening to and reading the wide spectrum of authors we publish; and above all, daily contact with articulate, politically-aware Catholic colleagues. Publishers are professional users of language and we're constantly inspecting apparently inert words and phrases for hidden detonators. For example, I had no idea why Catholics dislike being called Roman Catholics until a very cross Catholic editor put me straight. If we are to deliver our implicit manifesto at Blackstaff – books on Northern Ireland that explain ourselves to ourselves, to the 'other side' and to the outside world, this sort of discussion and the personal shifts in attitude that it generates has to be unceasing.

I've left gender to the last, not because it's the least important ingredient in my identity – after all, it's the first and sometimes the only thing that people perceive when they see or hear me – but because it's the least compartmentable element of all. It underpins and overshadows the other categories of religion, class and politics. To take one instance, I've spoken about the anti-Catholic discrimination in the Northern Ireland Civil Service in my day. But this was at a time when it was an absolute rule that women were dismissed on marriage; this practice continued until the late 1960s. The Protestant/Catholic balance in top management there is now improving, but we have yet to see a woman Permanent Secretary and women are still shamefully under-represented in the top tier. Gender for me and I suppose for all of us, male or female, is the fundamental shaper of both our identity and our destiny.

It certainly strongly influences my politics in this respect; I would like to see a united Ireland but it is as a woman, far more than as a Protestant, that I find the power and influence of the Catholic Church in the Republic an almost insurmountable barrier.

I hope I've shown that I see my present self as the result of hundreds of diverse influences, dynamic in the sense of constantly shifting attitudes and stable in the sense of retaining some unchanging core elements. However, this self-examination would be profitless for our present purposes if I were in any way unusual in this diversity. I believe that I am not and that there is actually no such thing as an uncomplicated, unchanging individual or tribe or society. All of us are aware, however dimly, of our attitudes and beliefs shifting under internal and external pressures. This movement, this lack of fixity, is alarming; that is why we try to resist it by presenting a rigid identity of ourselves and by projecting a similarly rigid identity onto others.

Stereotyping other people is a way of diminishing and dehumanising them, but even more damaging is its self-perpetuating and self-reinforcing nature. For instance, if the world sees you and your group as intransigent, it's easy to take a perverse pride in that intransigence and consequently very difficult not to feel threatened by any impulse towards movement in yourself, let alone in your friends or leaders.

The realisation that individuals and group identity is not fixed but rather contradictory, fluid and dynamic, is unsettling in a chaotic world where all of us crave order and certainty. But it is also liberating; the fact that individuals do change, and change all the time, means that their groups and tribes not only can but must change to accommodate them.

Of course, the danger is that changes will be for the worse and we've seen enough in the north this year to make us fear just that. But we've also seen Dublin government ministers at Stormont at the height of the marching season with barely a murmur of protest from the unionist community. Even more unthinkable, we've seen Unionist MPs at Dublin Castle.

Against all expectations and all the pressures of history, it is the unionists who are now moving towards an accommodation, however slowly. There is a danger that the stereotype of unionism is preventing people from appreciating the real progress in Unionist thinking and consequently from feeling appropriately angry at the unwillingness of Fianna Fáil and the SDLP to recognise and honour that courageous change. Perhaps a rainbow coalition will be more sensitive and constructive.

Because of the complex, elusive nature of personal and group identity, rigid definitions are bound to be inaccurate; in the case of Northern Ireland they are potentially and actually lethal. If the fact of attitudinal flux can be recognised and, more importantly, accepted, the fear of betraying one's religious, class, political or gender group by the slightest movement towards other groups can at last loosen its stranglehold on us all.

PART III

REGIONS IN TRANSITION

THREE PAPERS

GENERAL DISCUSSION

CHAIRPERSON

The second series of workshops will address a set of topics, all of which relate to 'Regions in Transition'. To help the groups to focus, we start with three short talks, which concentrate on the relationships which have to be negotiated internally in the regions, and with those external relationships which connect local areas to the larger political entities which contain them.

Máire Uí Shíthigh will consider the inter-relationships between a language community and its environment, and the holistic approach necessary for the expression and survival of both.

David McConnell will focus on minority interests and their relationship with central political agendas, and Tony Kennedy will address issues of marginalisation and empowerment, dealing with the democratic deficit in Northern Ireland, and the centralisation of state power in the Republic.

MÁIRE UÍ SHÍTHIGH

HERITAGE AND ENVIRONMENT

Tá traidisiún i gcainteanna poiblí sa tír seo tosnú as Gaoluinn agus athrú go Béarla chomh tapaidh in Éirinn agus is féidir leat. Tá súil agam go maithfear dom nuair a dhéanfad an rud san go díreach ar an ócáid seo inniu.

Is ar phobal Gaeltachta a bheadsa ag tagairt – Corca Dhuibhne in Iarthar Chiarraí. Tá cáil idirnáisiúnta ar áilleacht na leithinise, agus maraon le feirmeoireacht agus iascaireacht, 'sí an turasóireacht anois príomh-thionscal an cheantair.

Bunaíodh Comharchumann Forbartha Corca Dhuibhne i 1967 agus Oidhreacht Chorca Dhuibhne mar fho-choiste i 1980. Táimse fostaithe ag Oidhreacht Chorca Dhuibhne ar thionscnamh oideachais oidhreachta ó 1988 i leith.

My focus here is Corca Dhuibhne – or the Dingle Peninsula in West Kerry – a place renowned for its extraordinary beauty. Like many communities along the western seaboard, the main occupations are farming and fishing with tourism almost taking over as the main source of income in the 1990s. Comharchumann Forbartha Chorca Dhuibhe – or the West Kerry Co-operative – was founded in 1967 to tackle the area's social and economic problems and Oidhreacht Chorca Dhuibhne came into being in 1980 as a subsidiary of the Comharchumann to deal exclusively with the heritage of the area.

Heritage is a legacy that has been passed on from generation to generation. Knowing ourselves, our background and locality well, gives us confidence to study the rest of the country and the world at large. It is easily forgotten in today's competitive world that our basic needs on this earth are food and shelter and to achieve this for everyone, all the resources handed down to us must be used. Our forbears lived on less than we do, they lived within their means and they were more in tune with their surroundings.

We see heritage in three main components. Firstly the physical environment – over a period of at least five million years huge changes occurred that have left us with the landscape we have today; the second aspect is nature – the flora/fauna of land and sea and thirdly there is the man-made heritage which includes language, music, archaeology, art, folklore etc.

I am employed with Oidhreacht Chorca Dhuibhne on its Heritage Education Project since 1988 through grant-aid from the National Lottery, received from Roinn na Gaeltachta. A vast range of scholarly work has been done on the area's heritage down through the years – much of it published and some ready for publication. This scholarly assembly of knowledge is crucially important, but the question is, who is reading it? Our project is about the communication of this heritage to the whole community – all age groups.

As Oidhreacht Chorca Dhuibhne devoted the early eighties to archaeology, culminating in the publication of the *Dingle Peninsula Archaeological Survey* (1986) we have given priority to other aspects of the heritage since 1988 – mainly the Irish language and the environment – one project being a scholarly study of the plant life of the peninsula – with plant and herbal and folklore included.

'Sí an Ghaoluinn ceann de na tréithe is tábhachtaí i saol Chorca Dhuibhne. Is teanga Cheilteach í atá difriúil ar fad leis an mBéarla maidir le gramadach, ord na bhfocal agus fuaimniú.

The following are some observations of my own on Corca Dhuibhne. The fact that the most westerly part of the peninsula is a Gaeltacht – where Irish is still widely spoken – is of utmost importance. The Irish language is a Celtic language completely different from English in grammar, word-order and pronunciation. It is through the Irish language we gain a greater understanding of the landscape – names of cliffs, rocks, field-names, place-names, folklore, music etc.

For years, young people from all over the country have come in their thousands learning Irish, and the large numbers of adults from within and outside this country coming to adult courses is very encouraging. But of greater importance is that the language stays as a living language within the Gaeltacht community.

Looking at the title of this paper, 'Heritage and the Environment' makes one wonder a little why the language hasn't been more popular with conservationists, as precious and worthy of support as the flora and fauna. Perhaps the language revivalists, the much-derided Gaeilgeoirí, who sometimes came on too strong, had something to do with it. Perhaps the language's association with remoteness and poverty did not fit the 'green wellington' image. Perhaps too, the new state's commitment to Irish as an integral part of our self-image as a people crowded out voluntary enthusiasts.

The new state placed great emphasis on the place of Irish in education, but not enough on the language in other spheres. The schooling system was expected to save the language, too much to expect of them. On their own, the schools could neither kill nor save Irish. But in the nineteenth century the schools were accused of 'killing' Irish by not educating the Irish in their own language. Since the 1920s in the Gaeltacht the emphasis was reversed. Indeed the question of the teaching of English in Gaeltacht schools has often come up in discussions with primary school teachers and is worth mentioning – because there is no doubt that there was more emphasis in the primary school curriculum on the teaching of Irish in Gaeltacht schools than vice versa. It is probably true that the official feeling was that Gaeltacht children would just pick up English and it was contrary to the notion of a Gaelic Ireland to spend a lot of time on English in Gaeltacht primary schools. This resulted in vast numbers of Gaeltacht people arriving in New York and London and even Dublin with no confidence in their spoken English. They were competent in reading and writing the language but at a loss with words. Some of these same people, their families and friends are now rearing their children completely through English in the Gaeltacht today. This feeling of hurt and panic is deeply entrenched and nothing will convince such people that Corca Dhuibhne is now a bilingual society and that the situation has now almost gone full circle with English now in danger of becoming more dominant. Of course there are other reasons also for this phenomenon – English language television, and the increasing numbers of people with English only who now live in the area – being but a few. However a lot of people with Irish have also moved in; I am an example myself, being originally from Dublin, but married into the area.

Historically, the conservationist groups have been loosely associated with the more well-off echelons of our society. The perception was that most conservationist groups and individuals interested in the country's artistic, environmental and architectural heritage were often not remotely interested in the language – indeed they were sometimes even opposed to it.

This had the effect that the value and beauty of the language was lost to many conservationists. Things are not as bad today but we still have a long way to go. There is goodwill towards the language outside the Gaeltacht, and there are signs that Irish is becoming 'fashionable' with some younger people, in a post-nationalist 'green' sense, but you can still spend a spell in Dublin without hearing a word being spoken naturally. It is still difficult to do business anywhere in Irish. We organised a course titled 'The World in which we live' last Spring, in conjunction with Co. Kerry VEC. Most of the talks were in English because we failed to get the people we wanted – good communicators with known expertise in their respective environmental fields – who could deliver comfortably in Irish. Unless Gaeltacht people are recognised as having language rights, more and more of them will see the language as being increasingly irrelevant and this seems to be particularly true of people who left school early with a feeling of alienation and disenchantment with the competitive school system. It strikes me that on occasions such as this conference, in the future, instantaneous translation for Irish speakers would be an idea, as there are so many Irish speakers present.

Is ceisteanna móra iad ceisteanna oidhreachta, timpeallachta, teangan agus fostaíochta ins na Gaeltachtaí agus ar fud chósta Iarthar na hÉireann inniu. Heritage, language, environment and employment are huge questions in the Gaeltacht today, and indeed all along the west coast.

To survive as a Gaeltacht with the development of the '90s and the upsurge of tourism will be a challenge. Help will be needed from outside – but there are many optimistic signs and Údarás na Gaeltachta must be credited with a lot of fine projects achieved down through the years.

We are just getting over hosting An tOireachtas in Dingle last month. This is Ireland's most important annual, cultural, Irish language and Gaeltacht festival. Our biggest problem was crowds – far more people came than we expected – and I suppose that really was a healthy problem. Liam Ó Cuinneagáin, this year's Oireachtas National Chairman, who is present here today, will bear me out on this. But at a time of rising world popularity for genuine, uncontrived traditional music – note the interest of Paul Simon and David

Byrne – the surprise is that the *sean-nós* has not already become more popular. A case in point: most of you will have noticed the TV ad for a certain cider from Clonmel which uses unaccompanied traditional music to make a point about the purity of its product – but the singers in the commercial live a long way from Tipperary, they are three traditional singers from, of all places, Bulgaria.

Fós tá cúrsaí níos fearr anois ná mar a bhídist. Chuala le déanaí gur iomaitheoirí is mó a bhí san lucht éisteachta do chomórtas Chorn Uí Riada an Oireachtais ins na caogaidí. Sí Corn Uí Riada an duais is clúití ins an sean-nós. I mbliana sa Daingean bhí breis is ocht gcéad sa halla agus chloisfeá biorán ag titim 'fhaid is a bhí duine ag canadh ar an stáitse. I mbliana leis bhí mórán iomaitheoirí óga ann agus triúr ban a bhuaigh an trí dhuais.

I heard recently that the competitors made up most of the audience at the Corn Uí Riada Competition at the Oireachtas during the fifties. Corn Uí Riada is the coveted *sean-nós* singing award. This year in Dingle over eight hundred were in the hall and you could hear a pin drop while someone was singing. Many of the competitors were young, and as far as I know for the first time ever, the three winners were women.

Ceal ama, caithfead stopadh anseo agus tuigim go gcaithfear leathnú a dhéanamh ar roinnt pointí, ach tá súil agam go mbeidh am ins na ceardlanna. I have to leave it here, some points have obviously only been touched upon, and I hope that can be rectified in the workshops.

DAVID McCONNELL

REGIONS AND MINORITIES
The Adelaide Hospital – the last Protestant general teaching hospital in the Republic of Ireland

Introduction

The Adelaide Hospital, Dublin poses some important challenges and opportunities as we are taking a more confident interest in the diversity of our culture. William Bateson, Balfour Professor of Genetics at Cambridge, and a leading exponent of Mendelism in the early quarter of this century advised, 'Treasure your exceptions'. The Adelaide Hospital is a particular exception in Ireland as I will explain, one among many others which may now find themselves threatened by a creeping, centralising, homogenising form of government. This is a story about a hospital but it may also be a story about the attitude of local and central government, of officials and politicians to minority interests of many kinds.

The questions are two – in what form will the Adelaide survive and will it be treasured? Putting it another way, will the Adelaide struggle on because it cannot or will not be destroyed, or will it prosper through a wholehearted belief by society that it must be sustained and enhanced precisely because it is an honourable exception.

With the recent closures of Sir Patrick Dun's, Dr. Steeven's, Mercer's, Baggot Street, Monkstown and Barrington's (in Limerick) Hospitals, the Adelaide is the last voluntary Protestant general teaching hospital in Ireland. It has been apparently rather easy to close Protestant hospitals – the Adelaide has learned from the experience of the others and it may now be opportune to tell all other voluntary organisations what is in store for them if they do not fit the mould of the mandarins of Hawkins House or for that matter of Marlborough Street. As John Hume implied we may want unity but we must not ask for uniformity and that injunction applies equally north and south of the border.

The Adelaide Hospital, founded in 1839 is located in the Liberties in the historic centre of Dublin close to St. Patrick's Cathedral, and it is a charitable institution. It is governed by a Royal Charter, given in 1921 and amended by the Oireachtais in 1981, which states that the hospital should be a religious and essentially Protestant institution. It is a public hospital, dedicated to the care of the poor and managed by a board of Governors, drawn from the member of the Adelaide Society. It receives most of its monies from the Department of Health in Hawkins House and is answerable to the Department for its expenditure, its services and in every other respect.

The hospital also receives substantial charitable support from every county of this island, especially but by no means only, from the Protestant community. It is widely regarded for its caring Christian ethics, and for its insistence on the privacy of the relationship between doctor and patient – the Adelaide has no ethics committee. In a country where public medicine is a religious matter these qualities distinguish the Adelaide from all other major general teaching hospitals in the Republic of Ireland. Happily there is widespread support for the hospital from people of all religious persuasions and none.

It is by modern standards a small teaching hospital, with an agreed bed complement of one hundred and ninety and it is housed in very old buildings. It has for many years been closely associated with the Medical School of Trinity College where the medical consultants have academic appointments. It has a well-known nursing school and it also teaches students of physiotherapy, dietetics and other paramedical subjects. The Adelaide in association with the Meath and National Children's Hospitals is part of the MANCH Group, one of the six major acute hospital units in Dublin. (The others are St. Vincent's, the Mater, Beaumont, St. James's and Blanchardstown.) About eight thousand inpatients are treated each year and forty thousand outpatients in the Adelaide.

Plans for development of the small hospitals associated with the Medical School of Trinity College
In 1955 the Trinity College Medical School had seven small teaching hospitals including the Adelaide, all more or less strongly associated with the Protestant community. Led partly by Adelaide

consultants these hospitals formed an association, which was formalised under the 1961 Federation Act, with a view to amalgamating in one major modern hospital. Four of them (Baggot Street, Sir Patrick Dun's, Mercer's and Dr. Steeven's) eventually combined to form St. James's Hospital. Three others, the Adelaide, Meath and National Children's Hospitals were not accommodated at St. James's. Today these three are still run under the terms of the Federation Act and are co-ordinated to some extent by the Central Council of the Federation. Unlike all the other major hospitals in Dublin, they have not been developed, they have not been properly re-equipped and they are still housed in small, mainly Victorian, buildings.

Tallaght Hospital
Tallaght, the new suburb to the south west of Dublin, is larger than Limerick but has no hospital. The Department of Health proposed in 1977 to amalgamate the Adelaide, Meath and National Children's Hospitals which together would move to form the core of a new seven hundred and fifty bed hospital in Tallaght. Worryingly, the task of planning Tallaght was not given to the Central Council of the Federation but to the Tallaght Hospital Board which was formed in 1980 with strong powers reserved for the Minister for Health. This was a clear signal that powerful interests intended that the new hospital would not be managed as a 'voluntary hospital'.

The Adelaide was given representatives on the Tallaght board and looked forward to moving to Tallaght with enthusiasm. Tallaght should be a fine new hospital and it would be appropriate for a charitable foundation like the Adelaide to join thus providing medical facilities in a rapidly growing part of the city.

The Adelaide could not make an absolute commitment to participate in Tallaght until many matters concerning its management became clear. Mr. Barry Desmond as Minister for Health agreed that there would be a number of places reserved for Protestant trainee nurses in the new hospital which was helpful, but the Adelaide board always recognised that this was not sufficient to ensure the continuation of the Adelaide tradition at Tallaght.

The planning of Tallaght was delayed for many years, but as soon as it was appropriate the Adelaide board initiated discussions with the Department of Health, in March 1988, on the management structures of Tallaght, emphasising that the Adelaide wished to move to Tallaght. It believed that the Protestant community would like to play a significant role in supporting and governing the Tallaght Hospital. It introduced the idea that Tallaght should be a 'public voluntary hospital', governed by an independent board, with a continuing role in management for the Adelaide. This was apparently acceptable to the Minister for Health in 1990 (see below). In 1988 the Adelaide believed that a minority role on the Tallaght board would be sufficient to ensure a continuation of its tradition. However it learned in the next two years that there was substantial opposition to the Adelaide tradition – minority representation for the minority on the board of the new hospital came to look more like a prescription for slow extinction.

The design stages and specifications for tendering for the Tallaght project were competed by the Tallaght board in 1990. However the government did not include the Tallaght project in its budget for 1991 or 1992 due, it was said, to financial considerations. This was a severe blow to the Adelaide which had waited more than thirty years for the development of modern facilities. The delay led to suggestions that the government wanted to downgrade Tallaght or even to cancel it altogether. Doubts about the real reason for the delay intensified in late 1991 and early 1992 when the Adelaide came under strong pressure to withdraw totally from the Tallaght project. It seemed that government interest in Tallaght was waning in proportion to the insistence by the Adelaide that it should have a significant role in managing the new hospital. It would perhaps be more convenient, from the government point of view, to keep the Adelaide in Peter Street. From the Adelaide's point of view such an outcome would have amounted to the end of the hospital as a teaching institution – it would have withered away in its old and small premises.

Financial and political pressures in 1987–88
Atrophy seems to have been in the government mind for a number of years. In 1987–88 the Adelaide had been placed under severe financial and political pressure by the Department of Health and by the Minister for Health, Dr. O'Hanlon, to amalgamate with the Meath and National Children's Hospitals. The Adelaide, underfunded for many years, had accumulated a deficit of about £1 million by the end of 1988. This was not a promising position in which to discuss its future with its paymaster, the Minister for Health.

The minister made it clear in 1988 directly, and indirectly through his Department, that unless the Adelaide, Meath and National Children's Hospitals amalgamated they would receive no budget for 1989. The Adelaide objected strongly to this proposal for amalgamation. The minister also proposed, without consultation with the hospitals, to alter the structure of the Central Council of the Federation, which still had an important role in co-ordinating the activities of the three hospitals. He decided to replace the Chairman, Dr. Watts, Provost of Trinity College, without consulting Dr. Watts, and to remove the right of Trinity College to nominate members of the council. The board of the Adelaide believed that the combined financial and political pressures were intended to close the Adelaide as an independent institution and, of course, to separate the new hospital structure from Trinity College. It was suspected that Dr. O'Hanlon intended to link the new hospital group to the College of Surgeons, a very fine institution in its own right but not appropriate for the Adelaide in the circumstances.

The pressures were somewhat crude, clumsy and they were certainly hurtful and worrying. They need to be seen in the light of the political situation at the time. Two referenda had been held, on 'the right to life of the unborn' in 1983 and on divorce in 1986, and in each case the results had demonstrated, what Garret Fitzgerald has noted in his autobiography, 'the sharp swing to the right in religious as well as political affairs'. Protestants in the Republic were gravely disturbed by the tone of both debates and most were dismayed by the outcomes. In this climate the Adelaide was very anxious indeed, apparently bracketed by conservative politicians and nervous bankers.

Nevertheless the Adelaide board politely but firmly refused to accept the minister's proposals to amalgamate with the Meath and National Children's Hospitals, and it objected, as did Trinity College, to the minister's proposals for reorganisation of the Central Council (which in particular respects were believed to be *ultra vires*).

Although the Hospital had no formal budget as of January 1989, it continued to function, somewhat anxiously making the assumption that the Department of Health would not or could not close it down. This turned out to be a correct reading of the situation. The Department paid the hospital monthly at the same rate as in 1988 but maintained the pressure on the board by refusing to give any assurance that it would continue to do so. The board was taking a considerable risk as it was continuing to enter into routine contracts without being sure that it could honour them and members of the board were informed by Senior Counsel that they might be personally liable for any failures to meet obligations.

The board was however quite determined in its reaction to Dr. O'Hanlon. Eventually, with important firm support from the three main Protestant Churches, and after vigorous public debate and private negotiation, a device was arranged which allowed the Department to agree a formal budget in the middle of 1989. The proposal to change Central Council was temporarily dropped, and there was no further discussion of amalgamation of the Adelaide, Meath and National Children's Hospitals.

Public debate 1989
There was considerable public discussion in the press, on radio and television, and at the Church of Ireland Synod, the Presbyterian General Assembly and Methodist Conference in 1989. There was widespread support for the Adelaide. Indeed very strong support came from the liberal centre of Irish society, possibly drawn from a coalition similar to the one which showed itself to be in the majority at the time of the election of President Robinson. An excellent editorial in the *Irish Times* (June 1, 1989) and an article in the *Belfast Telegraph* (July 7 1989) give the flavour of the discussion.

Consultation with the Church leaders 1989
In January 1989 when the situation was most tense, the Adelaide sought advice jointly from the Archbishops of Dublin and Armagh, and from the Moderator of the Presbyterian Church and the President of the Methodist Church. The Adelaide explained the seriousness of the financial situation at a meeting in March 1989 and being a small organisation the board asked whether the Protestant Churches considered the Adelaide to be important. If so the Adelaide hoped for support from the Churches in putting the case for the Adelaide to the government. The Church leaders were extremely concerned, partly because of the closure of several other Protestant Dublin hospitals in recent years with very little consideration being given to the interests of the Protestant community, but mainly because the Adelaide was in fact the last one which could possibly ensure that the Protestant community would have a dis-

tinctive and honourable role in a health system. The hospital was most grateful for the strong support of the leaders, and the board was even more determined to stand its ground.

Discussions between the Church leaders and the Taoiseach 1989
The Church leaders believed that the situation was so serious that they arranged to meet Mr. Haughey in September 1989. The Taoiseach was most helpful as the record of that meeting shows. The minute notes that 'he would wish to see that the ethos represented by the Adelaide Hospital was maintained as an integral part of the hospital system'. He undertook that the Adelaide would not be placed under 'such financial pressure that its board would be significantly reduced in its capacity to negotiate the future of the hospital' and he asked the Church leaders to ask the board of the Adelaide 'to present to the Department of Health a detailed plan of what they would regard as the most advantageous future for the Adelaide Hospital.' The leaders met the board and passed on this welcome encouragement and asked the board to write its views to the Taoiseach.

Proposal by the Adelaide to the Taoiseach September 1989
The board wrote to the Taoiseach explaining the aspirations of the Adelaide to play a significant and determining role in running a major teaching hospital. It pointed out that it could not stay in the small and old premises of Peter Street. The board stated that it would welcome an invitation to run the new Tallaght hospital which it had been involved in planning for several years. It believed that it could adapt to this larger role, and it believed it could provide for appropriate participation by the Meath and National Children's Hospitals in the new institution. After all, both of these hospitals had historical associations with the Protestant community, though the Meath, governed under the Meath Act of 1951, was by now strongly influenced by local politicians.

The Adelaide board thought that the government might consider it highly desirable to respond to the growing if hesitant pluralism of the Republic by agreeing that one of the more than twenty major hospitals in the Republic should be managed with significant Protestant participation. The memorandum of the meeting between the Church leaders and the Taoiseach, quoted above, seemed to indicate this would be possible.

The Adelaide received no written response to its letter to Mr. Haughey. Nor did it receive any comfort from the Department of Health with regard to its financial difficulties which Mr. Haughey had undertaken to deal with. Essentially nothing came from Mr. Haughey's commitments in the next three months.

Public debate 1990
The Adelaide's position caused further public anxiety in early 1990. The financial situation was still desperate, in spite of the Taoiseach's undertaking in September 1989. The Archbishop of Dublin and the Chairman of the board met with the Taoiseach in January 1990 to discuss the financial crisis again. This time some action was taken and the crisis was partly relieved by monies paid in subsequent months – but the Adelaide is still in 1992 owed £182,000 for work carried out in 1989!

The miserable nature of the Adelaide situation led to public outcry and there were debates at the annual meetings of the Churches, and in the media. There was a second editorial carried by the *Irish Times* on 19th May 1990 which specifically referred to criticism of the Adelaide by Dr. Newman, Roman Catholic Bishop of Limerick. Dr. Newman was believed to have been influential in the closure of another Protestant foundation, Barrington's Hospital in Limerick, and now seemed to have the Adelaide in his sights. An interesting letter by Rev. G.B.G. McConnell (*Irish Times* 4 June 1990) pointed out that the Anglo-Irish Agreement in Articles 2(b) and 5(a,b) may allow for consideration of the protection of human rights in the Republic.

The Adelaide was debated in the Senate on the 1st May 1990 on foot of a special motion put down by Senator Norris. The Minister for Health, Dr. O'Hanlon, reiterated the commitment made to the Church leaders by the Taoiseach and called the Adelaide to a meeting.

The Kingston Group 1990–91
Dr. O'Hanlon, set up a working group under Mr. David Kingston, Chief Executive of Irish Life, to 'consider possible future management arrangements for the new public voluntary hospital with nursing school at Tallaght.' The Group had two members from each of the three hospitals (Adelaide, Meath, Children's) and was given specific terms of reference by the minister. These terms were clearly

designed to take account of the national importance of the Adelaide. The Minister's terms stated that the management board might operate 'under an adapted Adelaide Charter' and that the 'position of the Adelaide as a focus for Protestant participation in the health services and its particular denominational ethos must be continued in Tallaght.'

The Kingston Group met many times for several months and worked quite harmoniously. Eventually it agreed a scheme for amending the Adelaide Charter as the legal instrument for Tallaght. The new board for Tallaght would be elected by three foundations (Adelaide, Meath and Children's) and by Trinity. The foundations would also act as trustees for the assets of the old hospitals using them for the benefit of the new hospital at Tallaght. The representatives on the new board would be in the ratio of Adelaide : Meath : Children's : Trinity = 5 : 4 : 3 : 1 giving the Adelaide a significant though a minority position on the board. The new hospital was to be called the Tallaght Adelaide. There were to be other safeguards for the Adelaide's interests in the mechanism for election of chairman and president.

The Kingston plan was put to the Adelaide, Meath and National Children's Hospital Boards in May 1991. The Adelaide and Children's Hospitals agreed to it in a spirit of optimism and goodwill, but the Meath rejected four key provisions, all of which were well-known to be vital to the interests of the Adelaide. The Adelaide board – knowing that the Meath representation in the Kingston Group had accepted it – was deeply shocked. More than that the Meath board had picked out items of critical importance to the Adelaide and dismissed them as 'minor'.

Many attempts in the summer of 1991, partly at the behest of Mr. Kingston, failed to repair the breach between the Meath and the Adelaide. Indeed the situation actually worsened when the Meath appeared to misrepresent the proposals of the Kingston Group and repeated that the only differences between the Meath and the Adelaide were minor. The effect was to undermine the goodwill which had developed between the two hospitals, and to suggest that there was strong opposition to the Adelaide, especially among the local politicians who appeared to control the Meath board.

This rejection shocked the Adelaide board; it confirmed the views of a number of experienced members, which had been discounted for years by newer members of the board, that the Adelaide ethos would not be safe without Protestant control. The newer members learned their lesson.

The crisis in December 1991 – the end of the Adelaide?
The Department has consistently underfunded the Adelaide. The allocation for 1991 had initially been less in money terms than the hospital spent in 1990 – after strenuous negotiations it was improved somewhat. Nevertheless the Adelaide had a budget overrun of £200–300,000 for 1991 as it negotiated its allocation for 1992. Worse was to come.

For 1992 the Adelaide was given a quite derisory allocation. The Adelaide needed £11.5 million for 1992 – it was allocated £9.13 million. The secretary-manager advised that the board would have to lay off up to one quarter of the staff in 1992 and to reduce services to patients, if it were to stay within this allocation. The capacity of the hospital to train nurses, undergraduate and postgraduate doctors as well as paramedical students was seriously threatened. The secretary-manager advised the board that the hospital would soon become suspect 'in terms of its ability to train', and 'therefore recognition for training in medicine, surgery, nursing, and paramedical disciplines would be re-examined and in some cases recognition would inevitably be withdrawn.' The medical consultants advised the board that the Adelaide would cease to be a teaching hospital.

In effect the 1992 allocation meant the end of the Adelaide Hospital, a fact that was well-known to the Department of Health – the Department had been told as much in meetings in the last quarter of 1991 during the negotiations for the 1992 allocation.

The board decided to take the case once more, for the third time in three years, to the Minister for Health, and then if necessary to the public. Pending the minister's reaction, the board decided to run the hospital at the same level as 1991 – staff would not be laid off while the case was made.

The determination of the board to assert that the Adelaide had a future and to stand up to the Department was of course tested at each monthly board meeting in early 1992 and at many sub-committees. The board is composed of more than thirty members who are seasoned businessmen, lawyers, engineers, some retired nurses and doctors, a few churchmen and other and thoughtful citizens. They were astonished at the way in which the hospital, and especially its staff and patients were being treated by the Department of Health. But they were by now also seasoned in the new brand of Irish politics. The board was absolutely united and insisted that it would fight.

The Archbishop of Armagh, the Archbishop of Dublin, the Moderator of the Presbyterian Church and the President of the Methodist Church had been briefed at a meeting in Dublin by the chairman and vice-chairman of the Adelaide on the November 18th 1991. The chairman wrote to the new Minister for Health, Mrs. O'Rourke on December 2nd 1991 to explain that the situation was very grave indeed. He sought an early and positive response.

The minister was asked by the chairman to proceed with the Tallaght project in 1992 and to announce that it would be completed and commissioned on a normal schedule. Her reply was non-committal and did not reveal any sense of urgency. She set up a committee, under Dr. David Kennedy to assess the Tallaght project. It was suspected that Dr. Kennedy's committee was being asked to find reasons to downgrade Tallaght.

The appalling allocation to the Adelaide for 1992 was the subject of a further letter of January 31st to the minister. It protested the clear indication that the Department of Health was intending to close the Adelaide. It was not possible to draw any other conclusion from an allocation which would have led to the laying off of one quarter of the staff. Difficult meetings followed and revealed that the Department indeed was not at all sympathetic to the Adelaide.

In the political turmoil following Mr. Haughey's resignation, a new Minister for Health, Dr. O'Connell, was appointed. A letter (February 24th) to the minister asked for assurances both on finance and on the Tallaght project. The Adelaide was invited at a more or less public discussion on March 2nd 1992 to withdraw from the Tallaght project. The Adelaide quickly emphasised that Tallaght was the best solution to the Adelaide's future and it could not withdraw in the absence of an equivalent alternative development. The Adelaide believed that an alternative development was impossible unless Tallaght was reduced to a cottage hospital which was certainly not appropriate for Tallaght. In its submission to the Kennedy Committee, the Adelaide (March 18th 1992) gave strong support for the full Tallaght project, especially emphasising the large children's unit which was under specific threat. In April the Taoiseach also encouraged the Adelaide to withdraw.

Financial matters and the Tallaght project had by this time become so serious that the Adelaide called a press conference on May 11th. On the May 19th the Archdeacon of Dublin spoke at the Church of Ireland Synod that the Protestants were being edged out of the hospital system and the Archbishop of Armagh, Dr. Eames, said concerning the Adelaide 'We are an angry people'. On the same day the Minister for Health met the Adelaide.

Finally in May, five months into the year and only after the Adelaide press conference, the minister promised to be helpful on the financial problems of the hospital. He accepted that the hospital should not lay off staff and he undertook to seek ways of improving the basic funding for 1993. He appeared to accept that the long saga of underfunding should now be stopped and indeed reversed. He gave no useful undertaking about Tallaght. When approached by the Church leaders, the Taoiseach was unable to give any substantial help. The Minister for Health on July 21st expanded on his commitment to the funding of the Adelaide and he gave some cautious indications that Tallaght would be built essentially as planned. Once again he was evasive about the management, but the Adelaide emphasised the need to resolve the management question by government decision one way or another before Tallaght was announced. The Minister did however say in a letter of July 28th that he would meet with the chairman 'in the coming weeks in regard to the other matters'. In the context of the discussions and correspondence this meant that the Adelaide would be consulted further about management before Tallaght was announced. In fact the minister did not meet with the chairman of the Adelaide in the next three months in spite of many attempts by the Adelaide to obtain such a meeting. The next public information about Tallaght came from the Taoiseach's speech on November 6th 1992 in which he said that Tallaght would be built essentially as planned – management would be decided later 'with the necessary goodwill on all sides'. The Adelaide was delighted for the people of Tallaght and hugely disappointed that the Taoiseach and the Minister had ignored the interests of the Protestant community in the management of this great project.

The election November 1992

On the announcement of the election the Adelaide immediately asked each of the political parties about the role of the Adelaide in the management of Tallaght. Mr. Spring and Mr. Desmond of the Labour Party, Mr. O'Malley of the Progressive Democrats and Mr. de Rossa of the Democratic Left, wrote in strongly sympathetic terms. Fine Gael wrote briefly in more general terms. Fianna Fáil repeated its commitment to the Adelaide which amounted to 'trust us'. The Adelaide in a message to the people of Tallaght said 'We now need to make sure that the promises made in the heat of an election are fulfilled. With you we want to make Tallaght one of the best teaching hospitals in Europe'.

Conclusion
The Adelaide is determined that its traditions and ethos should be maintained in an identifiable and secure way. We have tried over many years to resolve the matter with the government and the Department of Health. Apart from the fact that we still exist, we have quite frankly got nowhere. We suspect that the way we have been treated is but part of a much wider question which affects the future of all voluntary elements of the health service and other social activities. This is the question of government against the people. The Adelaide is but one of many excellent religious and non-religious voluntary foundations contributing to the wellbeing of our people. In our own small way we are making a case for all such institutions to be allowed to develop and continue to play a part. These are the exceptions, each in its own way, which would be treasured in a truly pluralist state.

TONY KENNEDY

POWER TO THE REGIONS

Since we have been talking on the subject of our of backgrounds I should mention that until four months ago I was Chief Housing Officer with a local authority – council employees and perhaps council house managers are not known for their culture so I speak to you with a degree of apprehension.

In a conference entitled 'Regions: Identity and Power' we have been spending much more time talking about identity than power.

In part this is because of a feeling that we should somehow clarify our terms; in part because we can gain endless entertainment from exploring definitions which differ not only between us but within us according to time or issue; in part it's a recognition of the real powerlessness of regions.

However the issue of power is of course central. Without power, either direct or indirect, we cannot achieve our goals.

In Co-operation North we aim to promote practical co-operation and respect between the people of Northern Ireland and the Republic of Ireland and an essential part of this is the importance of people as individuals. If building bridges between people and communities is to mean anything, these people and communities must feel empowered – they must feel that they are in control of their destinies, or at the very least that they can have a real influence on issues which directly affect them, their families and their futures.

The topic was addressed in part by a Co-operation North conference earlier this week which looked at the position of people in our communities who are unemployed and who feel at the mercy of unyielding state bureaucracies, but the issue is just as valid for the communities as a whole.

In both Northern Ireland and the Republic of Ireland there is a serious lack of local democratic control over services which have a real day to day impact on people and their lives. Decisions on allocations of resources are made in the absence of local political responsibility. In Northern Ireland items of fundamental local importance such as education, housing, health and social services are managed by bureaucrats who are to all intents and purposes unanswerable to the local political process. While we all know the historic reasons for this we cannot afford to consider this as a normal state of affairs.

There are long term dangers to our attitude to democracy in these arrangements. Decisions are made away from public scrutiny and questioning, politicians become merely processors of complaints, and the public lose faith in the services, in their ability to influence them, and in the political process. The greatest worry must be that a vicious circle develops with talented people being unwilling to serve as councillors, councillors becoming happy with their lack of responsibility, and public opinion of councillors further declining.

In the Republic it is again striking how little real power is in the hands of councils. As in the North, many of the main functions of what should be local government are administered away from local control, with the most glaring example of powerlessness being the inability of local government to raise its own revenue independent of the centre.

This is an issue of fundamental importance. As Bernard Cullen said in this morning's workshop, 'No matter where we live, it is local politics in which we get most involved and most excited politically'.

Unfortunately for these islands, the trend continues to be away from local control. In Great Britain in recent years, central government has steadily eroded the powers of local government, reducing it to local administration or less – even going so far as to abolish councils which are felt to be too much of a challenge. We need to be clear on the results of this – people and communities do suffer. I have experienced the despair felt by council tenants who feel that gradually and inevitably they will have to change their landlord against their will. Or the dismay felt by miners as their work, and with it their whole position in society, is taken away.

While I appreciate and welcome the growth in community arts projects and in local history societies, I do question whether they are wholly positive, or whether they use defensive reactions as people reach for some certainty in difficult times, reacting to a loss of power or confidence. As long as the miners were an industrial elite, there were no mining museums and precious few local history groups in industrial west Yorkshire. They have only grown with the collapse of the coal industry.

Though a knowledge of roots is important, people need to look forwards as well as backwards.

And there is an alternative. As we have heard, elsewhere in Europe local government and regional government has real powers. The constitution forced on Germany by the allies after the Second World War would never allow their government to work as ours do. Democratic Spain has devolved power from the centre, and even France now has regional government with real powers.

However, in Northern Ireland and Republic of Ireland we should initially concentrate on restoring local government because I believe we are more likely to achieve change through what exists at present rather than establishing new structures. Devolution of other central government powers to regions could and should follow as and when they are established. But to the proposition 'power to the regions' my comment is yes, and beyond. But within basic standards established sometimes at national, sometimes at international level and including a Bill of Rights. We have to learn to trust local communities in the government of their affairs; I don't care about a definition of subsidiarity, but I do care about the idea of giving people and their representatives the power to make decisions at the most local level possible.

If we don't how can we seriously expect people to respect other cultures, if they can't even respect themselves.

GENERAL DISCUSSION

Martin McLoone (University of Ulster)
Dr. McConnell, I was most interested in your detailed history of the Adelaide hospital controversy and I have the deepest sympathy for you and the case you have presented. I was unaware of this controversy but it does remind me of the very similar arguments surrounding education in the South. I wonder if the case of the Adelaide hospital is similar.

In education, one commonly finds that the educated Catholic, or ex-Catholic, middle-classes support the denominational status of Protestant schools because these provide them with the possibility of a non-Catholic-controlled education for their children. This is the best option in the absence of non-denominational schools. Is this, I wonder, the case with the Adelaide hospital? That is, is it supported by the Catholic middle-classes because it offers the best option to those seeking non-denominational health care?

David McConnell
Much you have said rings true, especially the similarity drawn to the Protestant schools. However the Adelaide, in the heart of old Dublin, is not a middle-class hospital – the support for its role comes from all sections of society. While it may be perceived as non-denominational, or attractive to people who want non-denominationalism, the charter states that the hospital must maintain the fundamental principle namely that it 'should be and remain an essentially religious and Protestant institution'.

The board has interpreted this principle in the broadest possible way as times have changed. Thankfully, Irish people of different persuasions have realised there is much more in common than divides us, and the Adelaide has happily and quickly become a hospital for everyone. Like Protestant schools it is definitely 'inclusive' rather than 'exclusive'. Of course the hospital has for many years treated patients, taught medical students and employed staff regardless of religious affiliation. It does give preferential admission to qualified Protestant student nurses, following principles similar to those used by Protestant schools in the Republic. Qualified Protestant applicants are admitted first. While there are no religious qualifications for membership of board and no church is represented on it, it has been considered wise in the present circumstances to ensure that the great majority of the Adelaide board are members of Protestant churches. This is likely to continue until the future of the Adelaide tradition is secure. As Protestant schools welcome Catholic involvement, they also try to ensure that these schools retain those characteristics which make them attractive to non-Protestants, so the Adelaide wishes to ensure that its ethos is perpetuated.

In a country where health has unusually important religious dimensions, due partly to the strong interest of the Catholic Church in medical services, and its quite reasonable insistence on the exercise of its authority as widely as possible within its own institutions and by its own members, the position of the Adelaide as the last of the Protestant general hospitals has three important consequences.

First, the Adelaide is the last remaining institution of its kind through which Protestants can support the health services in an effective and distinctive way. In this support Protestants seek to emulate their Catholic fellow citizens who do the same for virtually all other public hospitals over which they have effective management control. The Protestant community has often – wrongly – been accused of not taking part in the Irish state. In fact it plays its part and wishes to do more, but without always losing its identity. Insofar as the health services are concerned, the Adelaide has a key role in this endeavour.

Second, the Adelaide is probably the only public hospital in which patients can be sure that they are being given medical treatment which is decided completely within the context of the unencumbered professional relationship between the patient and the doctors. No medical procedure which is legal within the state is precluded in the Adelaide. I think this is very important to many Catholic patients.

Other public general hospitals are *de jure* or *de facto* strongly influenced if not completely controlled by the Catholic Church. They have ethical committees to which procedures such as sterilisation must be referred. In practice it may be more important that staff are sometimes unwilling to advise on or carry out such procedures. Some hospitals have recently altered their attitude to certain operations. Notably, the National Maternity Hospital at Holles Street and the Coombe Maternity Hospital have modified their rules governing tubal ligation (sterilisation). These changes in a way emphasise the quite different situation in the Adelaide. Old ethical dilemmas will continue to cause difficulties outside the Adelaide; new ones will pose new problems for most hospitals, but most if not all will be dealt with as before by the Adelaide. New medical procedures will be offered to Adelaide patients if doctors believe they are in the interest of the patients' health.

Third, the Adelaide nursing school is, all things considered, the one to which Protestants prefer to send their sons and daughters. They are confident that its teaching, including the ethical teaching, is consistent with the Protestant emphasis on personal responsibility.

So, in summary, the Adelaide case does resemble that of the Protestant schools. As Protestants prefer to think of their schools as having become to a great extent multidenominational rather than non-denominational, so I have made the point about the Adelaide being 'inclusive' rather than 'exclusive'. We hope every patient in the Adelaide feels cared for, *as they would like.*

Catholic support for the Adelaide has been crucial to its survival. I think this has come as much from a belief that there should be at least one teaching hospital associated with the Protestant community as it has from a recognition that this kind of hospital meets the needs of many people who are not Protestants. As Noel Purcell said to the ambulance driver who asked him where to go: 'To the Adelaide of course'.

Paul Sweeney (Northern Ireland Voluntary Trust)
I would like to thank Dr. McConnell for his excellent presentation. It never ceases to amaze me – the extent to which we mirror issues on both sides of the border – often conversely. For example, in Northern Ireland the Mater Hospital in Belfast has over the years been engaged in a similar relationship with the state in Northern Ireland. I was really struck by David McConnell's refusal to allow this to become an overtly sectarian issue, but could I ask David to clarify if the issue is not one of narrow sectarianism, what are the key issues involved?

David McConnell

The Adelaide has tried very hard indeed not to interpret the issue in sectarian terms. That has not been easy, because it is hard to explain why the Adelaide has been so badly treated. But I must emphasise two things above all else. First, as I have said we have a huge amount of support from Catholic people, including of course our own staff. I am convinced that the great majority of the people are very sympathetic to the Adelaide. Second, if we do not have clear evidence of crude sectarianism, we must seek alternative explanations before accepting that bogey. I will offer some alternatives. Political confusion: the Department of Health may not have received or may not have understood political directions from Mr. Haughey or from the various Ministers for Health that the Adelaide must be properly financed. No one should believe that governments are usually well run. Local political opposition: hospitals are very important in Irish local politics (through the local health boards) and local politicians may see the Adelaide as thwarting their interests in getting control of the new hospital at Tallaght. Political misjudgement: the Fianna Fáil Party may not believe that the Adelaide has wide popular support. Opposition by the civil service: the Department of Health may want to control all hospitals directly through pliant boards appointed by the Minister for Health rather than have to deal with independently-minded apolitical boards like those which run the majority of the Dublin teaching hospitals. My own view is that these, and other factors which I do not have time to go into, have contributed to the outrageous treatment of the Adelaide.

I suspect however that the main reason for this treatment may be quite different but very disappointing – the majority of Irish politicians who have been in power for the last five years, and I suspect the majority of civil servants, have little or no meaningful interest in cultural diversity. Minorities, especially small ones, have few votes! Running a major department of state is difficult enough for civil servants without the irritation of minority interests. In the turmoil minorities need their champions. In spite of occasional public statements of support, the Adelaide has not had influential champions in Fianna Fáil or in the civil service. I suspect that many politicians simply could not care less whether the Protestant community (or any other minority for that matter) disappeared. This attitude is short-sighted, narrow-minded and irresponsible but I do not see it as bigoted or malignly sectarian. I would be extremely reluctant to conclude that the treatment of the Adelaide is more the result of wilful attrition than the consequence of political and bureaucratic negligence.

Whatever the reason, the Adelaide has stumbled from crisis to crisis. This cannot go on. If pluralism is important in modern Ireland, then it is extremely urgent that the government work with the Adelaide to solve the hospital's short-term financial problems (the Department owed the Adelaide £2.5 million in December 1992), restore the hospital to full activity, re-equip some essential departments, and therefore make good the professed intentions of Mr. Haughey, Dr. O'Hanlon, Dr. O'Connell and others. These steps must be taken as soon as possible in order to reassure the Protestant community of the good intentions of the government, and to restore the confidence of the staff and patients of the hospital.

It is also essential to decide whether or not to respond to the aspirations of the Adelaide for development as a modern teaching hospital with a nursing school, the whole to be *guaranteed by the Adelaide.*

The government needs to find a way for the Adelaide to participate in the Tallaght project. The Adelaide hopes that public opinion will in the end persuade the government to honour its commitment, through participation in Tallaght, to ensure that 'the ethos represented by the Adelaide Hospital' is 'maintained as an integral part of the hospital system.' (Mr. C.J. Haughey, TD, Taoiseach, September 1989). Otherwise the Adelaide will remain puzzled. Just what is the difficulty in allowing the Protestant community a controlling interest in the management of one teaching hospital in Ireland, an interest which would be exercised by the Adelaide Hospital according to an inclusive and evolving Adelaide tradition? The Adelaide Society only wants to have a similar role in governing its hospital as the Sisters of Charity have in running St. Vincent's Hospital.

The Adelaide wishes every success to the people of Tallaght for the new hospital as announced by Mr. Reynolds in November 1992. The Adelaide has fought for this hospital for nearly twenty years and has helped to plan and design it. The staff of the Adelaide have been appointed to staff Tallaght. The Adelaide dearly wants to be a part of it, thus fulfilling part of the commitment of the

Protestant community to our country. The Adelaide believes that it would be accepted by the people of Tallaght in the same way that it has been warmly accepted by the people of the Liberties for more than a century. We are not foreigners in our own country.

If we have not been foreigners, we may have been blind. I hope that the difficulties were not due to the 'Adelaide factor', and I have suggested some reasons. But perhaps there was more to the problem, of much greater general significance, perhaps relating more to the nature of modern government. It may be that we have stumbled on a particular form of government that could not accept the Adelaide because that would represent a very strong decision to allow voluntary organisations including *all Churches* to participate in social services for the foreseeable future. Exceptions of any kind may not have been treasured by this government; if the Adelaide experience has been anything to go by, exceptions were not even to be tolerated, they were destined to disappear, whether by attrition or neglect remains to be seen.

John O'Connell (Dublin Travellers Education Group)

Travellers are one of the most despised, marginalised and socially-excluded group in Irish Society, both North and South and generally when we raise this, very often the response is that travellers must act responsibly and behave and conform and so on, because their identity has been systematically denied and undermined down through the years both by the state and by the voluntary sector and indeed by the general public and I think what that fails to do is acknowledge the reality of nomadism in their way of life and certainly not resource that, and secondly it doesn't acknowledge the reality of power, that the onus is put back on travellers to behave and to conform and so on rather than on the dominant sector, sedentary society which systematically excludes travellers from participating as equals in society and retaining their culture and indeed their own language. I was wondering if Máire saw any possibility of an alliance there?

Máire Uí Shíthigh

Speaking for myself, I can't see why not. I think minority groups should work very closely together and I think that has to be the way of the future with minority groups. It's very important that minority groups know each other and understand each other and gain strength from each other, because we are talking about such a massive culture out there and if minority culture is to survive, I think we can only survive by supporting each other and helping each other. I can see no difficulty with that myself.

Brian Walker (Institute of Irish Studies, Queen's University Belfast)
As an historian and political scientist I find Dr. McConnell's remarks very interesting. I admire his efforts to try to keep this matter free from sectarianism and not to make it a sectarian issue, but it does have such very severe sectarian consequences. Because what happens to the Adelaide is noticed in the North. Many people in the North see the conflict in Northern Ireland and in Ireland as a religious one, a lot of people in the South think that's just boloney, it's some myth in Protestant minds. But Protestants are conscious that in 1911, 10% of the population in the twenty six counties was Protestants and it is now 3%. There are some forecasts which say that this may disappear altogether and in these circumstances, what happens to the Adelaide is very important, because what has happened to Protestants in the South has been closely watched by Protestants in the North. In all talk of relationship between North and South, between Catholic and Protestant, this fear of numbers diminishing under the stress of sectarian issues like this are very much to the forefront of Protestant consciousness.

David McConnell
If today the Adelaide is taken as a test case of the pluralism of the state, then the state must fail.

The Adelaide has been kept in a desperate yet awkward situation for many years, hardly what might be expected given its unique position and role. The hospital has sought to explain to the Department of Health and successive Ministers for Health that it is important for national and international reasons to find a solution to its problems – the Protestant community and the many other members of society want the Adelaide to be supported. Mr. Haughey as Taoiseach, Mr. Reynolds as Taoiseach, Dr. Fitzgerald as a senior politician, Mr. Dukes (when leader of the Opposition), Mr. Spring and Mr. O'Malley (when Minister for Industry and Commerce in the present government) have been briefed likewise, as have other senior politicians. Everyone seems to agree that the Adelaide tradition should be maintained, and some even have said it should be strengthened. The Taoiseachs and the Ministers for Health have appeared to be helpful – but in practice *only* in response to the pleas of the Church leaders and sustained public outcry.

The board of the Adelaide has done everything possible within the guidelines set by the ministers. It initiated discussions about management of Tallaght as early as 1987 and participated wholeheartedly in all efforts to resolve the matter. For nearly three years (1988–92) we sought to play down in public the difficulties we faced day to day, allowing the government time to act, especially because we know the Adelaide is important to the Protestant community in the North. The Adelaide behaved as carefully and responsibly as possible – even in the face of swinging public accusation by the Catholic bishop of Limerick which amounted to the implication that the Adelaide facilitated abortion. While the Kingston Group was meeting (October 1990–October 1991) the hospital had been conscious of the Brooke initiative and of the interest being taken by Northern politicians in the Adelaide as a kind of test case – Mr. John Taylor once raised the matter in Westminster. At one stage in the early summer of 1991 the Kingston Group seemed to be breaking up without agreement. This was a time when bad news from the Republic could have been unhelpful in the North; whether the Adelaide would have made any difference there is a matter of judgement, but it was of concern to the hospital in the event the chairman might have to comment on the future of the Adelaide while matters were delicate in the North.

The policy of the Adelaide was this: while progress was being made, or was likely to be made, it was extremely important to maintain a steady display of confidence in the ability of the government to reach a solution. *But the fact was that the hospital lost confidence in the government in late 1991, leading to the press conference of May.* Confidence has been further undermined by the failure of the Minister for Health to meet again with the Adelaide prior to the announcement of Tallaght in November.

The situation has to be seen in perspective. The frank view is that the Adelaide has had to fight for any crumbs that have fallen from the government's table. The polite, constructive and respectful attitude of the Adelaide has been rewarded with astonishing rebuffs, year after year, and most recently in the allocation for 1992 and the decision not to decide on the management of Tallaght.

On reflection it is sad to be able to state that the Department of Health has not taken a single substantial initiative in catering for the interests of the Protestant community in the Adelaide or favouring the development of the Adelaide. In contrast it succeeded in closing three other hospitals with historic links to the Protestant community (Barrington's in Limerick, and Monkstown and Dr. Steevan's Hospitals in Dublin) without any consideration for Protestant interests, and there is no doubt in the minds of the Adelaide board that the Adelaide was to have gone the same way. The Adelaide only exists today because it has fought every inch of the way against the sustained bureaucratic and financial pressure apparently designed to force its amalgamation with the Meath on terms which would have led to the disappearance of the Adelaide tradition. Now it is fighting against exclusion from Tallaght, or arrangements at Tallaght that would make it meaningless for the Adelaide to participate.

The treatment by the government amounts to indifference to the interests of the Protestant community represented by the Adelaide. Were one to examine the history of the relationship between the Department of Health and the Adelaide in the last five years it would be astonishing to find any evidence within the Department of Health of an intrinsic desire for or commitment to a pluralist society. Instead one would find letter after letter from the Adelaide pleading for fair play, many of which were never even replied to, interspersed with occasional letters of gratitude for small mercies which it was thought, wrongly as it turned out, might lead to a more conciliatory attitude in Hawkins House.

In asking why the Adelaide has been ignored, and why it has been so undermined and discriminated against, the possibility of sectarian reaction to an independently-minded Protestant institution has been raised from time to time. That was inevitable. There are other possible explanations as I have said – a drive for centralisation of power by the bureaucracy, powerseeking by the civil service or by local politicians with an eye to patronage. But even if these do not seem to be sufficient to some observers, it must be said that there is no direct evidence for active discrimination on the basis of religion. Warm support from the general public and extraordinarily kind letters from Catholic clergy show that any surreptitious sectarian antipathy to the Adelaide is far outweighed by widespread and generous goodwill.

But if there has been no evidence for sectarian illwill from official or political sources, where these things count, neither has there been any substantial sign of innate official goodwill towards a minority. The best that can be said for the civil service and the politicians of the last governments is that they do not understand, much less empathise with the Adelaide, hardly an indication of a pervasive commitment to pluralism in the corridors of power; they simply have not thought it necessary to pay any particular attention to the Adelaide on account of its special position as the last of the Protestant general teaching hospitals.

We are going to be measured as a people – in respect of our commitment to pluralism – by how the Adelaide is treated. It is the most important single issue facing us with respect to the treatment of religious minorities. The extraordinary lack of comprehension by our senior politicians in one major party stands out as an incredible indictment.

But I want to repeat, I do not think the main opposition is coming for crude sectarian reasons. There may be some antipathy for the Adelaide as a voluntary hospital, there may be a simple incomprehension of our community, a narrowness of outlook, an attitude which just does not see the larger issues. This is the same kind of blindness that many minorities or disadvantaged groups find in government, whether they are women, or travellers, or linguistic minorities. The large questions are just beyond the comprehension of many ordinary members of the civil service, or of local politicians, or of one the major parties.

Mary Freehill (Dublin City Council and The Labour Party)
I'm a local politician – I am not a member of the Voluntary Hospitals Board, or of the Eastern Health Board. What I really wanted to contribute to the discussion, I think it's significant that so many of us want to talk about the Adelaide, because we feel very strongly about it but when you spoke, Dr. McConnell, you talked specifically about the concerns of the Church of Ireland and all of our concerns about the ethics committees in Catholic Hospitals. There is a whole other constituency out there, of those of us who would have been reared in the Catholic tradition but no longer practice that religion and who also hold very dear to us to have the right to be able to feel that we can go to a hospital and that the medical profession is not controlled by another body, and that group is no longer a minority in this country, in fact that group is now second

largest to the Catholic Church in Ireland. Therefore, you are not a minority, but I think we probably need to talk about it more, people need to know about it more. At least we in Labour had it as an item on our manifesto that the Tallaght Hospital would be protected in that sense.

David McConnell
Thank you very much for your support, and for the support of the Labour Party which I greatly appreciate. You have indeed put your finger on a very important point. There are two reasons why the Adelaide is still open today, treating nearly fifty thousand patients per year. *One* is the marvellous support we have had from the leaders of the Protestant Churches and from that community. *The second* reason is the support we have had from the group of people who you refer to and represent, that is the great number of other citizens of our country who think that institutions like the Adelaide are important. I believe like you that together we are in the majority. That is why I am confident that we will succeed in the end, and that is why I do not want people in the North to be pessimistic. We are building a new Republic and it will be one which is much more acceptable as a neighbour to all who live in the North.

Terry Clare (Wexford Centre for the Unemployed)
As a Catholic myself, I would certainly like to support the stand being taken by the Adelaide and I would like to make a practical suggestion; as a sea-farer, we had a seaman's hospital, the Dreadnought in Greenwich and we were under a lot of pressure to have it closed and we fought that particular issue and we had it transferred to St. Thomas's, but the problem about the Seafarers' Hospital was with seaman you have to have instant admission and that was under Royal charter, that was a condition at the Dreadnought. What happened to us was, after a long struggle, we got recognition from the British Department of Health that we could operate as a separate unit with its own administration, its own budget, in St. Thomas's. The suggestion I would like to make would be that you retain your ethos within the Tallaght Hospital, as a complete separate unit, a complete group within that particular community.

David McConnell
Thank you very much for that interesting suggestion. It is something we have thought about. For a variety of practical reasons it

is not possible. Nor is it the way we want to participate. I used the word 'inclusive' earlier to describe the Adelaide in the sense that everyone is welcome, with no assumptions made about people's beliefs. I hope that we can have a hospital at Tallaght which completely reflects that idea.

Larry McCluskey, (Co. Monaghan VEC and Arts Council)
As a bureaucrat with a local education authority in the South I am a little confused because one of the speakers said that elected representatives ought to have more direct control and authority and power, and then I think David McConnell suggests that the control by politicians of some health boards or hospitals can be a problem. Now, I notice that in the arts, in education, in health and in many other spheres very few people are in favour of political control of these 'specialist areas' and I just wonder if they could clear up that confusion. One seems to favour more control by the elected representative and less by the bureaucrats and the other seems to be afraid of political control.

Can I just make one other point? I think for the people arguing David's point in relation to ethics, it is their problem if so many people don't seem to understand. I find that people who argue about the ethos of schools and the ethos of hospitals are not very clear in their analysis. I think the ethos argument needs to be made more explicit and in the public domain. It is the job of the proponents of the ethos argument to persuade and convince the larger public. Very often I find that if one scratches that argument, it conceals prejudice. I'm not suggesting in this case that it does, but I think you must bring your argument into the public domain and then you will find that politicians of all kinds and the public generally will be persuaded more to your point of view.

Tony Kennedy
Just very quickly, I think your confusion arises from a false idea that there is supposed to be unanimity on the panel, I don't think that was every required of us, and I don't think we intended to achieve it. Could I say from my experience that in the real world decisions have to be made about priorities, about who gets what. I didn't mean to be pejorative about bureaucrats, since I have been a bureaucrat myself most of my life, I think they do an admirable task, but I do believe that, at the end of the day, people expect

someone to be politically answerable for the decisions that are made, and expect to be able to influence them. I'd like to mention an event that brought it most fiercely home to me, I was Regional Director for the Housing Executive in Derry, in 1983. We had a target, if you applied for an improvement grant, our target was that within six weeks, if your documentation was in order, you could start that work. I was going to the local Councils and because the Councillors had no responsibility, they were kicking me all around the room, because of the alleged bureaucracy that meant that people had to wait six weeks before they could start work. I went to Wakefield Council as Chief Housing Officer. The waiting list there for an improvement grant was four and a half years. When people complained about it, the councillors who had to make the decisions about priorities, explained to people that this was, of course, because there was only a certain amount of money around and decisions have to be made, and one of the decisions was that the money wasn't going to go to improvement grants. The councillors having made the decision had to stand over it; people respected that decision, they didn't read in the papers daily that I was an incompetent bureaucrat who couldn't do anything: In fact, they read that I was a very noble servant of the public who was trying my best under very difficult circumstances. This was despite the fact they were waiting maybe four and a half years. The lesson I learned from that, is that when the local politicians have to accept the responsibility for the decisions, the local community learns about the decisions and learns about the priorities that have been made. The phrase I would use is dependency culture. In Northern Ireland, in particular, people believe if they shout loud enough for something, no matter what it is, they will get it, and if they don't get it, it's because either the bureaucrats are being malevolent, or because the politicians aren't shouting loud enough. That is an unhealthy state of affairs; we need a state of affairs where people have to answer publicly, openly, and at as local a level as possible for decisions they make which affect other people's lives.

David McConnell
To reply to Larry McCluskey, and say more about ethos and other differences, of course we are bound to try to explain as much as we can, and hopefully to convince people of the specific qualities of a particular ethos, ethos being the 'total character' of a place. I

think if you look at the full text of my paper you will see we have been working very hard to persuade people and what really does puzzle us is that we have failed to make what seems to us to be a reasonable case.

If you take the ethics of the Adelaide, then I think you must consider them as different from the ethics of virtually all other public hospitals. I will give you a contrast. The Sisters of Charity who run St. Vincent's Hospital, have a philosophy and code of ethics from which I would like to quote one sentence. 'Procedures which are judged immoral according to the teaching of the Catholic Church may not take place in any facility under our care'. I wholly support that code of ethics for St. Vincent's Hospital. I believe that it is entirely proper for the Sisters of Charity to ask that the hospital which they founded and maintained for many decades, and which they still manage, should run under their code of ethics.

Our code of ethics is completely different. We only ask that our doctors behave professionally with respect for their patients, caring for them in the best interests of the health of the patients as the patients themselves would wish. This code emphasises entirely the personal and private relationship between the doctor and patient, without any external moral interference from outside that relationship.

The question is quite simple. Why can our ethics not be accepted in just one major Irish teaching hospital, and why can the Adelaide Society not be accepted as the trustee of that hospital and the guarantor of those ethics?

Chairperson:
Thank you very much, I think that the code phrase from this session is obviously the one that we've got perhaps ironically from an English geneticist, via David, 'Treasure your exceptions' which covers very well, perhaps the first two presentations and if we can as it were through the suggestions that have come from Tony, find a way to fund our exceptions and to move the path towards them, then this particular session will have set us on the way for another direction that was suggested at one of the workshops this morning, a phrase which is very practical: that what we need is an imaginative Ireland. I hope that in the next six workshops you get a chance to re-imagine Ireland, and we look forward to hearing the outcomes tomorrow morning.

PART IV

REPORTS ON WORKSHOPS

REPORTS BY WORKSHOP CHAIRPERSONS

GENERAL DISCUSSION

CONCLUDING REMARKS BY CONFERENCE CHAIRPERSON

LOCALITY AND DIVIDED HISTORIES

WORKSHOP 1

Chairperson: Helen Lanigan Wood

Reporter: Deirdre McKervey

The members of the workshop introduced themselves and the session began with a discussion of a comment made by Kevin Whelan in his introductory address, about the extraordinary growth of local history societies in Northern Ireland being a product of the 'Troubles'.

It was agreed that this widespread interest in the past appeared to be stronger in the North than in other parts of the country. A community under stress, it was suggested, had a deeply felt need to sort out its identity. Both communities in the North, it was pointed out, were engaging in a sincere self-examination. Through a study of history, both were attempting to understand the other's viewpoints and great good was emerging from this exercise.

Reference was made to Myrtle Hill's keynote address and her comments about the changes in people's perceptions from birth to death. Anne Tannahill also referred to attitudes constantly shifting within Northern Ireland. A very optimistic view was expressed about this phenomenon. Through activities such as the study of local history, through individuals discarding stereotyped interpretations of their history, attitudes were beginning to change.

Not all were agreed that the current interest in local history was due to the Northern conflict, several commenting that this interest long predates the 'Troubles'. One speaker believed that to some extent the current interest in regional history might be seen as a reaction to centralised history, to history emanating from official sources. The same speaker felt that whereas formerly history had been transmitted orally from generation to generation, this oral tradition was now broken and people were beginning to feel the need to write down their histories. It was remarkable in the North that so many of the local history societies were publishing books and booklets about their localities.

Taking up the theme of local history being a reaction to official history, one speaker commented on the widespread growth of social history studies throughout western Europe. This was the history of people, of women, of workers, of everyday things and experiences. This kind of history was being reflected in museums throughout Europe and in numerous oral history projects.

Several speakers spoke of the value of local history and local environment studies in the education of children, particularly its useful role in encouraging self-confidence. The study of local history was also valuable in its potential to counteract dangerous over-simplifications of history; there are not, for example, just two traditions in the North but a much greater number and complexity of traditions.

The discussions then focused on what might be achieved through education. There was general approval of recent educational developments in Northern Ireland, programmes such as Cultural Heritage and Education for Mutual Understanding. These initiatives must continue to be developed and funded. With regard to the EMU programme, more contact should be encouraged between pupils of different religions. At present this element of the EMU programme was not compulsory but one of the speakers felt that this kind of contact was crucial to its success.

Several speakers felt that the South had much to learn from these educational programmes in the North. The curriculum in the South should embody more of the Protestant traditions. It could be improved by incorporating a new programme modelled perhaps on the existing Senior Certificate with its sound social and cultural content. Above all, more funding should be made available to encourage worthwhile educational initiatives.

Referring to Tony Canavan's keynote address, the discussion then moved to the possible dangers ensuing from the study of local history. It could be a reactionary force, a desire to escape, to bury oneself in a safe local world. There was also a risk, suggested another speaker, of expecting too much from local history study, of placing too much hope in its healing powers. We should, perhaps, continued the same speaker, look for other ways of living with our differences, with our conflicting prejudices.

Another speaker urged the need to integrate local with global understanding and to explore ways of achieving this goal. Commenting on the complex nature of local history, one speaker described it as political, apolitical and even anarchic. In response another speaker described local history as completely anarchic in that three thousand had died in Northern Ireland through people's misconceptions both of history and local history.

The discussion then moved away from local history to a consideration of other ways through which people could respond to their localities. The arts, and especially theatre, were considered to provide worthwhile and exciting avenues for exploring our identities, our differences, our histories. The discussion ended on a note of optimism with one speaker urging us to look to all the many imaginative forms embodied in music, theatre, the visual arts as ways of leading us to a new 'Ireland of the Imagination'.

Conclusions

The discussion centred first on the significance of the recent growth of local history societies in Northern Ireland. It was generally agreed that local history studies had the potential for improving community relations; through them shared traditions as well as more contentious issues could be explored, and important changes could be effected in people's perceptions. There was also a recommendation that people in Ireland should try to extend their understanding to world-wide as well as to local issues.

Several recommendations concerned education. The value of programmes such as Education for Mutual Understanding and Cultural Heritage in the North was recognised, and further development and funding of these was urged. The group felt that much more could be done to improve the school curriculum in the South and it wished that more emphasis should be placed on Protestant traditions and on local environmental and history studies.

A more novel approach to the subject of divided histories was in the recommendation that we look to the arts for ways of expressing and resolving our differences. Music, theatre and the visual arts could provide the creative framework to guide us, less painfully than by local history, through all our difficulties and divided histories.

An Assessment

The topic, Locality and Divided Histories was understood by the group to refer to Northern Ireland. Because of the 'Troubles', those in the North were perhaps more concerned with facing the challenge of divided histories within communities. While there was an awareness that the South too had its inheritance of separate traditions, be it Protestant, Catholic, Gaelic or British, there was not perhaps so much urgency there to alter the status quo.

There was undoubted admiration for what was being achieved in the North in the field of education and many worthwhile suggestions were made regarding methods to improve the educational curriculum in the South. However one did not get the impression that any dynamic movement for change was afoot.

The discussion was conducted with courtesy, members listening attentively to what was being said, everyone participating, no one dominating. There was good representation from both North and South, and members spoke with clarity. Without any set agenda, the debate was able to flow freely, and while it may not have delved very deeply, it never strayed too far from the designated topic.

When the subject of the arts was introduced, there was a real enthusiasm, almost euphoria among the group. After such serious deliberations about history and divided communities, members began to feel that music, theatre and art provided real hope for resolving communal difficulties, and far more easily and effectively than local history studies.

WORKSHOP 2

Chairperson: Gearóid Ó Tuathaigh

Reporter: Eamonn Hughes

Introduction

The workshop sought to address a number of basic questions regarding the role of local/regional history in informing and shaping a sense of community. The particular circumstances of the divided community in Northern Ireland inevitably figured prominently in the discussion. The participants in the workshop tried to find ways of assessing the significance of the growth in recent years in the number (and the activities) of local historical societies and groups, throughout the whole of Ireland but particularly throughout Northern Ireland. Among the questions which emerged in the discussion were the following: Whose curiosity and interest were these societies serving? What was their impact on local community relations and on the collective well-being of the communities whose history they were exploring and discussing?

A key concept for discussion was the concept of local history as 'living history'. On the one hand, the concept of local history as 'living history' might, in a benign sense, be taken to mean that 'immediacy of reference' which local history enjoys in stimulating and enriching historical and cultural curiosity within a local community. But, on the other hand, it must be recognised that 'living history' can be highly problematic in a divided community, where historical memory sustains (and is invoked as sanction for) entrenched positions of suspicion, prejudice, hostility and confrontation. This dichotomy strikes us forcibly when we turn to consider the thorny question of how long an interval must elapse before contentious (i.e. socially divisive) historical episodes can be said to belong 'safely' to the past of history. How many years must pass before a particular historical period or episode can be discussed and interrogated within a divided community without causing further division, rancour and conflict within that community? This question is burningly relevant to Northern Ireland. Why is it, for example, that dark and contentious issues in the Irish land war of a century ago are now generally 'fit matter' for historical investigation and discussion in most local history societies in the Republic (though the descendants of many of the participants in that conflict may still reside in the same localities), while the commemoration of historical episodes far more remote in time (e.g. 1641, 1689–91) continue to fuel division and hostility within the communities in Northern Ireland? Clearly, the answer to these questions relates to the different senses in which history, at a local level, remains 'living history'.

Workshop Discussion
The questions of what stimulates historical curiosity, how widely dispersed it is within a community at any given time, and how best to enrich and to focus it constructively, were some of the main questions discussed. It was suggested that, among the factors which had led to a quickening of interest in local history in recent years (notably, but by no means exclusively, in Northern Ireland) were the following: – a growing awareness that in a rapidly-changing society (with increasing mobility, economic and technological transformation etc.) there is a danger that a sense of rootedness and continuity (cultural and physical) may be ruptured or seriously weakened. A Northern participant expressed the view that the surge of activity in local history societies in the North was, in part at least, 'a response to the erosion of heritage'. A County Clare view was that 'it is sad when young people in rural Ireland don't know their neighbours, or the names of the people in the houses they pass on their way to school'. It should be added that the issue of whether the response to the perceived erosion of heritage could or indeed ought to be distinguished from a fear of change and development was raised by a number of speakers.

The second factor cited for the increasing interest in local history was the growing realisation among alert but ordinary people that, as social geographers and historians maintained, an immediate and vital 'sense of place' is an important part of individual and collective identity. In this context, several speakers suggested that local history (social history in particular) was seen as a way of overcoming the idea, which school and textbook history had fostered for many people, that history was something which happens 'somewhere else'.

Thirdly, it was suggested that there is a growing demand from various groups or sections of the community (e.g. the handicapped; those whose parents or neighbours or kin made no public speeches; most especially, women) hitherto excluded from or marginalised in the 'official histories' of the textbooks and the schools, that their voices be heard in historical narratives, so that their contribution to the story of humankind and its progress should be recorded and acknowledged. Fourthly, reference was made to the fact that in a more information-driven society, and with ever-widening access to formal education at all levels, there is now a more widely-dispersed capacity within local communities to undertake historical enquiry (i.e. locate and use documents, research family and public records etc.). In this particular context, it was suggested that very often the returned emigrant seeking historical information (for family or more general reasons) provided an important stimulus to a sharper historical awareness throughout a local community. The fact that many recently established local and family-records societies were making a particular effort to meet the curiosity of the Irish of the diaspora was also seen as a significant development.

Turning to the different roles and functions which local history societies were seeking to discharge, there was a clear difference of opinion on whether these roles/functions differed depending on whether they operated in a rural or an urban setting. On the one hand, it was contended that there was no essential difference between urban and rural dwellers in respect of their need for (and entitlement to) an historically-informed 'sense of place' (though it was acknowledged that in a more shallow-rooted suburban setting the 'creation' of such a meaningful sense of place would require greater effort from the leaders of the community in partnership with the 'professionals' – geographers, historians, archaeologists). Others insisted that there was an enormous gulf between a rural community, with a rich matrix of reference available to it in affirming continuity between the generations, and the sprawling suburbs of Dublin or Belfast, with recently-settled or transient populations, where 'creating' an authentically historical 'sense of place' might not be the best, or indeed even a viable, option in the formation of some kind of community cohesion. Several speakers emphasised the fact that gender or social class or ethnicity would, for different individuals and groups, be more powerful determinants of their 'identity' than a sense of shared community based on 'place'.

There was a lively discussion of the impact which active local history groups can have on a community. There was evidence from Co. Tyrone of the potential of an active local history society to generate and inspire other and wider community action in, for example, tourism, crafts, heritage, and general community-based development. Speakers from other areas confirmed that the Tyrone experience was not uncommon. However, a number of issues emerged from this discussion of the 'organisation' and 'professionalism' of local history and related activities. In particular, concern was expressed that the 'communal story' of memories, folklore and local history might become 'too bureaucratised' (in societies, committees, formal lectures, learned papers), to the detriment of the sense of 'ease' which ordinary people ought to feel in contributing to discussions of local history and folklore. In the same vein, it was suggested that the process of local historical research/enquiry is at least as important as the findings, and that an excessively 'bureaucratised' or overly co-ordinated approach might exclude people from the process and thus devalue the individual perspective and the individual voice. Even those who defended the need for professional standards in researching and presenting local history agreed that facilitating the widest possible access and accommodating the widest possible plurality of perspectives were both highly desirable objectives for any community-centred local history project. For some speakers the ideal 'commune of learning and knowing' which might constitute a community's response to its own local history was at the opposite pole from the highly-commercialised 'heritage industry' which was being advocated by certain influential voices involved in cultural tourism in Ireland, north and south.

The practical proposals which found general support in the workshop included the following:

(i) There was a particularly vital role for the schools – from the primary level forward – in encouraging a healthy historical curiosity among children. There was agreement that a variety of strategies should be employed in the schools; bringing in guest story-tellers, doing field-work – in its widest meaning, individual or group projects, role-playing and drama, using films with 'historical' themes as stimuli. It was stressed by several speakers that the rigidity of an examination or test-driven curriculum was not conducive to cultivating a healthy historical curiosity among school-children of any age.

(ii) Local history societies should, as far as possible, try to act as resource centres for historical records and related materials for their local communities (where appropriate, in partnership with local libraries and museums).

(iii) The need to communicate historical information (and the activities of local history groups) as widely as possible could be met through the effective use of local newspapers and radio, and through popular as well as specialist/learned publications. It was suggested that some lessons might be learned from the experience in Holland (described by Rienk Terpstra) of trying to attract attention to the importance of a sense of history and of cultural continuity in a society where many (especially young) people seemed at best indifferent to the concept of 'continuity'. Assuming that those who were already interested in local history were, in a cultural sense, already 'saved', and could be depended upon to fend for themselves and generate their own activities, Rienk Terpstra described how in Holland they tried to capture the attention of the historically indifferent by organising popular events, concerts and entertainments centred on an historically-significant monument or building, thereby focussing attention on the building/monument, and (hopefully) raising historical consciousness thereby. The group found this imaginative suggestion an interesting example of one way of promoting 'living history'.

WORKSHOP 3

Chairperson: Tony Canavan

Reporter: Sean McGearty

I had the misfortune to chair a very good group. I say misfortune because it meant that a great number of issues were raised and a lot of very relevant points made by the members, making it very difficult to sum up in a brief time. And so perhaps I should begin by apologising now to the members of the workshop if I have left anything out or not spent enough time on any particular issue.

The first question to which our group addressed itself was that of definition. We felt that we had to know just what we meant by locality or region before any worthwhile discussion could take place. After an initial exchange of views, one of our group came to the conclusion that 'definition can be paralysing', a sentiment with which we all agreed. Nevertheless from what was said, we recognised that two distinct concepts on what was a region were emerging. One was a structural or administrative region, that is one used by government to define an area for the purpose of administration such as a county or a constituency. It was recognised, though, that this did not always coincide with the 'regions of the mind', those areas whether large or small with which people identified, and this gave us an alternative definition as being that place or district with which an individual could identify. We concluded that it was the sense of identity which was crucial to a definition of a region in the context of our discussion. Two provisos, or addenda were added. Firstly, that it was not just a question of identification with, but also participation in by an individual that defined a region, and also that someone could identify with different or even overlapping regions. The example was given of the Aran Islands which were part of County Galway, of the Gaeltacht and of the Diocese of Tuam. Having taken this as a working, but we hoped not paralysing, definition we proceeded with the workshop.

In this the question of locality and its relationship to history was discussed. In particular we were asked by one of our members to look at the mechanisms of local history. Calling on the experience of members of the workshop, we identified these mechanisms working through local history societies as follows. Firstly, the process of research and exploration of history, and by implication of cultural identity, in the local context. This was important as it entailed people learning where to find sources of information, how to gather it and analyse it; which would not only improve their knowledge and understanding of the past but would also enable people to bring these skills to bear in other areas.

Any process of examining and learning about history must result in discussion and debate. Realistically, it was recognised, this would for the most part be within a particular community, but could eventually lead to discussion with other communities, and those with other identities. As most of our group came from or worked in Northern Ireland, this was viewed very much in the northern context and the question was raised of how far local history societies contribute to the debate in Northern Ireland and what contribution, if any, they have made to dialogue in a general sense there. The point was made that many societies do actively engage in interrogating the past. The recent two hundredth anniversary of the founding of the Society of United Irishmen had been used by a number of societies throughout Ireland to take a new look at the principles of the United Irishmen, the events of 1798 and their significance to modern Ireland. Similarly the anniversary of the rebellion of 1641 had also seen discussion at a local level based on the events of that year.

However the actual efficacy of such things was questioned on the basis that not only did they often involve only those who already had an open mind but also that the exploration was often confined to just one community or one section of the community with little opportunity for divergent opinions to be expressed. In effect, that history conducted at the local level was in danger of reinforcing prejudices and preconceptions. In response to this, it was said that a 'non-verbal' debate was being conducted through the media, which had an important role to play. Television and radio were obvious means by which the issues in history could be popularised, but local history publications – from the established companies and local societies – were also an important way of conducting the debate. A person might be wary of going to a history seminar in, for example, South Armagh or Ballymena, but he or she would willingly read the papers from a seminar when printed in a conference report or a local history magazine. Although it is difficult to quantify, there does seem to be a market for local history publications well beyond the area in which a history society operates.

The workshop was unanimous in emphasising the important role of the media, and urged that more programmes bring history to a wider audience. An example of media power was given in reference to the Aran Islands, where a TV programme had soured relations between the indigenous islanders and newcomers, but a subsequent programme had helped to heal the rifts created by the first. It was felt by all that more local community input into television programmes on historical topics could only be beneficial to Ireland, north and south.

Television is usually seen as something neutral, and this raised the question of the importance of neutral venues in Northern Ireland. While people from either side of the community there were willing to get together to explore the past there was often a problem of finding a safe or non-offending building in which to meet. This was highlighted as a practical problem for the chances of meaningful discussion in Northern Ireland, and it was felt that more support should be given to the opening of community centres, libraries and similar venues that people felt safe in going to. This was a very important consideration in the context of Northern Ireland.

Neutral venues took on another connotation in a metaphorical sense when it was realised that certain topics could be seen as neutral or safe to discuss and explore. For example, archaeology is often seen as a safe topic because it pre-dates the history that leads directly to the present. Other topics might be certain local personalities who have made a name for themselves in the fields of science or literature. On the other hand, political figures and certain aspects of local history are often sidelined in order to avoid arguments. This issue was further discussed because, as someone remarked 'sectarianism had to be tackled at the source'. It was felt that the sharing of the past, or a mutual exploration, should be encouraged when possible. However there was also the recognition that in some contexts sharing could be viewed as theft – the tercentenary celebrations in Derry when many of the Protestant community within the city felt that this was a nationalist attempt to hijack their heritage was given as an example.

It was agreed that there could be other issues or other catalysts which could also help to explore or redefine the sense of identity. Prominent among these were women's groups – and not just the groups themselves with the important community issues they tackle but also the role of women in the community and in societies of which local history societies were an example. On the whole area of community issues, it was felt that action at grass roots level was a way of participating in and reinforcing a sense of identity.

In attempting to draw some conclusions of a wider relevance from our discussions, we felt that policy and decision makers should recognise that Ireland is a changing society and this calls for a response, a strategy to meet the challenge of change. Any such strategy, however, should begin at the lowest level, and by this we mean not just the lowest administrative units but by consulting ordinary people, asking them their concerns and finding out their interests. In other words, any strategy to meet the needs of modern Ireland should begin from the bottom up. In this, we felt that what has happened in history, where local studies conducted by local people has transformed in many cases how we view national history, could be viewed as a pattern and as a metaphor for what could happen to society as a whole.

If recommendations were to come out of our workshop, then our chief recommendation was that funding, whether from government, the EC, or other agencies, should be directed towards people and communities rather than just buildings. In other words that money should be there to empower local communities to improve their quality of life and to tackle the problems they face. As a corollary of this, there had to be a recognition that success has to be judged by different criteria – that helping communities means that results may take years to emerge or may not be amenable to quantitive analysis. Success should not be measured in pre-set criteria based on buildings, whether heritage centres, enterprise units or community centres, and the numbers involved – a simple 'bums on seats' approach, as they say in theatrical circles – but it should be recognised that community projects grow organically and that solutions to problems should be sought in the same way instead of a bureaucrat or politician deciding on 'the solution' and then imposing this on a community.

Finally, our group tried to draw all this together and see if we could come up with any conclusions of relevance to Northern Ireland – which took up some time in our discussion – but also to the Republic. We decided on the following, I hesitate to say rules, but recommendations. The fundamental problem was how to come to terms with confrontation and exclusion: the confrontation between Protestant and Catholic, between regions, between the central government and the regions. We felt it was important to emphasise those things which we hold in common in our heritage and in our concerns on social issues. As well as this, we felt it important to celebrate the diversity we have in this island and not see differences between people of one region and another in terms of confrontation and rivalry. We also came to the conclusion that it was important to recognise that the pace of growth was going to be different in different parts of the country and among different sections of society; and so we must make allowances for this. And, what we hope is being complementary to this rather than being paradoxical, that growth is necessary to a healthy society. We cannot turn our back on change and should recognise that dynamism is essential to our survival as a society. Finally, if less concretely, we believed that we ought to seek ways to avoid confrontation over these very issues of identity, heritage, rivalry and so on. Whatever works in this area ought to be encouraged, and, like the community itself, a solution to this problem is perhaps better left to work itself out organically rather than trying to come up with a hard and fast solution.

INGREDIENTS OF REGIONAL IDENTITY

WORKSHOP 1

Chairperson: Terence Brown

Reporter: Desmond O'Rawe

The workshop began by considering whether Kevin Whelan's model of the rural region constituting itself from 'the bottom up' had any relevance in the city. Was the city excluded from such regionalism? Discussion focused on the ways in which in the city issues of wealth, class and family tradition created complex cultural points of personal identity and made for variegated forms of social allegiance. Participants in personal reminiscences were sensitive to the ways in which snobbery, elitism and matters such as accent and educational experience in the urban context militated against any comfortable cultural identity for many people. Attention was drawn to the interfacing of family, class, regional and national factors in both the urban and the rural setting. Some participants questioned whether the idea of belonging was not a myth or social construct. Others considered that a sense of belonging, even if it was always a mediated set of assumptions that were open to question, was a powerful social cement that set more firmly in the rural situation where it supplied a basis for consensual attitude to law and order and to socialisation in general.

In response to the chairperson's query as to whether different models of rural and urban communities are necessary it was suggested by one participant that a theoretical distinction could be drawn between a Burkean and a Jacobin approach to the idea of community itself. The Jacobin sense of social organisation would emphasise the modernising and centralising processes of the modern state, national and trans-national. It would privilege such concepts as citizenship, abstractly defined individual rights, as core elements in identity formation and cultural commitment. By contrast the Burkean sense of community would emphasise concrete identities with their sources in paternalistic, conservative notions of socialisation and would privilege geography, history and tradition as its core elements in communal identity and would sponsor a vision of communitarian obligation. The Jacobin model was more likely to be found relevant in the urban context, the Burkean in the rural. This conceptual dualism stimulated a good deal of debate with numbers of participants expressing concern that the rural, Burkean model of community was often an ideological justification for the coercive and repressive aspects of local, rural communities. It was by no means clear that the extended families of many rural communities and of some urban communities were necessarily preferable to the more fragmented, often liberating forms of family and social life in the cities. It was strongly argued by some members of the workshop that gender and language issues challenge conventional pieties about community and region as does the perennial phenomenon of emigration.

The workshop then considered whether Kevin Whelan's model with it's 'Chinese boxes' notion of regional identity was not too static. In both the countryside and in the city regional identity was reckoned a more fluid, mutable reality; though some participants were at pains to remind the workshop of the strength of local feeling, of the kind that resists administratively convenient name changes that defy local histories and long-established loyalties.

Much of the rest of the discussion focused on the ways in which the globalisation of culture through all forms of communication had complicated the context in which ideas of regional identity had to be defended and developed. In this discussion it was suggested that some of the assumed differences between urban and rural identity had diminished and that in the rural world as in the urban, complex forms of identity had now begun to develop where a region of the mind to which people (Whelan's *pays*) felt they belonged was open to many national and international influences which allowed people also to identify with such things as youth culture, gender-based social action and environmental crusades. In this context there were those who expressed doubt whether the idea of the region was in fact really useful in considering the relationship between the individual and state power while others were concerned about a certain sentimentality which sometimes accompanies talk of regional attachment while disguising a complacently conservative outlook. In the main, however, participants wished to see real decentralisation of power in Ireland to the regions that were becoming marked by rapid social change (the changes in family life, work patterns and in the roles of women were noted as particularly salient in this respect) and by complicated forms of loyalty and identity formation. It was thought that the model within the state and within the EC of centre and periphery with an implicit set of hierarchical assumptions about power and significance would have to be broken down in any true decentralisation. In this the radical potential of information technology, its capacity to establish networks and to make available educational resources, was considered most important. Indeed if the region is not to become, as one participant warned it might, just another building block in an unwieldy hierarchy of power which stretches from the individual to the EC Commission, then exploitation of such technology and the creative use of local radio stations must become elements in a genuine process of democratisation and local empowerment. It was felt that as yet the implications and potential of the communications revolution at the local level were improperly understood. This is an area that needs further research and thought.

WORKSHOP 2

Chairperson: Edna Longley

Reporter: Kevin O'Neill

To judge from this workshop, the regional groups who feel most threatened, the exceptions that, in David McConnell's genetic metaphor, ought to be treasured, are Ulster Protestants and west-coast speakers of the Irish language. It was also said that 'liberal' or non-religious constituencies don't receive the attention their numbers warrant.

1. Place:
Perhaps encouraged by Anne Tannahill and Dermot Healy (whose talks were much praised) the workshop began with strongly autobiographical statements from each member. Nearly every statement included a declaration of allegiance to place – or places: often a combination of urban and rural loyalties. One speaker urged us not to fear remote control from Brussels, since local politics would always engage our real interest and energies. Another insisted that local attachment involved not merely physical belonging, but 'mystery... the being of all generations that expresses ourselves'. However, it was also argued that we were in danger of idealising 'little localities' and 'rural idiocy'. 'Claustrophobia called community' was the main cause of emigration, and we should beware of recreating the monster which had destroyed us. Ireland is short of ideas rather than of roots. There was disagreement as to whether city-life conferred a liberating anonymity or whether it, too, broke up into distinctive villages that served a continuing need for affiliation. Someone suggested that Kevin Whelan's socio-cultural model was unduly rural and Catholic (as well as male) – it lacked intermediate levels between the kinship-network and national or universal systems. A more graduated and self-conscious relation to place

(local history etc.) was largely a Protestant invention. A museum worker spoke for that tradition when he said that the conference should be paying more attention to regional material culture.

2. Place and Politics:

We noted various effects of politics on the understanding of place: the sectarian maps internalised by Northerners; the practical difficulty and hazard of crossing ghetto-lines in Belfast – for instance, to learn Irish; the additional hazards for women; the relative obtrusiveness of army or police presence in different areas (a class-issue too); the false consciousness encouraged by the term 'two traditions'; 'the formalisation of the Border'; John Waters's representation of male Fianna Fáil Roscommon; the retreat of Ulster Protestants to the bawn – to mono-cultural districts. It was said that some Protestants simply did not want to live alongside Catholics, and this refusal pre-dated the 'Troubles'. However, political violence, in conjunction with the rise of the Catholic middle class, has led Protestants to retreat even from Belfast itself; the area behind Balmoral Golf Club is now known as Vatican City. South of the Border, the workshop picked up some east–west tensions. One important question was asked but not answered: is the Border felt as an artificial cleavage through communities, or has it now acquired its own shaping role?

3. Language:

The theoretically bi-lingual Republic was found wanting in its care for the Irish language. Where was the long-promised TV channel which might both help to bind communities and display the language's diversity? It was also impossible to receive certain services – even to be buried – through the medium of Irish. One disenchanted enthusiast said that he now envied the language provision in Northern Ireland – a tribute to recent government policy as well as to the efforts of various groups (though we were reminded of the long Unionist taboo). However, regional factionalism within Irish-language circles was also noted: as between Munster and Ulster variants; between Dublin HQ and Gaeltachts; or between Belfast intonation and the purist insistence on a Donegal *blas*. One member observed (neutrally) that Irish was a 'peasant dialect': i.e. its native speakers had long ceased to be anything other than rural workers. Thus certain contradictions should be admitted. So should the dubious package-deal which – not only in Ulster Protestant perceptions, but in Nationalist assumptions and rhetoric – continues to link Catholicism/Nationalism/Irish. For instance, republican remarks by Proinsias MacAonghusa, head of Bord na Gaeilge, a state language body, had not helped those who were trying, with some success, to de-politicise the language in the North. There is also the 'chill factor' of mono-lingual Irish street-names (though bi-lingual inscriptions might be extended, e.g. on historical monuments) and of the mono-lingual signs in Queen's Students' Union. These send a disturbing territorial message to Protestant students, one in which the Irish language is implicated as a 'weapon of aggression'. It was said that this spilt over into the resonance of the term 'Irish Studies', for which there were far more Catholic than Protestant takers at Queen's, whereas 'Local Studies' did not suffer this imbalance. Nonetheless, attitudes are changing, and Unionists like Chris McGimpsey have done their bit. As for the English language in Northern Ireland, the BBC, last bastion of so-called 'good English', has now fallen to a range of regional accents – despite teachers' complaints that proper 'elocution' is no longer on offer, and that 'Sammy' has ousted 'Julian' . . .

4. Gaelic Culture:

One speaker, a researcher into Protestants' relation to traditional music, said that there were three main branches of Gaelic culture: sport, music, language – in descending order of influence. Of these, traditional music (usually a separate sphere from the language orbit) had proved the most inclusive, flexible and mobile. Musicians introduce local styles to new places, new places present new stimuli. Irish music abroad is not the property of expatriates, but an international idiom. The Co-operation North conference *Whose Music?* had been mistaken in its premise that Protestants/Unionists did not participate in traditional music, though the 'Troubles' might have curtailed their involvement. (Note: This illustrates the tendency to read cultural history back from the polarised present, let alone from the 1920s. Cf. Aodán Mac Póilín's articles in *Fortnight* which set the historical record straight about the role of Northern Protestants in the Irish language movement.) The all-Ireland organisations charged with promoting Gaelic culture were generally criticised for exclusivism, inflexibility and lack of local sensitivity: the GAA ruling on the RUC, the identification of Comhaltas with Catholic moral teaching. Years ago, a Protestant Irish-dancing champion had given up when told not to dance at concerts where 'foreign' national anthems were played. And although Unionism is held wholly responsible for the past failures of the BBC to disseminate Gaelic culture, when it came to the crunch, the greatest resistance often emanated from the monopolistic and secretive reflexes of institutions like the GAA. Hierarchies were said to be 'almost universally pernicious'.

5. Religion:
All the Protestant autobiographies stressed religion – which seemed less visible to the Catholics present as a marker of identity. One speaker talked about the powerful influence of evangelical Protestantism. Despite its bigoted and puritanical aspects, it should not be ignored as a cultural force and a communal prop for Protestants who feel lost and forgotten. The Glengormley churches are full. At the same time, 90% of church-based activities have not a political dimension. A Church of Ireland speaker reminded us of the variety of Protestant culture – his own background did not include 'conversion-experiences'. Two members of the group emphasised changes in the Catholic Church and its context. One said he wished that Northern Protestants would realise how society in the Republic has rejected authoritarian Catholicism. (Someone asked whether the Northern Catholic Church realised or relished this.) The other said that respect for different spiritual convictions should be paramount. However, a historian told us not to forget the very sharp divisions of forty years ago: 'All Catholics are damned'; 'Protestants cannot be part of the Body of Christ'. It was said that a political institution like the Catholic Church has to do more than lower its public profile and soften or privatise its language: it must genuinely give up power – e.g. over education. It is by no means clear that 'spiritual paramilitary' groups such as SPUC are utterly distinct from the institutional Catholic Church. They were sparked off by the Pope's visit to Ireland in 1979. Protestants need proof that the Church is not threateningly monolithic. A united Ireland holds little attraction for Protestant women, even if fundamentalism is just as anti-feminist. However, as elsewhere in Europe, it looks as if religious difference is here to stay, and it's high time that we 'learned how to manage it'.

6. History:

Throughout this session we became aware of our historical situation. On the one hand, we could measure progress in cultural understanding over forty years or ten; on the other hand, while 'movement' was claimed on behalf of both Protestant Ulster and Catholic Ireland, that movement seemed rather imperceptible or insignificant to 'the other side' – in the group and on the ground. The phrase 'gestural politics' was used. It was also evident that at least two Ulster Protestant generations had been denied access to historical elements of their identity in Ireland – a deficiency now being supplied in the schools and through adult education. The historian stressed how we write history according to contemporary needs. Certainly, the Unionist and Nationalist narratives are being modified, together with their supporting cultural ideologies – often from a local or regional viewpoint. For instance, Fethard-on-Sea in Co. Wexford, once the scene of a boycott on Protestants which gave Ian Paisley his first platform, is today marketing its Anglo-Norman heritage. But, someone asked, why should history still loom so large when we define identities in this electronic age?

Suggestions and Conclusions

1. The predicament of Ulster Protestants recurred in this discussion – perhaps a reflection of the group's make-up. Working-class Protestants in particular were said to feel abandoned, even to have 'given up real resistance'. One speaker was acutely aware of the gulf between the university and the housing-estate. Meanwhile, many middle-class Protestants – the non-chattering sector of their class – had retreated into private life, as well as into the bawn, thereby, renouncing political leadership and disclaiming responsibility for a situation which their abdication helps to perpetuate. It thus seems very important to involve both groups in processes of cultural discussion and education. Education 'should be spread at all levels of the community'.
2. On the wider Irish front, our job is to spread the idea of cultural diversity 'into communities throughout Ireland, and that is a long, hard task which we're scarcely beginning on'.
3. Many cultural special-interest groups operate on a cross-border basis: could these be identified (perhaps by Co-operation North) and to some extent used as a bridgehead for further advance? Museums will be working together on the bi-cente-

nary of 1798. New technologies facilitate inter-regional communication.
4. Ideally, cultural bodies should find a *via media*, a mode and scale of operation, between centralist arrogance and the parish pump. Similarly, traditional music affords the most attractive model of how to combine local or regional affiliation with a more fluid and cosmopolitan consciousness. Inter-regionalism within Ireland and Europe?
5. The withdrawal of Protestants from rural Fermanagh, or from parts of Belfast, or from the North altogether, diminishes the number of culturally diverse environments in this country. The Cultural Traditions movement is, in a sense, rediscovering the complexity of pre-partition Ireland. But is it a race between that rediscovery and the Northern war?
6. This workshop confirmed my personal view that we will never change the political culture of Ireland until we directly tackle the divisive religious culture. The churches have proved unable or unwilling to do it on their own account.

WORKSHOP 3

Chairperson: Proinsias Ó Drisceoil

Reporter: Jane O'Neill

Our workshop concentrated on power and its relationship to identity and how the expression of that relationship ought to be given political and geographical expression. The discussion developed from the premise that both regions and regional identities are human constructs rather than facts of nature but it was nonetheless conceded that a continuum exists going from geographically and environmentally self-explanatory regions to political entities created to fulfil bureaucratic requirements or sustain funding applications. These latter were seen to be most glaring in the case of structures such as the North-Eastern Health Board which owe their configuration more to the exigencies imposed by partition than to any geographical coherence or identification with the structure by those living in the region. Many of the local government structures in Northern Ireland were also seen as being on the arbitrary end of the continuum and it was held that for all of history nobody will ever describe herself as a Mourne and District Council woman!

Identities are multiple and overlapping and imagined communities such as Derry and Londonderry can co-exist imaginatively with the interplay between their political expressions as the dialectic of history. It is not possible to have a political correlative for every identity, any more than it is possible to have a state for every nation. Political boundaries inevitably tend towards the arbitrary and are a compromise which may be unsatisfactory for many inhabitants but rather than seek national or regional expression for every imagined community, the emphasis ought to fall on the need for all political constructs to offer equity and democracy and not to stifle the imaginings of any community. In this context, the notion of the 'progressive' was seen as having a continuing relevance in terms of the reconciliation of competing identities through mutual struggle to achieve social and democratic goals.

It was felt essential not to situate the debate on regions and power solely within the regions themselves. The centrality of the central in this debate was emphasised: decentralisation of power is only achievable through political decisions made where power is currently centralised and the tendency to blame the absence of regional power on those living in the regions was regarded as badly misplaced. The intense centralisation at EC and governmental level was accompanied by a rhetoric of regionalisation, but the minimal EC budgets for the regions gave sobering evidence of actual EC priorities. Where local identities are insecure, as in Northern Ireland, a political resolution at central level would necessarily determine the extent to which an amelioration of insecurity at local level could be achieved and similarly at EC level the power to substantially alter the relationship of core with periphery was vested primarily in Brussels.

The weakness of local government structures had fuelled a myriad of voluntary groups seeking to compensate for the absence of an effective expression of local power, particularly in areas such as Tallaght and similar new suburbs. However, they had failed to fill the vacuum and no substitute exists for effective local government if people are to achieve control over their own localities and, equally importantly, express themselves effectively to central government. Weak local government had considerable potential for damage and demoralisation when the centre which purported to substitute for local democracy was itself weak and ineffective and the emergence of Tallaght as what one participant described as 'the Irish Soweto' bore eloquent testimony to these intersecting forms of ineptitude.

Local identities not only overlap each other but are shifting under pressure from demographic change. This is particularly the case in Northern Ireland where the most recent census gives grounds for a fear among the Unionist–DUP block that over the next two local government elections their majority will be permanently lost. Such fears are likely to be given a political expression premised on notions of regional identity which are unpredictable in their consequences.

A more invigorating consequence of local government weakness was seen as the extent to which local communities have sought to evolve avenues to Brussels which by-pass existing paths. The office opened in Brussels by a variety of agencies working in the west of Ireland was given as an example, as was the Catholic Bishops' campaign for the West – although the view was offered that this was essentially a campaign to maintain the springs of clericalist conservatism and that it was significant that no similar campaign had been initiated in relation to deprivation in urban areas.

One participant held that arbitrarily designated regional identities could eventually win acceptance and he cited the instance of the huge Mayo official Gaeltacht which although not Irish-speaking had been designated a Gaeltacht for political reasons in the 1950s. In his work with Údarás na Gaeltachta, he found that this area now had a largely similar character to other, more historically-justified Gaeltacht areas and had taken on the imposed identity.

Any sentimentalisation of the local was tempered by reference to the extent to which improvements in the status of women had been won at EC level in the face of opposition from local and central government. This appeal to trans-national solutions was in line with the way in which women were rejecting the identities available to them regionally and locally in favour of cross-cultural action on political and feminist issues. Women had traditionally been the conservers of regional culture, language and dialect through their full-time presence in the home and now that this was decreasingly the case, social and linguistic consequences were likely and it would be necessary for administrative structures to take account of these changes.

Similarly in the field of visual culture it was felt that the trans-national nature of television and film while a homogenising force, disrespectful of local identities, was also a liberating force for the young and the curious within regions, given the absence of other forms of visual cultural expression. It was felt to be particularly significant that those listed by Dermot Healy as painters of the North-West were all landscape painters and that their pictures were largely devoid of people – a possible indication that landscape lends itself more readily to regional expression than do the inhabitants!

One person's identity can be another's alienation and the tendency to describe regional and local communities, particularly in rural areas, as socially and culturally coherent ignores the extent to which the communities, whether urban or rural, are riven by divisions of class, by issues of gender and by increasing poverty. In rural parishes labourers and the unemployed and their families are likely to be as alienated as their urban equivalents – perhaps more so given their relative lack of opportunity for group solidarity and class identity. The much-vaunted Irish sense of place could be a force for alienation, rather than identity, when acting to demonise areas of high unemployment such as South Hill, Ballymurphy and Tallaght.

Consensus on the points made was not sought but the following conclusions might be tentatively offered:

(i) access for women to points of decision-making beyond the national should be extended;
(ii) local power needs to become an issue in central politics;
(iii) some measures of compatibility ought to be sought between administrative structures and geographical and environmental entities;
(iv) the continued debilitation of communities in the new poverty-ridden suburbs ought to be countered through the creation of structures at local level capable of addressing their crisis.

For my own part, I found it extremely significant that participants were either hostile or indifferent to local elected politicians (an attitude which suits these politicians in many respects) while simultaneously very alive to politics and the possibilities it brings for regional renewal. This is perhaps an indication of the extent to which Irish intellectuals have managed to foreswear participatory politics while themselves offering analyses which are deeply political. It is also symptomatic of a dangerous gap between local need and its political articulation, a gap which unelected and sinister political forces, often describing themselves in terms of local identity, are only too willing to fill, particularly in a context in which poverty and alienation are increasingly in parallel.

HERITAGE AND ENVIRONMENT

Chairperson: Lelia Doolan

Reporter: Jane O'Neill

In order to stay within the editor's space guidelines and still give some of the flavour of the proceedings, I have shortened some direct contributions and, in other cases, summarised the speaker's main points. I trust that I have not seriously damaged the sense of what was a very open and lively exchange.

To begin with, I asked Máire Uí Shíthigh to expand on any particular topic covered in her talk to the full conference.

Máire Uí Shíthigh:
When I started working with Oidhreacht, a load of work had been done on the history and archaeology and not very much had been done on the flora of the area, so I devoted a lot of my time to that and also to the whole question of the language. They are really the two aspects I have given my energy to.

With regard to the flora project, the scholarly work is done. We've had this project going on for three years and now the job is to communicate it. I am working on it with teachers; at the moment I am working two days a week on the 'béaloideas' collection, about presenting the information that was collected all over the country in the thirties in the schools and in the curriculum. It is no good having a survey sitting on a shelf unless people are reading it and know what is in it, particularly people who have land or have access to land.

Chair:
Right. You were also talking about the [Irish] language being a main mode of communication and saying that the 'green wellie brigade' hadn't taken much of an interest?

Máire Uí Shíthigh:
Yes, I think it is true the language has not been huge issue with conservationists and I think, going back thirty or forty years, it might have made a difference to the state of the language today if it had been seen as being of real importance in terms of the country's heritage.

Leo Hallissey:
I would like to start by broadening out a bit from that. I believe that our country is up for sale and it seems to me that money is coming from Europe and this can be misappropriated and will not get into the cultural heritage area but into the business area. I think it is important for people who are involved in the heritage and cultural area to quantify and quite clearly state what is important to us, to our identity as an Irish people. Because I feel now that gombeenism is having a field day and it is masquerading under the benign banner of creating jobs. So a very sacred part of our culture is under attack. I think a conference like this must address the facts and get out into the public arena what is important for us as a nation, that we are not going to be strangled by gombeenism and petty politics, and that the money that is for culture and heritage is actually spent on culture and heritage. That's an important debate that we could talk about.

Mary Banotti:
Could I marginally disagree with you? The money is not for culture and heritage, it's for tourism and regional development. Culture and heritage are only just beginning to creep into post-Maastricht Europe and there isn't any discussion on culture and heritage, on the way that this money is actually being used; and those of us who have warts on our palms from the great fight about Mullaghmore and the other centres and what they represent will be aware that there is a kind of spurious language going around which tells us that this is vital to a) our tourist interest; b) to jobs and c) to the local community.

I mean we look at this hotel here. By all accounts this hotel is defining the culture of Cavan at the moment, it is being seen as the greatest thing that has happened to Cavan and it is not here just as a hotel but as a way of mopping up Regional funds. You have to find a little label and send your shopping list over and we are told subsequently that this thing is vital for our national heritage. You would be surprised at how quickly unvital something becomes once the ability to draw down those funds is stopped. What we are beginning to see is that various state organisations regard the drawing down of these funds as vital for their institutional future. In other words, the jobs within particular areas of the civil service depend on whether they can justify their existence by bringing down this kind of money. So I agree with Leo. I think that the country is up for sale and it is being sold by people who are not publicly accountable, who don't feel that it is important to come along to something like this to explain to us why they decided to do this.

Pat Cooke:
I work for the OPW, which is a big, nationwide organisation. Many parts of it are effectively decentralised. It just isn't one big centralised bureaucracy. All kinds of people work for it: archaeologists, architects, scientists, and people like me; I'm a literary historian.

I like to think that I have a free mind and that if I didn't have a free mind I wouldn't be of any use to the Office of Public Works, which now has such a key role to play in the cultural life of this country. For many of us within the organisation the present controversies about the various interpretative centres have been a cause of anxiety. I feel that those of us who work at a decentralised level, within some local context, managing specific heritage amenities, see the OPW as most effective when it works at this level, when you have people out there based in the local scene, acting as a pivot between the organisation and the community, taking seismic testings, if you like, of what effect a particular proposal might have on the people of the area.

The OPW itself, I would say, was taken aback by the virulence of the reaction to its interpretative centres because, for about ten years, we were on a rising curve where everything to do with heritage was popular and we couldn't do wrong. Maybe we should have seen it coming because it had already happened in England around 1985. The defining moment of critical reaction there was a book by Robert Hewison called *The Heritage Industry,* which started a whole wave of critical reflection on the heritage business in England. It is interesting that the trigger for this reaction in Ireland has been the interpretative centre issue.

Now this is not an easy issue. It is complex and I don't think there is any generic case to be made about these centres. They are all unique. You can't say all interpretative centres are bad. Each one has to be looked at individually: Luggala, the Blasket Island Centre, Mullaghmore.

In the case of the one I happen to be involved with, the Blasket Island Centre, I know that there was a great investment in dialogue with the local people. I think there is immense potential in this building to be a prestige building for the people of the Gaeltacht. With an auditorium that seats one hundred and fifty people, things like a Pan-Celtic congress can take place there. National organisations concerned with the Irish language can meet in the heart of the Kerry Gaeltacht and discuss issues in an area and a context that means something. There is positive potential there, but most of it is, as far as I can see, a community-development type of potential.

I feel that the business of treating these heritage amenities as solely commercial propositions is a complete delusion. There was a key conference held by Bord Fáilte about three years ago, which was amazing in the sense that we had a group of mostly English consultants telling us about our history, as if nobody here had worked in that area. Here were these guys lecturing us about our history. With the emphasis on tourism, no reference was made to the role of these things in community terms. In the most obvious and practical sense you've got a tourist season lying largely between the months of June and September. What are you going to do for the rest of the time? Let all these things moulder away on the landscape all winter? Unless there is a positive community involvement in the management of these facilities, they will fail miserably; they will be the new Ballrooms of Romance on the Irish landscape.

Chair:
Thanks very much for that frank and illuminating contribution and a very welcome one since it gives a good deal of intelligent background to what we've all been through in the recent past. Does anyone else want to comment on that? The phrase 'heritage industry' seems to be a danger area.

Pádraig Ó hAoláin:
At the present moment, there is an intense debate going on within our organisation (Údarás na Gaeltachta) in relation to this whole issue. This relates to how the organisation is to work in closer part-

nership with local communities in relation to developments such as these, and on the other level, it's the type of discussion that needs to take place between state agencies, our own included, and our masters, if you will, in relation to expenditure of exchequer money and, indeed, European funds on what we would see as the enhancement of income and part-time job opportunities in local communities which are of enormous importance in rural communities but which may not meet the criteria expected of us in our annual returns – that is, full-time jobs or full-time job equivalents. There is enormous pressure on the development agencies to be seen to deliver in terms of full-time jobs and there is big pressure to get involved in the cultural tourism area on the basis of it delivering jobs or delivering enhanced income to local communities. The question I would like to raise is: to what extent can these problems be resolved by partnerships between the development agencies, the state agencies and the local communities and are there objective criteria by which heritage and heritage-related projects can be evaluated? Is the local community, for instance, entitled to be sometimes wrong about what can or should take place in their localities?

Susan Christie:
I agree that there is danger to the environment, but there can be a good side to it as well. Yes, tourism is a bandwagon; yes, culture is the big buzz word that means we can get money from Europe. We have to be very careful about how exactly we go about that. If we can do something that is going to create jobs, is going to be a nice tourist resource in the summer and in the winter is used for public meetings, is used educationally so that children can learn about their environment; and in the meantime that we are not destroying what we are putting interpretative centres there to look at – that's fine. We have to make sure that we look at the effect, in the short term and the long term, of any development that we are pondering.

Chair:
Upon whom?

Susan Christie:
Upon local residents and on the environment: things like an interpretation centre in the Burren, where you are going to be putting

more and more people through a delicate ecological community, there is a very great probability that you are going to destroy the very thing you are trying to attract people to see. There is a good side to it because, if the planners see that, in order to encourage tourism, we are going to have to do something about the whole environment in general, it will go back to more sympathetic planning that could be very good.

Chair:
Well, given that everyone accepts there should be great care that communities should not be damaged – even though, as Pádraig says, they may not always be right – how can we create structures of partnership between them and, say, the OPW, Bord Fáilte, Údarás, the educational system and so on – so that we get a 'gush up' effect rather than the 'trickle down' one?

Leo Hallissey:
I was just thinking that, at the moment, there is a Green Paper on education which is to be discussed throughout the country. I feel we're now at a crisis in culture and heritage terms and we need something similar. We need it to become the concern of everyone so that some are not isolated and called names – like 'Dublin 4' 'blow-in', 'yuppie' and 'hippie'. Local history, the language, the music and folklore are precious and important to us all as a nation and I'd wish that this weekend could somehow spark a national debate which would be open, democratic and accessible to everyone – and then linking that debate into a coherent education policy, involving all the relevant state agencies.

Leo Hallissey went on to say that the OPW doesn't have an educational philosophy nor linkages with local communities and he expressed wariness at one organisation having control of heritage and of employment in that field – to the extent that potential employees were intimidated from making public criticism of the OPW.

Pat Cooke agreed with the point about education, adding that the OPW had developed hugely into the heritage area within the past ten years, having been mainly a maintenance and preservation operation up to then – and pointing to EC money as a large factor. He went on:

Why is it that we don't seem to have the political will to stand up to and challenge the terms on which money is given to us by Brussels? We should be able to say: 'Look, we are going to build something for one and a half million but give us one and a half million to invest in a trust fund which actually is an investment in the human resourcing of that building, structuring the human dimension into the thing from the start. There is only an investment in bricks and mortar. Even the OPW finds itself caught by this – unable to recruit fulltime professional staff to build up a body of experience and expertise. I'd like to ask Mary Banotti – isn't the formula fundamentally wrong?

Mary Banotti:
Yes, it is. The formula is inscribed in the Treaty of Rome. Call it *training and information* and just don't talk about it and you will get the money! Every system has its formal way of doing things, but much more powerful is often the informal way in which things are done. Notwithstanding all the nasty things that are said about the bureaucracy in Brussels, they are actually much more open and, dare I say it, transparent, than our own bureaucracy. You certainly get in to see a senior official on the Commission quicker than you can here.

Flann Garvey:
I think that we are adept at knocking, if you don't mind my saying so. When we have the OPW and Brussels to have a go at, I think we lose track of where we are ourselves. I live on the edge of Mullaghmore and I wonder what all this talk is about. The interpretative centre is going to be built roughly a mile and a half from Mullaghmore itself. There are two sides to the story. One thing that's missed out on is the desecration of the Burren by the hippies – and that's what I call them – and there was no word then from people outside the county about those people absolutely defacing the surface of the Burren for years.

Going back to another point that Máire made about the schools collection in the thirties – that's a positive thing that could be done now in every school in the country. I remember when I was a lad, people played Irish music in a house or a pub. In a house they were respected but in a pub they were laughed at because it wasn't popular at the time; they were the gombeens from the west of Ireland who were thick and probably poor as well. But, suddenly, it became fashionable, and then set dancing came back too. It's wonderful to see who's learning to dance now! But the kernel to me is the language. I think people are now beginning to see, at last, that the other pieces – the music and dancing – were certainly part of our way of life, but the language is the kernel. Why do you go to a country? You go to see and hear what is different. I admire Séan Quinn for putting his money into this hotel. He is putting life back into a part of Cavan that was as good as stone dead. There is an investment of six million in this building here and the canal, the Ballyconnell Canal – wonderful! But the point about the language is vital and important. I think people are beginning to see that now. So I am more hopeful now.

Chair:
But I assume you'd make a distinction between what some residents – 'hippies' – may do to the environment and what the state is doing?

Flann Garvey:
Yes, Okay. The point I am making is that we shouldn't spend so much time knocking institutions. Okay, if they are doing something wrong then challenge them, but rather spend more time lighting the candle than cursing the dark.

Pádraig Ó hAoláin:
One last comment. It is obvious that Oidhreacht Chorcha Dhuibhne has a very important educational function and recognises that as part of its own role, and to universalise that is one of the things required throughout the country whereby we have some mechanism by which educational awareness programmes can be run at community level. I would suggest that, in relation to what Leo said, perhaps no white or green paper for this particular area is needed but we should stitch this into the Green Paper on education and make that an important aspect of our educational system so that it will get the recognition that, for instance, Enterprise Technology will get in future according to the Green Paper.

Denise Ferran:
I would just like to make an observation about heritage and environment. About twenty five years ago, we went to Donegal – North-

ern people going in search of roots. We went to a very beautiful place called Gleanncolmcille which was scattered with thatched cottages, whitewashed everything and gradually these started to disappear. Now I remember being down at an art event in Dublin and talking to Jack Lynch and, of course, when I started to say to him I would like to take up an issue with him, he thought this is the Northern 'Troubles' and I said: 'Would there be any way of giving people grants for thatches?', and he was taken slightly aback. I said 'You know they are putting asbestos slates on roofs, and they are ruining them', and he said, 'From whose point of view', I said, 'True enough, I am the person who is going and enjoying the environment'. He said, 'You are not living there all year round, they are damp cottages for the people living in them' – and I had to agree. We were through all the years with Fr. McDyer, the co-ops, the failures, the factory, all that. Then someone over here started a culture centre and Irish language in the schools and a comment was made that the only tourists in Gleanncolmcille this year came because of the Irish language and they were there and the step dancing was there and the fiddle-playing.

Liam Ó Cuinneagáin:
I am involved in this a number of years in Gleanncolmcille. We started ten years ago with thirty people learning Irish. Last summer, we had eight hundred people from twenty different nationalities learning Irish, including Chinese and Japanese. Now it is a community where English is spoken by most of the people but most of them can still speak Irish. That language change-over happened unknown to them because of all the influences: tourism, emigration, media, education, the church, political, commercial influences and this gave the people low self-esteem. But my analysis is, if we can increase this self-esteem and instil some kind of sense of pride in the local people about what they have, and put across the message that Flann was talking about, that if you are different, then you can be economically successful with tourism, and people will come here because we are different. I have absolutely no hesitation in justifying in the local pub that they are making money from the Irish language. I say to them that there is nobody in my valley who can't turn around to me after ten years in operation, and say that the Irish language is no good, because I can point to a relation who has made a few bob selling jumpers, etc., to people. We

have to keep local control over the development of cultural tourism and heritage. Okay, we may be wrong in some cases, but unless we have local control and avoid the 'money from Europe' syndrome as it so often happens in my own place – there's money there: what idea can we come up with to get a few bob – rather than being convinced that there's a real need and then going and getting the money.

Chair:
What means do you think can be put in place in order to strengthen local regional control, the control of the ideas, the notion of partnership, the actual power to create and to stop, how do you think this is going to happen in our centralised system?

Pat Cooke:
I think there has been a tendency all weekend to put things too much in opposition to each other. I mean, there are obvious reasons why people think nowadays about the centre and the region as totally in confrontation. What I tried to show at the beginning is that there are whole areas of the OPW's activities that are positively engaged at a local level. So it's the connection between the two that needs to be good, to have a positive relation between them. Let's face it, sometimes local authorities can be far worse bureaucracies than any centralised bureaucracy. They can be far less efficient and far more prone to petty politics and local interference than at national level. So let's not try to set the local and national at all times on a head-on collision.

Máirín Nic Eoin:
In the late sixties, a community development co-operative was set up in the west Kerry Gaeltacht and in 1967 another was set up in Erris, Co. Mayo. It was because of the initial success of these co-operatives that Roinn na Gaeltachta, the government department responsible, set up Scéim na gComharchumann Gaeltachta and afterwards about twenty-eight such co-operatives were established in other Gaeltacht regions, many of which were at the time still lacking basic services such as running water and electricity. The co-operatives provided a whole range of services and also provided much-needed employment, and I think they present a very good example of how central government could respond to local needs by channeling resources through a suitable local community struc-

ture. Many of these co-operatives have gone into decline in recent years and the range of services they provide has become quite narrow, in many cases being limited to the administration of the local summer college. But perhaps they could now be resuscitated to take on some of the functions in relation to heritage and cultural tourism we have been discussing here.

Chair:
Right. I think it is an interesting thing the way in which local initiatives can get a response and create an institute which may then become somewhat barren when its functions have changed.

Máirín Nic Eoin:
Yes. And a number of the schemes initiated by the development co-operatives became very successfully privatised, specialist projects such as Cniotáil Inis Meáin, for example.

Leo Hallissey:
A couple of final comments on the built landscape: we have a vernacular tradition of architecture and we are not ashamed of it. There *were* hard times in those thatched houses but they weren't all damp. They were organic – they came from the landscape and they fit into the landscape. It is indicative of where we are at that we are uneasy about them. I have in my house a stone floor and when Continental people come in, they say: 'isn't that beautiful and it must have cost a lot of money!' – And when the Paddies come in they say 'when are you going to get the carpet?'.

Now I have no argument about the man who wants to build a hotel, but I do have an argument with a man wanting to build a monstrosity. When I came around that corner, it certainly upset me as an Irish person. Fine – build a hotel – build three hotels – but build them with a bit of taste. If this is the best that Irish architecture can do and seal it with European money. . . . And as for the business of knocking. I think that to raise fundamental questions is not to knock – and I like to think I've lit a fair few candles in my own time – in my post-church period! – at a local level. I feel that we are at a crossroads with culture as a nation.

The discussion ended with a short exchange on the role of the church – priests and bishops – in connection with language and heritage. It was generally agreed that with some notable exceptions, the record was poor.

Recommendations
- A serious, open and accessible public debate on heritage, culture, tourism, the environment and the language involving the relevant local and national bodies and feeding into the educational system at all levels.
- The fostering and resourcing of initiatives at community level and creating workable, democratic connectors and partnerships between them and national institutions.
- A greater concern for training and information – as opposed to mere building funds – for heritage and environment from EC sources.
- A sense that these matters are now critical and urgent.

THE REGIONS AND THE MEDIA

Chairperson: Martin McLoone

Reporter: Kevin O'Neill

It is important, I think, to preface my report on the media workshop with a few observations on our agenda as it developed. After all, our discussions rarely touched on those questions which tend to dominate debates about the media in Ireland. We did not, for example, discuss in detail media coverage of Northern Ireland nor dwell on the related questions of censorship and government secrecy which remain, quite rightly, key concerns for those of us interested in the media in Ireland today.

Rather, our agenda followed the general pattern of discussion established by the conference thus far and we concentrated on the complex interconnections between the different media operating at local, national and global levels. Indeed by considering the media within this tripartite relationship, we were able to address the issues raised earlier by Dermot Healy in relation to RTE's role in the south. Was RTE the voice of a sectional interest group (closed-minded liberals, I think he called this) which foists its own particular metropolitan image of Ireland onto a rural population that neither recognises nor embraces this vision of itself?

The same kind of criticism is often levelled at the BBC, of course, though in this case the broadcasters are accused of peddling a London-centred view of Britishness which is barely recognisable outside the south-east of England, never mind in the more culturally diverse parts of the UK like Scotland, Wales and Northern Ireland. Indeed our discussions were also influenced by the recent publication in the UK of the Green Paper on the future of the BBC and we attempted to address this in relation also to RTE.

These preliminary remarks might suggest that broadcasting tended to dominate our discussions but we did manage to consider other issues as well, especially the role of the press and the general question of a global popular culture delivered through a variety of media forms.

We began our discussions, then, at the local level and considered first of all, the role of the local press, north and south, in promoting or cementing a sense of local or regional identity. There were conflicting opinions here. One contributor accused the local press of being the bedrock of conservatism in Ireland – tentative and cautious in its engagement with change and locked by history, family and/or money into the most conservative elements of a local community. In the North this was exacerbated because the local press tended to address either a nationalist or unionist constituency, rendering the other one invisible and thus underpinning long-standing sectarian division.

Another contributor, however, felt that the local press was an important conduit of identity. It spoke in a very local and idiomatic way a 'language of belonging' which people related to in their everyday life. It concerned itself with local news and gossip, births, marriages and deaths, the human concerns which form the bedrock of identity. That is why exiles tend to look for, or have sent to them, their local paper rather than the national press. The pity is that the local press in Ireland seems to be withering away (as it has done in England) under commercial pressures and increased competition from other media.

This theme was taken up by another speaker, who referred to the decline of the *Belfast Telegraph* as a factor in the 'democratic deficit' in Northern Ireland. The *Telegraph* has effectively opted out of the debate in Northern Ireland and is now content to peddle a consumerist message through advertising and banal popular features. Far from building, cementing or promoting a strong sense of local identity, the *Telegraph* had become an uncritical conduit for a global consumerist culture which is particularly debilitating. (Another person, though, ascerbically commented that this commitment to a consumerist culture does not prevent the *Telegraph* from expressing its unionist bias).

The notion of a democratic deficit might apply to the South in a similar way, it was also argued, though here it is not so much the decline of a vibrant local press that was the problem. Rather, compared to the 1960s, there was undoubtedly a decline in the quality, quantity and range of magazines available. And here, I think, we all recognised a basic paradox about the media today.

Despite the development of technologies which should render the media more accessible and more accountable, the opposite seems to be happening. We felt that new technologies should be used to give local communities greater access to the media – as a means of representing their own experiences, rather than to have these mediated or ignored by a remote professional bureaucracy.

In this regard, we discussed at some length the question of local radio and especially the success and failures of recently established commercial radio in the South. There was a fair measure of support for local commercial radio and one contributor in particular praised local radio in Kerry and Clare which, it was argued, had connected with the local community in imaginative and meaningful ways.

Others were less enthusiastic and felt that local commercial radio in Ireland was nothing more than a mechanism for 'delivering audiences to the advertisers'. Indeed the whole process militated against the development of genuine community radio and if one were to talk about empowering local communities politically, then the means of allowing them to express themselves culturally was a prerequisite.

This raised, then, the question of public service, or regulated broadcasting and there was a unanimous feeling that public service broadcasting was an inviolable principle that needed to be defended. Indeed one contributor likened public service broadcasting to public library provision or even public health and education – it was a basic right which should be demanded by all citizens.

A discussion followed on the successes and failures of both RTE and BBC as public service broadcasters. Interestingly, most contributors to this discussion praised both organisations in their achievements in radio. Indeed BBC's Radio Ulster and Radio Foyle were cited as good examples of the kind of regional and local radio provision that could never be delivered by a commercial broadcasting system. A similar point was made in relation to Raidio na Gaeltachta.

One speaker praised in particular the potent combination of telephone and radio which produced in Gay Byrne and Marian Finucane on RTE and *Talkback* programme on Radio Ulster, some of broadcasting's most exciting, challenging and influential programmes over the years. These had dared to raise issues and discuss topics which had been considered taboo until then. They had broken a silence precisely by giving voice to ordinary people, allowing ordinary people for once to set the broadcasting agenda.

Television fared less well in our discussions. Somehow all the issues which we had been discussing seemed to coalesce around our deliberations on television. The tensions, pressures, contradictions and paradoxes implicit in that tripartite relationship between the local, the national and the global became more apparent.

For example we discussed the often-voiced criticism that RTE imposes from its national citadel, a particular liberal agenda on the rest of the country – the 'Dublin 4 conspiracy'. I have to say that this accusation was forcefully rejected by the workshop. Indeed one person observed that this conspiracy theory represented the paranoid and dangerous delusions of the most right-wing, reactionary elements in Irish society.

(Since nobody in our group defended the thesis, we had to assume that such reactionary forces were not present at the conference, or else we were all, unwittingly or not, part of this liberal conspiracy.)

On the other hand though, RTE (and the BBC) are often condemned for allowing themselves to become conduits for the kind of mass culture that appeals to the most base instincts – a culture represented par excellence by *Dallas*. This kind of global culture is slowly strangling indigenous cultures everywhere and it is particularly regrettable that public service broadcasters are implicated in this form of 'cultural imperialism'.

There was some support for this point of view, although most contributors tended to argue for a more balanced perspective. One speaker referred to the liberating element in American popular culture, the best of which envinced a kind of populist, democratic thrust which blew away the stuffy, elitist 'official' cultures of the European nations in 1950s and 60s. (There were some nostalgic recollections of Radio Luxembourg at this point).

Another speaker referred to the pleasures which American popular culture offer, and especially the particular pleasures which women get from television's most characteristic form, the soap opera serial. Indeed given the diversity of opinion in regard to programmes like *Dallas*, it is impossible to define 'good', 'bad', or 'indifferent' forms of culture.

What was needed was not a rejection of global culture, but a negotiation with it through a commitment to developing and nurturing indigenous culture as well. There were impassioned pleas from numerous speakers for a commitment to low-cost quality television production, especially television drama. The proper structures to achieve such a negotiation, or balance, with global popular culture needed to be in place, hence our commitment to the principle of public service broadcasting. (This could also apply of course, to the notion of a national cinema, or a national production fund for film).

We felt that the broadcasting legislation in Ireland needed to be looked at again (one speaker referred to the 1990 broadcasting legislation as probably the worst and most contradictory piece of legislation ever enacted by a democratic state in regard to its own broadcasting service). Equally, this strategy demanded the preservation of public service broadcasting in Britain and we hope that all interested individuals, groups or organisations would respond to the British government's Green Paper on the future of the BBC.

Our discussions, then, were very broad, covering issues which are as central to our European neighbours as they are to us. If we are to manage successfully a new arrangement in the local, national and global dimensions of our media, then we would make the following recommendations.

- The principle of public service broadcasting must be defended.
- Public service broadcasting must itself change and begin to decentralise towards more regional and local structures.
- To achieve this, new technologies should be employed to democratise and diversify public service provision.
- In particular, there should be a commitment to high quality, low-cost indigenous production, in preference to a strategy of trying to compete with, or mimic, international styles.
- Given the nature of the debates about the role of the media in our society, the appearance of media education on new curricula introduced in both countries is to be welcomed. Media education, we all concurred, is a right and a necessity, not a luxury.

LOCALITY AND RELIGION

Chairperson: Joseph Liechty

Reporter: Deirdre McKervey

Judging by the number of conference participants who chose to preface their remarks with some statement of religious disaffiliation, said one workshop participant, 'we probably have here the greatest concentration of agnostics or atheists that Ireland has ever seen.' He added that this move away from traditional Christianity is not only an important current reality, it is probably a trend, with great significance for social policy, north and south.

These comments set the line of enquiry pursued by our workshop. Without in any way attempting to quantify the shift from traditional Christian allegiances, we accepted that it was significant and spent our time exploring the implications for social policy. Our conversation fell into categories as predictable as they are vital: how religion interacts with education and with medial ethics.

Workshop participants advocated a number of educational models. Some felt that state funding for schools should simply follow local support for particular options, whether that be for denominational, integrated, secular, or some other kind of education. If any religion is funded, all should be, said one person; another pleaded that society should allow for as many minority interests as possible, and do so generously. However, others were more sceptical about such an approach. One person sought some principle for evaluating diversity, fearing that embracing diversity for its own sake would reinforce existing social divisions. Others were willing to see some church influence in schools, but wanted control to lie elsewhere. State control raises another set of problems, one person pointed out, especially in nationalist areas of the North where the state is not accepted as legitimate.

Integrated or multidenominational education, as the main alternative to the traditional denominational model, was much commented upon. Two people expressed some irritation that integrated education in the North has become in some circles a benchmark of social and political correctness, while another person was disappointed that a multidenominational school in the South had been unwilling to accommodate Catholic parents who wanted Catholic religious education during school time. Several participants maintained that many who choose integrated schools actually want straightforwardly secular and non-denominational schools without any religious ethos, which the state should, but does not provide. No one argued that integrated education should not be available for those who want it, but some did warn against pretentiousness, while others wanted an additional and fully secular option to the denominational sector.

Our discussion of medical issues followed lines similar to our education discussion. Some people believed medical care should be provided under whatever frameworks citizens desire, whether that be Catholic, Protestant, secular, or other. For example, one participant described himself as a member of no church and in fundamental disagreement with aspects of Catholic medical ethics, but he also admired Catholic medical work and believed that Catholic medical institutions should continue to receive state support. Another person said that in the interests of accommodating diversity, tax-payers who want Catholic hospitals should have them, just as those who want Protestant or non-sectarian hospitals should also be provided for. But other participants were not so ready to accommodate every special interest or minority. One person argued that 'minorities that are exclusivist' should be excluded from state support, while another, reflecting on the code of ethics of a particular Catholic hospital, said, 'the idea that those people should, whatever their good intentions might be . . . get a penny of public money, I think is disgraceful.' The person who said, 'I disagree with the notion that the state or the public should actually fund any ethos', undoubtedly spoke for a portion of the group.

Running through our conversation was a commentary (sometimes explicit, sometimes implicit) on the role and significance of religion in Irish society, north and south. Three participants challenged the very idea of a Locality and Religion workshop. One believed that a workshop on religion gives credence to artificial divisions in society, another argued that any concentration on religion and what he called the 'two traditions myth' is actually dangerous because it 'reinforces whatever bigotry is there', and the third felt saddened and irritated that we should spend a lot of time talking about religion when there are more pressing social issues. Several people noted the close relationship of political, cultural, and religious identities in Northern Ireland and questioned whether social divisions are 'really' religious. One person identified a quandary he believed common in rural Northern Ireland, where people might be departing from the beliefs and practices of the churches, but cannot escape the churches' influence, because the churches are so woven into the fabric of rural society.

While some people clearly regarded the waning of traditional church adherence as a change to be cherished, others offered some cautions. One person challenged what he regarded as a widely-held and false assumption that people in the North are eager to throw off the shackles of their identities as Catholics and Protestants. Another person said that he was an agnostic, but he worried about where moral teaching would come from in a post-religious Ireland. He valued his own religious upbringing and feared that a huge reaction to negative aspects of religion's social influence might obscure appreciation of the churches' many positive contributions. Another participant felt insulted by this connection of religion with morality, which she believed were 'two totally different things', although occasionally coinciding. The first speaker accepted that religion and morality were not necessarily synonymous, but he wanted us to recognise their close relationship on this island, and he was concerned that as we move toward a more pluralistic society, we should not 'hold it against people because they happen to have strong religious beliefs'.

If the purpose of workshops was to set out clear policy proposals, we failed. What we did accomplish, however, was to shape a set of very important questions. The answers to them will indicate how we intend to handle diversity in societies where old unities are in decline.

In his address to the conference, Dr. David McConnell encouraged us to 'treasure your exceptions', and it was this challenge on which we reflected. What are the limits of liberalism and tolerance? When is diversity a social resource and when is it a problem? Do we in fact treasure all our exceptions? If not, by what criteria do we choose which to treasure? If treasuring involves state funding, one person was not sure he could treasure Free Presbyterian schools, others were not willing to treasure Catholic hospitals, and no doubt every one of us could identify the breaking point of our tolerance, that exception we simply could not bring ourselves to treasure.

One participant posed the problem with particular clarity. We disagreed about exactly what the recent abortion referendum in the Republic of Ireland meant, but for the sake of this argument, he assumed that the no vote on the 'substantive issue' was a rejection of abortion, a decision that abortion is an intolerable deviation from social norms. He then asked us to consider a situation more likely to arise in Britain: imagine that a Moslem school applies for funding, but the public body responsible refuses, because it believes that the treatment of and attitudes toward female students would fall outside socially acceptable norms. One of these practices, abortion, falls within the western liberal consensus about acceptable behaviour; the other practice, discrimination against women, is outside the consensus. We asked ourselves, are the two cases parallel? If so, is it legitimate to impose a social norm in one case but not the other? If a distinction is legitimate, by what moral/legal rationale? Our problem-poser identified himself as in favour of abortion (in some circumstances) and against discrimination against women, but he was troubled about how to justify favouring one exception to a social norm, but not the other. 'What', he asked, 'are the higher principles that allow us to distinguish between the kind of exceptions we tolerate?'

This question of 'higher principles' for evaluating diverse practices was a recurring problem in our workshop, and we offered a number of tentative solutions. In immediate response to the parallel cases of abortion and discrimination against women, one participant advocated a written constitution (framed in terms 'as vague and as enabling as possible') as an invaluable tool for maintaining consistency and fairness in the application of law. But a written constitution is a mechanism for applying higher principles, it does nothing to help us determine what those higher principles should be. Some participants did advocate or assume higher principles for governing the role of religion in society; religion should be private, not public; religion should be allowed social influence, but not control. We did not, however, debate the validity of these distinctions, nor did we attempt to set out the borderlines between public and private, influence and control. On the whole, our discussion faithfully reflected the difficulty facing Irish society north and south; old schemes for moral unity have lost some of their hold, and competing claimants clamour for attention, but no new consensus has yet emerged.

With the benefit of time to reflect on workshop proceedings, I want to make three personal comments.

The increasing numbers of Irish people deliberately outside or effectively disaffected from the Christian churches is a real and significant phenomenon. But for many people, affiliation as Presbyterian, Catholic, Church of Ireland, or whatever, is no mere sociological accident, it is what they choose to be and are very happy to be; it is not peripheral to their identity, it is central. This is likely to remain true for the foreseeable future, and any social analysis that ignores or underestimates this constituency will be as badly flawed as one that fails to take account of increasing numbers outside the churches.

Those who wish to correct what they see as the arrogance of the churches and their abuse of power must be careful lest they fall into the same traps. Secular liberalism is so much the consensus among educated western elites that its adherents can lose the sense that they are advocating one set of truth claims that competes with other truth claims, and come to think that secular liberalism somehow stands in an adjudicating position, above the sordid fray. It is difficult to avoid arrogance and intolerance even when fully aware of making truth claims. If truth claims are made without such awareness, the possibility arises of an unconscious and therefore insidious arrogance, and then we are faced with the spectre of an intolerant tolerance and illiberal liberalism.

While traditional ecumenism will remain an important way of dealing with an important set of problems; dialogue between those who define their identity in Christian terms and those who define it in other ways will also become increasingly important. It could be a bruising encounter – the abortion debate in the South reveals just some of the difficulties likely to arise. The prospect punctures any easy, romantic notions about cherishing diversity, but in fact this Christian/non-Christian distinction is one important aspect of the diversity from which a workable society must be forged. Failure to achieve such an accommodation could leave us with a new sectarianism, this time running along Christian/non-Christian lines, but potentially as debilitating as the old sectarianism.

SPORT AND CULTURE

Chairperson: Frank Short

Reporter: Séan McGearty

Initially I asked each person to give a brief description of the kind of work they were involved in. From this our first theme for discussion came. One participant outlined some of the difficulties encountered by the travelling community, and the kind of work done by the Dublin Travellers' Education Group. This was set up on the basic premise that if any progress was to be made towards the acceptance of their cultural identity, then travellers had to be involved at all levels. Their work focuses on education, enterprise and cultural heritage. Their incorporation into formal education has been a relatively recent occurrence, yet already there is evidence of a more positive attitude being displayed by the settled people they are in contact with. Travellers themselves demand the right to experience anti-racist policies, linked to cultural affirmation and identity and they rightly see education as the key to enhancing their self-understanding, self-image and levels of awareness. Other minority groups needed to legitimise their existence, therefore the immediate enactment of anti-discrimination laws was of the utmost importance. This, by law, would help to define traveller ethnicity.

The discussion then moved from cultural identity to cultural expression. Sport was seen as a powerful expression of popular culture, helping to focus territorial identity from parochial to national level. Quite often a parish defined its identity through support for its Gaelic football or hurling team. Although the formation of the GAA helped to concretise the old administrative county boundaries it also helped to unify those counties in a way that heretofore was never experienced. One participant described her almost tribal loyalty to her county when the team played in All-Ireland finals. It was also held that this sporting identity even transcended class divisions, as long as the player was a good footballer, it didn't matter where he came from. This was refuted somewhat by pointing out that at administrative and managerial level the parochial power-brokers – priest and teacher – were often in control. Belfast, it was said, did not experience this kind of control and therefore could be seen as being more 'of the people'. An example was given of a player who in the 1930s had been thrown out of one club for being a communist and subsequently welcomed with open arms by another Belfast club. He is celebrated in popular folklore as being the only card-carrying communist ever to play Gaelic football!

Identities other than territorial, such as class and gender, were discussed. Rugby was seen as an expression of 'the petit bourgeoisie' who were looking for upward mobility and establishing business contacts. Its social scene also generated contact between the sexes. Ireland was a rugby-playing nation until the banning of Sunday games with the formation of the IRFU in the 1880s. The GAA, founded in 1884, replaced rugby with the hybrid we know as Gaelic football. Popular sport began to focus nationalist and religious identity through a redefinition of Irish culture and particularly through banning foreign games and members of the Northern security forces.

These symbols of religion and nationalism, however were not potent enough for the Catholic and Protestant rugby-playing middle classes. Ironically this has been the reason why this sport has evolved as a thirty-two county organisation, a unity uncomplicated with the flag of cultural identity. However one participant pointed out that it was not true to say that rugby was exclusively middle class. Rugby around Limerick and Shannon if anything was a working class expression and was as equally popular as Gaelic and hurling. Soccer had an urban and working class base and from one point of view was seen as more malevolently factional than other sports. This view gave an English perspective on sport and soccer in particular. It was stated that 'sport was one of the greatest factors for evil in the world' and that the behaviour of English soccer fans at home and abroad was nothing short of tribal warfare. This was not the case in Ireland however where sport more often unified than factionalised, particularly on the international stage.

The exclusivity of sport was briefly explored. It was seen as a male concern where women were used as objects who would become partners for players. Women in general were alienated although it was noted that more women are seen at games today than ever before. This alienation first occurred at school where female access to sport was limited. The choices on the curriculum often defined the stereotypical gender role. This view was seen as being rather outdated and that there was movement, particularly at primary level, towards equality of opportunity for both sexes. The old male preserves such as golf clubs were now under constant criticism for their discriminatory constitutions and it was felt that widespread change was imminent. It was stated that the GAA were developing a coaching policy for primary schools. 80% of primary teachers are now female and the worry was that the quality of coaching would be diminished. Women were being encouraged to take coaching courses in Gaelic games and there were 'Mini-Games' played in Croke Park every year for both boys and girls. One participant felt, however, that women should not be coaching Gaelic to boys as competitive games reinforced gender roles.

Class was also seen as a barrier towards participation in certain sports. Rugby, golf, yachting were all perceived as being exclusive along class lines but such a perception may also be outdated. The rules of the GAA and its attempt to define a nationalist identity meant that many Northern Protestants could not participate in Ireland's most popular sport. This was reflected by the attitude of Belfast City Council towards celebrating Down's win in the 1991 All-Ireland. They refused to give the team a civic reception because of the GAA's ban on the participation of members of the Northern security forces, yet at local level, the Down County Board received many congratulations from members of the Protestant community. One participant felt that even if the GAA lifted its ban there would be no way that members of the security forces could join clubs given the current political climate.

It could be said, in fact, that all competitive sports were exclusive as only the athletic elite could participate. They were abilist and discriminated against people with disabilities. Yet, as previously expressed, sport has been a great unifying force in Ireland, crossing cultural barriers and celebrating Irishness in an unthreatening way. An Ulster Protestant became a fervent Irish supporter in Lansdowne Road and every time Ireland played in soccer internationals the whole country supported. Unfortunately these instances of unity are all too infrequent and the group felt that more should be done at community level to encourage cross-cultural and cross-gender encounters. Competition tends to factionalise, so it was felt that there was a need to develop non-competitive leisure activities and hone in on the general preoccupation with health and fitness. Youth clubs and sport centres should be funded to develop sports likely to draw a wide mix of people.

The question was posed as to why the calibre of academic discussion and writing on sport was so poor. Even literature paid scant regard to its popular significance. Was there a relationship between sport and higher forms of cultural expression such as art, theatre, poetry, literature, music etc. or was sport merely a plebian preoccupation? There were those in the workshop who voiced a total disinterest in sport saying 'it didn't matter'. These people were involved in the arts. One talked of traditional music and how it crossed the cultural divide. Literature too had similar qualities. A festival in Killybegs, Co. Donegal attracted ten Northern writers creating a new audience for their work in the South. So was sport not a valid expression of culture or could it and the arts be interwoven to give a complete sense of cultural identity? Before answering this question one participant pointed out that the antipathy earlier expressed went both ways. Often those involved in sport, 'the rugger bugger jock-strap types' sneered at and detracted from the importance of the arts. This was reflected in schools where a far greater proportion of time was given to sport than to any other peripheral subject. It was common for children to have to make the choice between music, art and sport. However it was expressed that the GAA promoted the arts, albeit a particularly nationalist perspective, through its annual Scór competitions. The recent Italian World Cup was a great example of a celebration of national identity, a sporting occasion which brought together many cultural disciplines such as fashion, architecture and, of course, classical music. This gave a greater number of people access to higher forms of cultural expression and as a result the sales of classical records have never been higher. It was felt that if this symbiosis was to be achieved in Ireland then the arts should be given greater importance at school and extra funding should be made available.

The discussion, nearing its end, briefly moved to defining Irish culture. There were great difficulties in coming up with a suitable one-liner. One participant described it as 'the learned and lived experience of people passed on'. Another quoted Kinsella, 'we are what we are, mongrel pure'.

It was a 'variety of non-static characteristics constantly changing over a period of time', another added. It was felt that these definitions were too vague and that there must be something that makes us uniquely Irish. It was a synthesis of our language, music, literature and our capacity for oral communication and willingness to celebrate our Irishness whenever it was non-threatening. Unfortunately and indeed rather unsatisfactorily we could not explore this any further as our time was up and the session ended.

Recommendations
In conclusion below are the practical recommendations which came from our discussions:
(a) There is an urgent need for anti-discrimination laws in Ireland to legitimise the rights and identity of the travelling community and other minorities.
(b) A wide ranging network of non-competitive leisure activities must be developed at local level to help create more opportunities for cross-cultural encounters.
(c) The poor representation of arts in education must be redressed and additional funding made available to achieve this.
(d) The arts provide an ideal opportunity for bringing people of differing cultural identities together so more festivals should be financially encouraged to develop along these lines.
(e) There is a need for an academic study into the significance of sport as an expression of popular culture.

Assessment
The discussion lacked a certain dimension and likely suffered for not having anyone to represent either the Protestant tradition or sporting organisations. Many people in the south of Ireland do not understand what 'makes' an Ulster Protestant. What is his/her sense of cultural identity? How does (s)he celebrate this? For some, it is hard to imagine that one can express loyalty to Britain yet claim to be Irish. It would have been interesting to explore this and look at what the different traditions had in common by way of cultural expression.

The workshop needed someone to counter the charges of exclusivity in sport and to express their view on the arts and whether there was any relationship between both expressions. This was discussed, to a degree, and it did bring to light how people in the arts view sport and vice-versa. The dismissal and disregard often shown, should be confronted and events where different cultural expressions were brought together organised to celebrate our shared sense of identity.

It was interesting to note the different perceptions of the value of sport as a vehicle for unity. In general those speaking held a benevolent view and many incidences were given describing loyalty and celebration. The discussion, however, did show that cultural identities other than the Protestant and Catholic existed in Ireland and in the case of the travelling community were struggling to legitimise their ethnicity.

The value and significance of sport as an expression of popular culture and how this could be harnessed as a force for unity and as a means of celebrating our Irishness in a non-threatening way, must be studied and acted upon. The calibre of academic analysis on this subject has been very poor to date.

LOCALITY AND ACCESS

Chairperson: Helena O'Donoghue

Reporter: Desmond O'Rawe

At the outset the workshop participants introduced themselves indicating briefly their interest in the conference topics. The chair took a few minutes to indicate the particular focus of this workshop and circulated a page with the issues and aspects which might be relevant to our discussion:

Issues: Marginalisation ....?
 Exclusion.................?
 Mobility..................?
 'Outsiders'...............?
 Rural edges...............?
 Urban ghettoes............?
 Size and scale of locality.................?

Aspects: – Access to services – education, health care, housing, law?
 – Transport structures?
 – Deterioration in provision of such?
 – Role of class or gender or other factor?
 – Centralisation?
 – Participation possibilities?
 – Access to funds – national/European/other?

Schemes? .... e.g. Postbus in West Clare

Initial banter by the participations on the word 'access' led to the first point for consideration – that of ACCESS IN, of the necessity for a 'visa' or permit to enter, at times, a particular region or locality! It was suggested that an area may sometimes distance itself from its significant people – writers, artists, musicians, others – and may resent the local image presented by such people, or that presented by outside journalists or television programmers. Questions around intrusion, pluralism and rural mythologising arise here. This problem is not peculiar to Ireland; it is experienced in other parts of the world too.

The rest of the workshop time focused on ACCESS OUT issues, which broadly related to different kinds of discrimination experienced by regions which were at a disadvantage in some way. The reality of centralisation, which is characteristic of both parts of Ireland, was seen to present serious difficulties in terms of equity. Social administration has a responsibility to get funds to the 'edges', whether these be distant rural margins or neglected suburban ghettoes. While a certain 'sensible deprivation' will be indicated in most areas, it is not acceptable that resources and services should be allocated on the basis of majority or other forms of clout.

Such patterns contribute to regional/area anger, lack of development, poor local image, depression and inter-regional aggression. In terms of basic standards it was felt that for education, arts, social services and other areas, access should be preventative and not ideological.

While centralisation and equity issues were seen to be closely interlinked, the workshop focused sharply on the need for access to information and training at local level. Without these any efforts at consultation and partnership are no more than cosmetic and token exercises. Information and training are most critical for access, for empowerment and for partnership. Responsibility for this lies very much with central government, as well as at other levels.

The dilemma of empowerment was then considered. What are we empowering people for? What vision of Ireland do we have? What are we trying to achieve? What model do we have? Is it an American one? In this context the issue of wealth creation versus social justice needs to be addressed. When stuck with a flawed capitalism how can equality and full access be achieved? We have to imagine a new Ireland, set goals in an Irish context, and address the planning questions which this entails.

One new factor in local regions which got some attention was the advent of local radio. Disappointment was expressed at the quality of local radio (allowing for a few exceptions) particularly in regard to its reflection of local identity, its potential to contribute to local development and its capacity to provide a voice and avenues to access. In some cases the local airwaves present 'wall to wall' music – country and western music! In counterpoint it was mentioned that this is what the people want! It was felt that there was something intrinsically important about public service broadcasting which ought to be encouraged and supported. In contrast it was noted that local newspapers were generally of a very high quality.

Conclusions
The two issues which emerged as strong recommendations were:

(a) that we look at the national goals we have set ourselves and that we begin to plan for equity in an Irish context;
(b) that local radio be invested in so as to utilise its potential for regional development in all aspects.

Value of the workshop:
The discussion was lively and ranged over a wide canvas. The points covered above were the more dominant ones. Other related aspects were touched on but probably none in sufficient depth. A strong sense of the need to pursue a coherent vision for region and country, together with equality of access, was present. In common with the other sessions of the conference, the workshop reflected the wide variety of experiences and concerns of the participants. Perhaps it is not realistic to expect a more coherent analysis and direction to emerge after such a short time together.

LOCAL IDENTITY AND LOCAL GOVERNMENT

Chairperson: Fergus O'Ferrall

Reporter: Eamonn Hughes

An Account of the Workshop

The workshop commenced with the chairperson posing some key questions for discussion: what structures in local government would facilitate strong local identities? How might new regional authorities take power from central institutions? Is that what people really want or is there a subtle complicity between people at local level and the central institutions? Is this indicated by the personalism in our political system and the role played by elected politicians? Is 'small town' government a liberal or an authoritarian idea? A wide-ranging discussion followed. The issues raised included:

- the best tiers at which powers might be exercised – whether at district, county or regional levels
- the role of local government authorities in reflecting, shaping or even determining local identities
- the relationship between revenue raising powers and the responsibilities exercised by local government
- the need for public debate on how local authorities might change so as to be more responsive to local needs or local voluntary organisations
- the role of party political representatives at local government level whether this role is detrimental or advantageous or even unavoidable.

A detailed discussion took place on the Local Government Act 1991 in the Republic and the report of the Barrington Committee. This report failed to agree on sub-county level structures but outlined two options – directly elected district councils or county councils electing District Committees. Both options would involve abolition of existing sub-county structures. It was felt that Urban District Councils and Town Commissions would resist abolition.

The Local Government Act 1991 is an enabling statute allowing for regional authorities to be established by the government. It is not prescriptive as to size or actual powers to be exercised. The Act widened the scope of county councils but decisions as to the new approach at sub-county level have yet to be taken.

The paradox was noted that Northern Ireland had fundamentally altered its local government structures while still part of the United Kingdom yet independent Ireland had essentially retained its British local government heritage and structure. It was felt that in Northern Ireland devolution of powers had occurred often without adequate resources or even the necessary competence in the local authority being present. One example was given of there being no central responsibility for training teachers in Education for Mutual Understanding as this was left to the Education Boards. The question was raised; is devolution of power and resources always an efficient use of resources or the best way to undertake certain activities? The question remains: what resources should be raised locally? What resources should be given from central government and for what purposes?

Assessment
The workshop did not reach firm conclusions. One issue was agreed however: it is vital for local authorities to be able to raise a certain proportion of their own resources. This will ensure exercise of responsible and developmentally-oriented local government. Also if local authorities can diverge on their spending by virtue of raising their own resources it follows that we must tolerate diversity of provision from one local authority area to another. For example, some may choose to raise and spend more on cultural programmes while others might not have the same spending priorities.

One key issue at the heart of the conference on 'Regions: Identity and Power' was that two opposing points of view were expressed on the relationship between regional or local government and identity. Some argued that local government to be successful must articulate, as a primary task, a clear local identity – each local authority must have a clear vision which will be at the centre of any successful integrated approach to local development or co-ordinated strategy for work in every area of its responsibilities. Local government must show leadership in identity formation and facilitate a deeper and wider appreciation and understanding of regional or local identities.

Others argued that this is not necessarily the case. In Ireland, where new regional structures might serve the purposes of more rational and efficient administration, it is not central that all local government bodies evoke a definite local or regional identity in the populations they serve. They are important for effective administration of services but not for identity formation. Such identities overlap and occur often at sub-county or cross-county levels and remain unrelated to increased powers for local authorities.

It is evident from our discussion, informed as it was by experienced people in local government – both elected and non-elected – who were involved, that much is unresolved in the debate on local government and local identity. Our social and democratic philosophy remains undeveloped at a popular level and we have not invested in people's education to give them the knowledge, skills and attitudes to transform democracy at local level. We seem to depend upon an external catalyst, such as the European Communities and their regional and structural funds, to initiate a process of change, simply in order to attract funds. This seems a very impoverished level of political and cultural thought in respect of how people should govern themselves and promote institutions which will allow their cultures and identities to flourish.

GENERAL DISCUSSION

Martin McLoone (University of Ulster)
Just to add to the media report, I did leave out one other ringing endorsement from our group which was brought up later by one of the other speakers. Obviously, it's a question of community radio and community television; I think in the future development of public service broadcasting, there was a general consensus that the movement away from the centre structure of public service broadcasting would indeed provide that kind of community-based television service and a community based radio service, but that could only be provided through the structures of public service broadcasting and would not be provided by commercial radio or commercial television. The priorities in commercial broadcasting are very different. So it's an endorsement as well of community-based-level radio and television.

Liam Ó Cuinncagáin (Oideas Gael)
I was unable, obviously, to be in every workshop, but was extremely interested in the one about Regions and Media and I would just like to support the last comment there. The major point that I would like to make is to underline the essential thing that the Gaeltacht regions would be seen as one specific region and that in order for the long term survival of the Gaeltacht regions and the language, the one essential need that we have at the present moment is a Gaeltacht or Irish language television. What struck me over the weekend talking to people, especially talking about European funding which came up a lot, the emphasis is generally on capital expenditure in heritage centres, so on and so forth, whereas I would like to see people-centred cultures being a priority and ensuring that, say, the ten million that needs to be spent on Irish language television would be spent and given a priority in comparison to money that is spent on actual buildings and treasuring of our heritage. I would like to see at the end of the con-

ference, it being underlined, that with Irish speakers, a lot of whom were present at the conference, that with all of us, this Irish language television station is seen as a basic necessity for the survival of the language into the next century.

Peter Jordan (Waterford Regional Technical College)
I would just like to make a comment on the provincial newspaper situation. Somebody in the media group was suggesting that there was a decline of the provincial newspaper; this might well be so in other regions, other areas, but I can say that in Waterford, and there are certainly two very strong local newspapers, the editor of the *Munster Express*, a larger than life character who died this year, John Joseph Walsh, partly maybe through his personality, partly for other reasons, established this paper and its very much a thriving organ of information in the Waterford region.

Lelia Doolan (Cultures of Ireland)
I just want to make a very short plea: we have a new arrangement of political parties. I would like to ask people who are here to speak to their local representatives in terms of looking urgently at the work of the Office of Public Works in the building of interpretation centres and specifically in calling for the relocation of the Mullaghmore Centre.

James Hawthorne (Northern Ireland Community Relations Council)
May I make an observation or two; first, on local newspapers. Provincial newspapers like the *Belfast Telegraph* and the *Irish News* are in decline by reason of their size. They are in competition with television and, because of that competition, they have had to readjust, not only in the face of falling advertising revenue, but to the more powerful influence of television news. To do so they have become more and more tabloid, more commercial. The so-called advertising feature often takes the place of real journalism and I see nothing but further decline and indeed I think they are doomed. But the small local newspapers have not been in competition with television journalistically. They reach parts where others cannot reach and they are likely to continue to thrive. In another area that I'm interested in, the area of health promotion, local papers are proving to be highly efficient conduits for new debates, new ideas and information – all for the public good.

PART IV — REPORTS ON WORKSHOPS   225

   May I say a bit about public service broadcasting, a phrase much bandied, especially now at a time of radical change and Green Papers? Public service broadcasting is not a synonym for 'decent' broadcasting or even for the BBC. It is a term which describes a system of broadcasting, an attitude to broadcasting, an understanding of the power and responsibility of broadcasting, broadcasting that is driven by judgements of what people require in terms of information and education and culture and entertainment. If broadcasting, directly or indirectly, is to be driven by other forces, by commercialism, by over-heated competition, by the economy then, by definition, public service broadcasting is no more. I see a world in which broadcasting organisations will be mere profit making institutions with video outlets! I am depressed because the ecology of British broadcasting – that essential balance between commercial and public service – is certain to be altered out of all recognition by hastily concocted theories – and they will influence Irish broadcasting – and the future is bleak. Commercial broadcasting, which had great strength in the UK, is now programmed on a ruinous course of decline from 1993 onwards. Most of the elements which made it superior to most other commercial networks have been removed. For example: Channel 4 has been forced into a new kind of competition for resources which is bound to inhibit its experimentation and its ability to cater for minorities. And for the very first time in our broadcasting history, the broadcasters will not simply be competing for viewers and listeners, they will be competing for advertisers – programmes designed to attract advertisers first and serve the public second. And there will be particularly fierce competition if Channel 5 ever comes on stream. And thus, after many years of high standards, we shall have produced the very formula which has shaped American television, with all its horrors and lost opportunities. And once that formula, that structure, is in place there can be no going back to that which once made our national broadcasting a matter of pride.
   Let's look at what is happening in the UK, using the terminology and values of the Thatcher era. As an industry, if that is what broadcasting is to be, then the British television industry has been manifestly better and more economically produced than the German or Japanese or Swedish or French industries. Imagine if the British motor industry were so highly rated all over the world – better, more efficient than all the competition – would anybody be so

stupid as to demand radical reform? And yet a government which expounds a philosophy of non-interference has continually had designs on broadcasting. The partial privatisation of both BBC and ITV production already in place does not have any sound economic rationale whatsoever. The changes have been enforced for political and ideological reasons. I would concede that, because of new technology and so on, broadcasting structures must be reviewed but I strongly suspect that there's an agenda to cut powerful independent broadcasting institutions down to size. The recent Green Paper on the BBC looks benign enough at this early stage – perhaps the conscience of government has been smitten after the absurdities of the new ITV licences. But beware. The BBC looks set to being substantially dismantled and that fact, coupled with the damage done to commercially driven television, which has attained such extremely high standards in the past, is certain to lead to a serious decline, if not to the end of television as we have known it in the United Kingdom. And you can be sure that all of these changes will influence the future of RTE.

Bernard Cullen (Queen's University, Belfast and The Irish Association)
First of all, I would like to support, in the strongest possible terms, the call for an Irish language television station. And can I add to that a plea: please beam it with sufficient strength, or better still beam it up to the Astra satellite, so that I in south Belfast can watch it. I was actually prompted to put my hand up by the last speaker, because, as I recollect, Dr. Hawthorne was also the first speaker from the floor on Friday evening, and he threw out a challenge which I don't think was taken up in the course of the weekend: namely, to define the word 'subsidiarity'. And it was either he or a speaker following him who reported Jacques Delors as saying that he didn't understand the meaning of subsidiarity and offering his job to anyone who could provide a definition of it. Well, I would like to make a bid for Jacques Delors's job here and now. It also surprised me at the time that Jimmy Hawthorne couldn't come up with a definition, but I shouldn't really have been surprised. His difficulty only served to underline the long-standing social divisions in Northern Ireland, and the fact that we were schooled in different traditions. Because I learned all about subsidiarity in the Christian Brothers in Belfast about 1965. Indeed, anyone who

learned Catholic social teaching in a Catholic school, and who read, as we were urged to do, *Quadragesimo Anno* should know all about the principle of subsidiarity. In fact, it could be said that the origins of the principle of subsidiarity in the writings of Thomas Aquinas and modern Roman Catholic social teaching only go to show that some Unionist politicians in Northern Ireland have been right all along: that the Treaties of Rome and Maastricht really are part of a papish conspiracy and that Monsieur Delors really is an agent of the anti-Christ. But whether you like the word or not, it denotes a brilliantly clear and simple idea. And my rough definition is that decision-making with respect to policies which affect people's lives should be made at the lowest practical level, by the people directly affected by the policy. End of definition. Of course, local decision-making can have cruel effects on individuals and those individuals must be protected by codes of human rights; and that's what we have codes such as the European Convention for. Mary Banotti is surely right: national governments will try to hijack this principle and will claim subsidiarity stops at Dublin or at Westminster. But that claim can and should be challenged. In the discussion in our group yesterday afternoon, something that was not, perhaps, adequately reflected in this morning's report was that we wrestled with the problem of regional power: how power is to be devolved, how far it is to be devolved, and to whom it is to be devolved. Now, the principle of subsidiarity is a double-edged sword. Let's not be too dewy-eyed at the prospect of bringing power to the people. For many of the positive social advances in the last twenty years in Ireland, North and South, have been forced upon us by Brussels. Let's not lose sight of that fact. Many of the positive social and political advances in Northern Ireland have been forced upon us by Westminster governments – and ironically perhaps, by Conservative Westminster governments. One of the participants in the group I was in yesterday morning reminded us of the fact that local communities can be exceedingly oppressive places. And he suggested an idea that I hadn't quite thought of before: that the hundreds of thousands of emigrants from Ireland over the years have mostly gone abroad to look for a job, but they have also to some considerable extent, been trying to get out of the very oppressive and claustrophobic atmosphere in which they had grown up. They went abroad (as I did myself) to get a breath of fresh air. Now, I think there's a lot of truth in that observation. I say that just to show that I'm not a dewy-eyed idealist on behalf of regional power. 'Power to the people' is indeed a double-edged sword. But in our group yesterday afternoon, we got into a discussion which was prompted, I think, by the story of the Adelaide Hospital, and we had a lively debate about the extent to which minority wishes and local wishes and regional wishes should be catered to (some would say pandered to). This was really a debate (although the term wasn't used) about the practical application of the principle of subsidiarity. If you take just one of the examples that came up in our discussion, and apply the principle of subsidiarity, I would suggest that the British government based in Stormont Castle should have the political courage to offer a local plebiscite to the people of Catholic west Belfast, for example, asking them to what extent they want their schools to continue to be controlled exclusively by one vested interest and to what extent they wish to have local democratic control over their own schools. If the principle of subsidiarity were applied in that way, my own hunch is that a very sizeable proportion would vote to have their schooling run and controlled by themselves and by local democratic management, to the exclusion of the clerical authorities who currently have effectively one hundred per cent control. And of course, there would also be a substantial number who would wish to maintain the clerical control. That would be subsidiarity in action; and on the basis of the results, government should then fund that proportion of people who wish to have that kind of democratic management of schools, irrespective of the church they may or may not go to on a Sunday morning. Subsidiarity is not a difficult idea. If we trust the people, the working out of the principle in practice may have some effects that many of us would rather not countenance. But on balance, if we're democrats, I think it's a challenge we have to accept and it's a risk we have to take.

Finbar O'Kane (Long Island University, New York)
I am in this country representing the American emigrants, during this political period and I drifted along in this direction and I think maybe it was a blessing, because I'd had enough of Dublin for those ninety six hours or whatever; I'm not listing you any more statistics or anything else, so I thought I'd get philosophical. 'Culture in Ireland' attracted me, and in particular I was attracted to the notion of identity and power, because what we are looking for is, believe

it or not, we're looking for the vote. Speaking of identity, we're looking for it on the basis of our Irish citizenship, which is denied when we don't get it and as a matter of power we don't have it. We're looking for empowerment on this basic issue. If a chain is as strong as its weakest link, I can tell you that your country's franchise system, as far as we are concerned, is invalid. We are a region, we are the diaspora and we are not in America because we were that bored. If we were bored at home, I can tell you there are a lot more boring places in these United States, in the last 12 years under Reagan/Bush. I got a very good response yesterday from your Patron, our president, or your President, my patron. For heavens sake, if you get us the franchise, we might be able to do something. I'm going back now and I want to take the most positive message I possibly can. I would really appreciate it. While there was no workshop on this issue, I'm suggesting that there might well have been, since there wasn't, I would like to put it on record and I would like terribly much to have the support of this conference and this weekend on our demand for the basic right of franchise.

Helena O'Donoghue (Cultures of Ireland)
What I would like to say follows quite naturally on the last speaker, because it was around the question of communication. In our workshop on locality and access, communication was one of the points which we raised and I didn't report on it that time. We talked about localities or cultures being able to exchange, being able to, somehow, communicate their particularities, one to another, and one suggestion was to invite people to travel to your place as well as having the possibility of travelling out of your place. It was also mentioned that communities quite close to each other can be disconnected, quite disconnected, if only because of the uncertainty of whether the train will run from your place to the place some distance away or whether it's unreliable. Communication between regions can quite literally fall apart, even though they can be quite close together. It strikes me, that one of the, I suppose, real concerns of such a body as this is to be able to relate together, and I found the speakers providing us with a very good model of communication, where we had a look at theory and data and personal experience in terms of getting a sense of culture, a sense of region and locality. If we are going to make progress in terms of understanding, in terms of tolerance, in terms of mutual support,

we need to develop a language of communication, a language that is non-judgemental, a language that is able to look at difference, even as we assess that difference in various grades. We need to communicate about it in a way that doesn't reduce people or groups simply because they don't measure up to a certain standard or they don't measure to a certain degree of development or progress, or whatever. That's a very difficult thing, I think, in the human endeavour, but if we're to make some progress and if this conference is to continue with an aftermath, in some way or another, I think communication and a language of communication is a really vital tool in terms of providing the road and the avenue to progress, whatever we all understand by that. But it certainly is related to our identity and our power as areas.

Constance Short (Cultures of Ireland)
I'm just taking up Helena's point, which was also mentioned during the workshop report backs. Someone said that we seem to have a great bunch of agnostics at the conference and at Joe Liecthy's workshop. Frank Short mentioned in his workshop that we only had very few people here interested in sport. Also somebody said to me last night that they would have preferred to see more Unionists here.

Tying all of that in with what Helena is saying, it is about communication, it is difficult to have communication if people actually don't come together to communicate. We were accused of this about the conference we had last year as well. For example, we were accused that we didn't have enough religious there. A bishop wrote to our honorary chairperson, and said that from what he had heard it was not Catholic-friendly. I wanted this man to attend this year's conference. We made every effort this year and last to make the conference Catholic-friendly, Protestant-friendly, Unionist-friendly, Nationalist-friendly, GAA-friendly, sports-friendly, you name it. I spent nine months encouraging people to come and unfortunately some of them just didn't.

Leo Hallissey (Connemara Environmental Education Centre)
Just on the question of communication, I'd have two questions just to raise. One is, I'd have a question over the venue or the location for this conference. I just wonder is this the type of venue that we should have? Secondly in terms of group dynamics, some of the

best talking happens at the end of the conference. I think that we should look at this notion of conferencing and the way we communicate. For the crack, somebody said to me this morning, maybe we should start off in a swimming pool, wouldn't it be very interesting. We are all down there without our clothes and we wouldn't be able to hide behind any masquerade, behind these masks and so forth. I know people who have done that, to be on a serious note and it has worked and also I would like to see the poetic and the philosophical running throughout the whole conference. I don't think that the music should be assigned to the bit at the end, musical entertainment or whatever sort of thing. I think the poetic, the philosophical should be running throughout the whole conference, if we are to talk about culture. On another note altogether, I'd like to endorse what some of the people have said about Green Papers, that there are serious threats in these Green Papers and one element that slightly escaped there was that there was criticism of our educational Green Paper in the twenty-six counties. There are very serious sinister ideologies involved in these papers, and there is a need for public open discussion on this whole business of culture and identity in Ireland. We need to quantify what is important to us as a nation and what we are not going to sell off, as the person who raised the hare, I want to ask, is the country for sale?, I think it's worth discussing that in detail in an open democratic way throughout the whole island.

Larry McCluskey (Co. Monaghan V.E.C. and Arts Council)
I would like to make two points, one in relation to 'identity', the other in relation to 'power'.

The role of the arts in forging community identity has been referred to a number of times. A very significant development all over Ireland in recent years has been the growth (in both quantity and quality) of local festivals, with a particularly strong emphasis on community arts. I believe that local communities are forging or developing their identities through these festivals. One thinks of Galway, Sligo, Kilkenny, Omagh, but there are many others, some quite small communities, and a complementary development has been the establishment of regional arts groups like Red Kettle in Waterford and others like Galloglass in Clonmel and Yew Theatre Company in the West – small and struggling to emerge as part of new regional identities.

We have talked about the other major power structures – the political system, the churches and organised business – these are highly established structures, with roots that go deep and whose resistance to change can be formidable. The arts on the other hand, being less established, are readier too for new constructions of local or regional identity, in my view. Their potential in this regard could be explored in greater depth and detail – I feel we only scratched the surface here this weekend.

Concerning 'power' I think we should recognise the clandestine power structures which exist in and around the political and bureaucratic systems in this country. I refer to the quasi-religious groups, North and South, whose power is considerable within government departments and other organs of state. Even major political changes leave these informal structures largely untouched – because they are not publicly accountable at all. It was interesting to hear (in relation to the Adelaide) that while the Taoiseach gave unequivocal assurances concerning the ethos of the hospital, the Department of Health effectively ignored him! You can be sure that other departments, on both the bureaucratic and political levels, have people who march to drums whose drummers are not publicly elected – or even visible!

Terry Clare (Wexford Centre for the Unemployed)
A previous speaker felt that this wasn't a proper venue for this conference, now let me say that I believe that it is an excellent venue, it demonstrates modern Ireland and the progress in modern Ireland in one aspect of that: tourism, and also it has brought together a lot of people from Northern Ireland and Southerners. I came from Wexford, which is five hours by road, but I welcome that and also I feel that I have served an unusual purpose. Some years ago, I was a visitor to Moscow, a guest of the Seamen's Union there and the conflict there was between the intelligentsia and the working class over their constitution. It was a workers' constitution, and the intelligentsia felt that they couldn't fit into it. How I became aware of that is because our guide was an English teacher in a Moscow University. Now there is such a wide gap here, although there is not a conflict in Ireland between the intelligentsia and the working class or the unemployed, but what there is, is a huge gap and I believe myself in this conference, by being here, that I have helped to contribute to create awareness of that gap. I would be quite happy

to go back to Wexford and to the constituency of the unemployed and say that I have spent a weekend in very nice company and in a very nice hotel and that something useful has been achieved on their behalf and I would like to say thank you to the chairman and the organisers for inviting me here.

Edna Longley (Queen's University, Belfast)
Just a point about the centre and subsidiarity. The Thatcherite juggernaut, which has not yet run out of steam, introduced a false subsidiarity or devolution, based on the parcelling-out of (inadequate) budgets – hamburger-franchises rather than true regional or local decision-making. This means, for instance, that Education and Library Boards have devolved budgets to schools in such a way that teachers cannot get leave to attend in-service courses because there is not money for a substitute-teacher. This actually sabotages government policy in Northern Ireland with regard to Cultural Heritage and Education for Mutual Understanding. On the press, I agree with what James Hawthorne says about other newspapers, but the *Belfast Telegraph*, which has a huge circulation, has shamefully opted out of political and cultural debate. It is part of the 'democratic deficit' that the north lacks a newspaper-forum such as that provided by the *Irish Times* in the Republic. There is no significant 'regional' tier between the parish-pump local newspapers or free-sheets (useful as these are) and the UK 'nationals'. This makes the survival of the BBC, especially in its regional function, all the more important.

Fergus O'Ferrall (Cultures of Ireland)
I should like to stress the role of adult education in developing a civic or political culture and in fostering local identities. The Folk High School movement since the nineteenth century played a major role in creating democratic society in Scandinavian countries. This is a classic example of the need for prolonged investment in a people's political and cultural education. Adults need educational opportunities to reflect upon and perhaps change their attitudes, to obtain participatory skills and to gain the knowledge necessary for authentic participation in politics.

The Green Paper discussions in the Republic on education provides an opportunity to insist that the self-financing rule for adult education be removed and that a positive commitment to shifting some financial resources towards adult education emerges in the White Paper. The network present here which is so representative and diverse could have a real role in lobbying for education for adults. This will be a real determinant of the kind of Irish society which develops in the next century.

Part IV — Reports on Workshops

CHAIRPERSON'S CONCLUSION

I want to thank, on your behalf, the staff of Project Planning, who have done all the crucial, but unnoticed things, which have ensured the smooth running of the conference, and have contributed to our enjoyment, as did the playing of Fintan Vallely and his fellow musicians last night. We are all grateful, too, to the Cultures of Ireland Group, the International Fund for Ireland, the Ireland Funds and Co-operation North, whose support has afforded this opportunity to debate issues which are important to us, and crucial to Ireland. In particular, can I thank Constance Short, whose energy, enthusiasm and determination has been the powerful force behind the conference. She could be a model of 'empowerment', so frequently mentioned in the workshops. Finally, can I thank all the speakers and chairpersons whose papers and direction both informed and focused our debate.

To conclude the conference, I would like to make four brief observations. Conferences have outcomes, as this one will, I hope, in two crucial ways. Firstly, in the faithful recording of what you have thought and said, which will appear as a publication. We should never underestimate the power of the book – as a source of forward-looking ideas, and as a resource which can widen our perceptions, through recording the priorities of others. The second outcome of this conference should arise from newly-established contacts, which have the potential for increasing our mutual understanding, that essential underpinning of book-knowledge. It is our individual responsibility to carry these ideas on wherever we work or live, and to maintain and strengthen the contacts – not to wait for the impetus of the next conference, but to act ourselves.

Our debates seem to me to have fallen, broadly, into concerns which relate to the past, to the present and to the future. We have pointed out the deficit in our knowledge and appreciation of all our local histories: those cultural expressions, not only emanating from different religions, but also from the diversity of class, gender and region. If we do not foster what we have we will lose our 'exceptions' and our diversity, leaving ourselves open to being defined by others – whose definitions are more likely to be based on their perceptions of our economic viability, rather than our sense of identity. We must foster our heritage, our arts, our regions – for ourselves. We must be the musician, the writers and the dancers, but we must also be the listeners and the watchers. We are both the creators and the audience: the validity of what we do lies in being both.

Opportunities for such self-determination are available. Our communities are all manifestly articulate, and, this conference has suggested, perhaps more liberal than is generally believed. There may be an impetus in the governments of both the Republic and Northern Ireland to support regional hopes and ambitions. While those in the Republic may come from the variety inherent in a 'rainbow' coalition, those in Northern Ireland come, not only from a community relations imperative, but also from the positive response from community groups to government initiatives. There are funding options outside central government – principally from Europe, but also from the major trusts which have interests in Ireland – and the independence such support can offer should empower local groups. The opportunities offered by increasingly accessible information technology have been frequently referred to, and the more traditional transmitters – the press, publications, and the broadcasting media, are also crucial. Most significantly, we all have interests in common: the natural, and the built environment, showing the traces of our ancestors, the imperatives of our generation and the contributions of our children, needs the same care in its protection and its maintenance, from one end of the island to the other.

Despite our emphasis during this conference on the pressing needs of regional identity and empowerment, the debate has throughout focused on the needs of the future, particularly on education and the economy, stressing the importance of imaginative educational programmes both within and outside schools. We have also pointed out the conflict between the needs of the unemployed, and the survival of cultural veracity. Like many other people in Ireland, I, also, struggle with both these constraints. My son has had to go for work to America, but wants to live in Ireland, as I wish he could. But, simultaneously, I am concerned about protecting the north-west coast from environmentally destructive development, development which will keep my neighbours' children living, as I feel they should, on the land on which they grew up.

Earlier this year I met a Croatian who was explaining the origins of the Serbo-Croatian conflict. He maintained that the years of communism had offered so little freedom in which to conceive a future that, when the tensions became unbearable, the contending groups could only look to the past for solutions – and these, as we know, were tragically bloody. This idea made a profound impression on me, as, immediately, I thought of our situation in Ireland, north and south. So, in conclusion, could I suggest most strongly, that we must be conscious of how our regional identities impinge on young people, and how they can empower them to work in, and have a vision for, an invigorated, diverse and imaginative Ireland.

Tony Kennedy (Co-operation North)
I don't think the conference should finish, chairman, without a word of appreciation for the way in which you have with good humour and firmness ensured that our debates have been valuable and productive whilst at the same time enjoyable. On behalf of everyone here I would like to thank you for chairing the conference over the last two days.

BIOGRAPHIES

SPEAKERS

Tony Canavan is a native of Belfast. Educated at St. Malachy's College and Queen's University, Belfast (MA thesis on the Hearts of Steel). Museum Officer for Newry and Mourne District Council; Development Officer for Federation for Ulster Local Studies. Author of *Frontier Town, an illustrated history of Newry*.

Dermot Healy. Born in Finea, Co. Westmeath in 1947. A member of Aosdána, his novels are *Fighting with Shadows* and *A Goat's Song*. Other work includes *Banished Misfortunes*, a collection of short stories, a film *Our Boys* and a collection of poems, *The Ballyconnell Colours*. He has written a number of plays and is editor of *Force 10*, a community arts magazine.

Myrtle Hill graduated from Queen's University, Belfast in 1983 as a mature student. She was awarded her Ph.D. in 1983 for a thesis on Ulster evangelicalism 1770–1850. Junior Research Fellow, Institute of Irish Studies, 1986–87. Currently a lecturer in the Institute of Continuing Education, Queen's University, Belfast. Author with D.N. Hempton, of *Evangelical Protestantism in Ulster Society 1740–1890*.

Tony Kennedy has been Chief Executive of Co-operation North since August 1992. Born in Belfast, he spent the nine years previous to his appointment as Chief Housing Officer with Wakefield Metropolitan District Council. From 1972 to 1983 he worked with the Housing Executive in Belfast and Derry.

David McConnell was educated at Sandford Park and Trinity College, Dublin. He has been chairman of the Adelaide Hospital since 1987 and Professor of Genetics at TCD since 1990, having joined the staff of the Department of Genetics in 1970. He was awarded his Ph.D. by the California Institute of Technology in 1971 for studies on the molecular mechanism of the control of gene expression.

Liam O'Dowd Reader in Sociology, Queen's University, Belfast. Co-author and editor of several books and articles including: *Northern Ireland: Between Civil Rights and Civil War; Culture and Ideology in Ireland; Ireland: A Sociological Profile; The State of Social Science Research in Ireland.* He is currently chairman of the Royal Irish Academy's National Committee for Economic and Social Sciences.

Frank Short Múinteoir bunscoile; iar-pheileadóir chlub is chontae; leaschathaoirleach CMÉ i nDúndealgan; ball de choiste Ghlór na nGael, Crois Mhic Lionnáin; comhfhundúir scoil Samhraidh Choláiste na Croise, Crois Mhic Lionnáin.

(Primary teacher; former club and inter-county footballer; vice-chairperson of Dundalk branch of INTO; member of Crossmaglen Glór na nGael; co-founder of Coláiste na Croise Summer school, Crossmaglen).

Anne Tannahill is managing director of Blackstaff Press, a member of the Cultural Traditions Group and of the Broadcasting Council for Northern Ireland.

Rienk Terpstra was a policy officer of the Department for the Preservation of Monuments and Historic Sites of the Province of Friesland. Now he is head of the Development Office of Cultural Tourism. An engineer, he has been involved in a number of important restoration projects and has carried out various archaeological–historic investigations.

Máire Uí Shíthigh. Rugadh i mBaile Atha Cliath í. Ina cónaí go buan i gCorca Dhuibhne ó 1981 i leith. Ag obair d'Oidhreacht Chorca Dhuibhne ó 1988. (Born in Dublin, resident in Corca Dhuibhne since 1981. Has worked for Oidhreacht Chorca Dhuibhne since 1981.)

Kevin Whelan is the Bicentennial Research Fellow in the Royal Irish Academy. He is co-editor of *The United Irishmen: Radicalism, Republicanism and Rebellion.*

CHAIRPERSONS

Terence Brown is Associate Professor of English at Trinity College, Dublin. He is a literary critic and cultural historian. Author of many books and articles, his most recent book is *Ireland's Literature: Selected Essays*.

Maurna Crozier is currently working on the Cultural Traditions programme of the Community Relations Council. She is chairman of Northern Ireland Environment Link; member of the Irish Heritage Education Network; the General Advisory Council of the BBC, the Historic Monuments Council; Honorary Fellow of the Department of Social Anthropology and former Junior Fellow at the Institute of Irish Studies, Queen's University, Belfast.

Lelia Doolan. Formerly Head of Light Entertainment, RTE and Artistic Director, Abbey Theatre. Film-maker, anthropologist, gardener.

Joseph Liechty is a Mennonite Church worker and an occasional lecturer in the History Department, St. Patrick's College, Maynooth.

Edna Longley is a Professor of English at Queen's University, Belfast. She is an editor of *The Irish Review* and author of *Poetry in the Wars* and *Louis MacNeice: A Study*. She edited the proceedings of the first Cultures of Ireland conference – *Culture in Ireland: Division or Diversity*.

Helena O'Donoghue is based in Ennis and is Superior General of the Killaloe Mercy Sisters. She is an ex-president of the Conference of Major Religious Superiors. She has been a teacher and school principal in Nenagh, Parish Sister in Shannon and for seven years was a member of a Lay Christian Community in Dublin. She has Degrees in Arts and Theology.

Proinsias Ó Drisceoil works for Co. Kilkenny VEC as Arts Education Organiser for the South-East. An honorary director of the Kilkenny Muncipal Theatre and of the Butler Gallery and a member of the VEC Adult Education Board, he has published articles on Irish literature in a variety of publications and was formerly Irish language editor of *Poetry Ireland Review*.

Fergus O'Ferrall is a native of Co. Longford. Educated at Wesley College and Trinity College, Dublin, his Ph.D. thesis was on Daniel O'Connell and he subsequently published *Daniel O'Connell* in the Gill's Lives series and *Catholic Emancipation – Daniel O'Connell and the Birth of Irish Democracy 1820–1830*. He has contributed articles and reviews to *Studies, The Irish Review, Irish Literary Supplement* and various historical journals.

Gearóid Ó Tuathaigh is Associate Professor of History and Vice-President for External Affairs of University College, Galway. His publications are mainly in the field of nineteenth and twentieth century history.

Helen Lanigan Woods. Formerly an archaeologist with the Office of Public Works and the Archaelogical Survey of Northern Ireland, she is now curator of Fermanagh County Museum. Author of *Images of Stone*.

REPORTERS

Eamonn Hughes lectures in the School of English at Queen's University Belfast. He edited *Culture and Politics in Northern Ireland 1960–1990*.

Scan McGcarty is a project leader on Co operation North's Youth, Education and Community scheme. He is a trustee of the British–Irish Exchange Scheme and previously worked as a Youthreach Co-ordinator of City of Dublin VEC.

Deirdre McKervey is a project leader of Co-operation North's Youth, Education Community Programme.

Jane O'Neill is a librarian at the Northern Ireland College of Midwifery.

Kevin O'Neill is an events organiser with Co-operation North in Belfast.

Desmond O'Rawe teaches in the Belfast Institute of Further and Higher Education and is currently undertaking research into a cultural analysis of contemporary Irish writing.

THANKS TO:

Mary Robinson, President of Ireland, our patron
The International Fund for Ireland
The Ireland Funds
Co-operation North
Central Community Relations Unit (Stormont)
Dept. of Foreign Affairs
Project Planning
All participants in the conference
Mary Wallace
Brendan Conway, Chief Executive Officer, Co. Kilkenny VEC
Frances Wallace
Jane O'Malley
Sheila Gallen, Computer Department, Carlow Regional Technical College

Epic by ***Patrick Kavanagh*** reprinted by permission of the trustees of the estate of Patrick Kavanagh c/o **Peter Fallon**, Loughcrew, Oldcastle, Co. Meath.

Welsh Testament is copyright property of R.S. Thomas